TENNYSON

THE
GROWTH
OF
A
POET

TENNYSON

THE
GROWTH
OF
A
POET

Jerome Hamilton Buckley

HARVARD UNIVERSITY PRESS

Cambridge, Massachusetts

1960

© Copyright 1960 by the President and Fellows of Harvard College

Distributed in Great Britian by Oxford University Press, London

Publication of this book has been aided by
a grant from the Ford Foundation

Library of Congress Catalog Card Number: 60-13298

Printed in the United States of America

TO
HOWARD MUMFORD JONES

PREFACE

DEDICATED from childhood to the poet's calling, Tennyson's life was his work; the story of his career — or all of it that he thought worth our knowing — is the bibliography of his published poems. But the poetry, often intensely personal despite appearances of objectivity, cannot be fully understood without frequent reference to the imagination that produced it. All students of Tennyson, therefore, owe a large debt to the monumental though loosely organized *Memoir* compiled by Hallam Lord Tennyson and to the more recent and wholly admirable biography by the poet's grandson, Sir Charles Tennyson. My own dependence on both of these will be apparent on almost every page of the present book. For it is my purpose to study Tennyson's developing sensibility as a guide to a critical evaluation of his accomplishment. But, though I have restored the poems to a biographical context, which throws light, I believe, on their intention and meaning and even their language, I have sought to make clear that each one must also be detached once again from its source in the imaginative life of the poet to be judged in terms of its own intrinsic qualities as a poetic unit.

In reviewing Tennyson's work from first to last, from *The Devil and the Lady* to *The Death of Oenone*, I have had the advantage of access to the great collection of unpublished notebooks and other Tennyson papers now in the Houghton Library of Harvard University. Since these materials were not available for examination until several years ago, no earlier general criticism has supplemented analysis with reliable evidence of the actual evolution of many of the poems. I am deeply grateful to William H. Bond of Houghton, who first directed me to the Tennyson treasure, and to the curator, Professor William A. Jackson, who has given me permission to make free use of the manuscripts.

Whatever may be its limitations in depth, my study with such support is therefore broader at least in scope than its predecessors. And it differs also rather sharply in tone from the only two book-length critical estimates of Tennyson to appear in the past forty years: Sir Harold Nicolson's brilliant but biased *Tennyson*, first published in 1923, and Professor Paull F. Baum's scholarly but hostile *Tennyson Sixty Years After* of 1948. It is frankly more sympathetic than either, for it rests on the assumption, which neither would allow, that Tennyson by endowment and attainment was a major poet (as I have tried to define such majority in my concluding chapter). Though the design of this book precludes sustained discussion of Tennyson's prosodic mastery, which is surely one of his claims to greatness, I have attempted to indicate throughout my argument, partly by liberal quotation, the quality of his technical achievement. And it is my hope that the chronological arrangement I have followed may place in clearer perspective the many gifts of sensibility and style that gave strength to his dedicated life in poetry.

I am indebted to the American Philosophical Society for a 1956 grant from its Penrose Fund, under which the writing of this book was begun, and to the Columbia University Council on Research in the Humanities for an award in the summer of 1958, which considerably abetted the progress of my manuscript. I should like to thank Sir Charles Tennyson for graciously permitting me to quote at some length from his editions of *The Devil and the Lady* and the *Unpublished Early Poems*, and the Macmillan Company of London for leave to cite a good many passages from the *Memoir*. I appreciate the courtesies extended to me over a long period by the librarians of Columbia University, Harvard University, and Victoria College, Toronto, and by the keepers of the Berg Collection, New York Public Library, and of the Pierpont Morgan Library. I am grateful in countless ways — for help, encouragement, and quiet suggestion — to many friends and colleagues, especially Marjorie Hope Nicolson, Helen C. White, Emery Neff, Howard Mumford Jones, Edgar F. Shannon, Jr., William Nelson, and Lionel Trilling; and to my many patient students, among whom I must mention Edward Engelberg, Martha Salmon, Patrick J. McCarthy, Jr., and John Rosenberg. I have received immeasurable editorial assistance from Joyce Lebowitz of Harvard University Press. And as always I owe an incalculable debt to my wife Elizabeth, whose good judgment and good humor have been abundant and abiding.

J. H. B.

New York
April 1960

CONTENTS

CONTENTS

TENNYSON

THE
GROWTH
OF
A
POET

❧ I ❧

THE EYES OF WONDER

Somersby, 1809–1827

ALL his life Tennyson remembered standing as a small child with outstretched arms on the gale-swept lawn at Somersby and crying in wild delight, "I hear a voice that's speaking in the wind." [1] The experience was scarcely unique, for countless children have given themselves to the wind's will; but the child Tennyson attached an unusual significance to the gesture. To him the voice was already the call of the imagination borne in upon his sharpened senses from some remote realm beyond all sensuous measurement; and the message that haunted his whole being was even then a cryptic "far — far — away," a challenge from time immemorial which filled him with what he came to call "the passion of the past." Toward the end of his long career, eager to explain to himself the unity and persistence of his emotion, he strove to weave a lyric around the incantation:

> Far — far — away.
> That weird soul-phrase of something half-divine
> In earliest youth, in latest age is mine.
> Far — far — away. [2]

Yet the "weird soul-phrase" was too vague, and the impression too private, to satisfy the poet who asked that vision be translated into the language of sensation and rendered in public symbols. Tennyson accordingly left the lines buried in his notebook as he reshaped "Far — Far — Away" first into a catechism in the second person and then, to make it appear more objective, into the song in the third person published in the *Demeter* volume of 1889 and carefully labeled "For Music." The revisions here and elsewhere suggest the method of the artist and the characteristic reticence of the man. But the essential impulse that prompted the lyric and that in a larger sense underlay a lifelong dedication to poetry arose from the depths of Tennyson's consciousness, from his continued and childlike interest in the problem of identity and his memory of a youth strangely animated by wonder and aloneness.

The Somersby environment fostered the boy's lonely sensibilities and at the same time provided the counterbalance of a small receptive audience for his first efforts at self-expression. "Well, Arthur," he told his brother with naive assurance, "I mean to be famous." [3] And recognition, though it might ultimately seem a delusion, first of all demanded communication, a sharing of idea, feeling, and insight. Almost from the beginning Tennyson was aware not only of the poet's necessary relation to a cultural heritage, without which there could be no conceivable poetic fame, but also of his own immediate place in a large family, a family to whom literature was a constant concern, escape, or example. In later years he would insist that no man could or should claim complete independence of his fellows, for "every human being is a vanful of human beings, of those who have gone before him, and of those who form part of his life." [4] In his ancestors as such, he had little apparent interest, though he sometimes spoke fancifully of the "black blood" of the Tennysons as the source of his recurrent melancholia. But he freely acknowledged a debt of affection to his somewhat passive mother, whose ready faith seemed far less precarious than his own troubled emotion. [5] And he knew at heart how much his thought and feeling owed to the eccentric cultivation of his father, who, dominating a highly literary household, behaved less like the country parson he was than like the hero of a tragic melodrama of dispossession.

As his most candid biographer has pictured him,[6] Dr. George Clayton Tennyson appears to have been a man of talent and versatility, a scholar who had mastered Greek and Latin, knew Syriac and Hebrew, and was familiar with several modern languages, an amateur of painting and architecture, a bibliophile, an adept maker of verses, a witty and wide-ranging conversationalist. Yet he allowed the deepening shadow of resentment to darken all his brilliance: his father, perhaps mistrusting his wayward will, had rejected him as a mere boy in favor of his younger brother Charles, whose hardheaded practicality promised better to preserve and augment the fortunes of Bayons Manor. He felt himself accordingly the victim of injustice and persecution, and his father's snobbish materialism served only to increase his own desponding introversion. Forced into the Anglican ministry to which he had had no real call, he remained temperamentally the nonconformist, rather heterodox even in his religious faith, restless, outraged, outcast, driven to a vicarious life in books and alcoholic reverie or to travel on the Continent and the telling (as a mode no doubt of self-justification) of fantastic adventures in which he himself played the intrepid protagonist.[7] Neuroticism, hypochondria, and ultimately physical violence [8] made much of his married life a prolonged incompatibility. His four beautiful daughters inherited his nervous disposition but something also of their mother's restraint and quiet endurance. And his sons eventually bore the scars of his instability; Frederick with difficulty and indifferent success strove to control a passionate temper; Charles surrendered for a time to opium as an escape from illness and his own dread of debility; Septimus yielded with self-conscious pride to a morbid languor; Arthur and Horatio entered their maturity without purpose or direction; and

Edward fell into permanent madness which made necessary his confinement from the age of nineteen until his death fifty-eight years later.

The blacker woes of the Tennyson family were, however, present only in embryo during the boyhood of Alfred, who was perhaps the most sensitive of the eleven children and surely the most gifted. The Somersby period of his life was in fact a relatively happy one, which he would always recall with a fond sad nostalgia. Yet he inherited his full share of the gloom that seemed to be the legacy of the Tennysons. As a young man he could write with feeling at the time of a second cousin's birth, "I hope for his own peace of mind he will have as little of the Tennyson about him as possible." [9] Even as a child he knew moments of profound despair. He suffered much for his father, to whom he was deeply devoted, and he shrank in terror from each display of petulance and scorn. Often he wished for complete removal from all the evils of unreason; and frequently he would wander off on all-night walks alone or yearn for death and burial in his father's churchyard. But he learned early in life to channel and to sublimate his melancholy, to ritualize his griefs in verse, to cherish self-possession as a necessary guard against self-betrayal, to live, in short, the ideals he would never tire of preaching — "self-reverence, self-knowledge, self-control," the virtues his father had neglected. Above all, he feared the insanity of violence, with a dread which was eventually to color his view of all unruly passion, whether religious, sexual, or political. Each of his many studies of madness implies the necessity of order and perspective, of self-appraisal and self-discipline. The half-mad hero of *Maud*, for instance, must rebuke his own rant in words which, despite their rhetoric, have a curiously autobiographical ring:

> What! am I raging alone as my father raged in his mood?
> Must I too creep to the hollow and dash myself down and die?

The memory of insane self-indulgence thus lingered as an admonition and a threat.

Fortunately Dr. Tennyson's most extreme wrath was inconstant and unpredictable. In spite of his grievances, perhaps in part because of them, he could inspire sympathy and a measure of respect. His children, who remained remarkably loyal to him, proved his most enduring satisfaction, and his concern with their education provided a considerable release for his frustrated energies. All of his sons received his earnest attention; but Alfred, in whom he found his readiest pupil, became his special pride. Of the child at six years old fresh from the village classroom and rigorous drill at home, he demanded an ability to recite by rote the complete odes of Horace before allowing him to enter the grammar school at Louth.[10] Four or five years later when the experience of Louth and its sadistic headmaster had become the substance of Alfred's nightmares, he brought the boy back to Somersby for private instruction. There he zealously inculcated an interest in the classics, history, science, and modern letters, and encouraged a talent already apparent for the making of verse in English and in Greek. If he himself had been spurned, his son was to be treated with an anxious solicitude.

At Somersby Tennyson learned the danger and the sanctity of the free human will. He acquired his father's impatience with his Calvinistic Aunt Mary who, consigning all her kin to perdition, was fervidly confident of her own election to eternal bliss. He came to distrust all theological or philosophical determinism and to charge himself with a constant, onerous responsibility for moral choice, in the full conviction, as he later said, that "it is motive, it is the great purpose which consecrates life." [11] But though he would one day believe nature quite amoral in its inexorable causation and its flagrant disregard of the individual, he found his first moral guide in natural science rather than in ethical theory. He saw in the great natural laws a rhythm, a design, and an adaptation to function all too often absent from the disordered lives of men. He studied in detail the habits of birds and small animals and pored endlessly over the intricate beauty of plants and flowers. At Mablethorpe on the coast, where the family spent several summer holidays, he discovered the vitality and vastness of the sea, in which he felt even as a child a rebuke to human pride. From the beginning he was fascinated by the mysteries of astronomy; he spent long hours scanning the heavens by night, and he read as widely as he could in the writings of the accredited astronomers. When his elder brother as an Eton schoolboy was self-consciously nervous about accepting an invitation to a dinner-party, he gave him the sophisticated if somewhat owlish advice: "Fred, think of Herschel's great star-patches, and you will soon get over all that." [12] For the young Tennyson had already learned the lesson of perspective, the message of timeless infinity, which could mock all illusions of self-importance.

But if his first concern with science was, broadly speaking, moral, it was also — and in larger part — aesthetic. The little world of Lincolnshire in its vast frame of endless space spoke to his unfolding sensibility and furnished metaphor and symbol for his early verse. Meanwhile, his reading in the old mythologies, the legends of chivalry, and modern fiction, especially the romances of Walter Scott, was opening to his eager imagination whole new countries of the mind. Like Thoreau in Concord, Tennyson traveled much in Somersby. Often his brothers and sisters joined in his exploration and adventure, for their games together were predominantly literary. They held Arthurian tournaments with wooden swords. They wrote tales [13] of daring and disaster to be hidden under the vegetable dishes and read aloud after dinner. They acted out Elizabethan dramas, and Tennyson in his time played many parts. So great was his talent as mimic and so resonant his voice that all felt he was destined to be an actor. In adult life, though far too diffident to mount a public stage, he could be persuaded readily enough to declaim his own poems before a small select group of well-wishers; and in his writing, even of highly personal pieces, he would strive always to wear the poet's "mask" as a means of giving his work an independent existence. But at Somersby, despite innumerable tensions, he had little fear of being misunderstood as artist; he had before him an audience predisposed to admire and to accept without question his dramatic renditions and inventions.

As we might expect, Tennyson's first poetry was literary and derivative. He remembered writing at the age of eight, for the approval of his brother Charles, a description (in Thomsonian blank verse) of the rectory garden. At ten he turned scores of Popian couplets. And at about twelve he produced an "epic" of six thousand lines in the manner of Scott. Inevitably much of his verse bore the impress of his strenuous training in the classics. His earliest extant poem, for instance, written before he was fourteen, is a translation of Claudian's *Proserpine*, the quality of which is evident from the invocation where the poet begs the "mighty demons" to explain

> How that stern Deity, Infernal Jove,
> First felt the power, and own'd the force of love;
> How Hell's fair Empress first was snatch'd away
> From Earth's bright regions, and the face of day;
> How anxious Ceres wander'd far and near
> Now torn by grief and tortur'd now by fear.[14]

This is a clever and rather precocious experiment in the vein of Pope and the Augustan translators, a fairly sustained exercise in rhetorical control, balance, and calculated euphony. But apart from a few standard stylistic devices and the theme — which recurs in the "Demeter and Persephone" finished nearly seventy years later — there is little suggestion in the verse of Tennyson's future development, scarcely a hint of the texture and cadence of his finely executed classical idyls. More revealing than the poem itself is an aphorism on the title page in Latin, probably the poet's own, to the effect that "Hope nourishes youth and poetry, abuse oppresses and injures them" — a reaction perhaps to the hostility of his grandfather at Bayons and an early suggestion of what in time would become an almost morbid sensitivity to criticism.[15]

The "Advertisement" to *Poems by Two Brothers,* dated March 1827, though issued late in the preceding year, both acknowledges the derivative character of the work and attempts, with a dash of boyish bravado, to disarm the reviewers:

To light upon any novel combination of images or to open any vein of sparkling thought untouched before, were no easy task: indeed the remark itself is as old as the truth is clear; and no doubt, if submitted to the microscopic eye of periodical Criticism, a long list of inaccuracies and imitations would result from the investigation. But so it is: we have passed the Rubicon, and we leave the rest to fate; though its edict may create a fruitless regret that we ever emerged from "the shade," and courted notoriety.

The two brothers were Charles and Alfred, though they were joined in their quest for fame by a third when Frederick agreed to add several typically rhetorical pieces of his own. In general, Charles' contributions are short and quiet, precise in detail, flat in diction, uncertain in music. Alfred's, more wide-ranging in theme and more accomplished in technique, are more heavily addicted to the sort of fashionable erudition we find in Moore's *Lalla Rookh;* they seek to establish their authority by frequent quotation, technical allusion, and recondite gloss. When Alfred draws an image from microscopic science, for example, he must refer the reader to "Baker on Animalculae." His description of death all armed on a pale horse impels him to explain: "I am indebted for the idea of Death's Armour to that famous Chorus in Caractacus."

And his comparison of a lady's tresses to "a midnight cloud with silver moon-beams wove" demands a footnote declaring the simile to be "elicited from the songs of Jayadeva, the Horace of India."

Since much of the learning so self-consciously displayed can be traced to random reading in secondary sources,[16] we should not assume that the youth's fund of information was truly encyclopedic. Yet the poems themselves imply an active interest in quaint and curious lore, and their very titles often suggest the strong appeal of the exotic and the antique: "Persia," "Egypt," "The Druid's Prophecies," "Lamentation of the Peruvians," "Mithridates Presenting Berenice with the Cup of Poison," "Written by an Exile of Bassorah, while Sailing down the Euphrates." But more significant than such subject matter is the evidence throughout the volume of Tennyson's deep familiarity with the conventions of English poetry and the manner of the English poets. The style is a medley of echoes: the Miltonic roll of proper names, the choral rhythms of Dryden, the factitious thunder of Ossian, and the nostalgic croon of Tom Moore. Like much minor romantic lyricism, the verse is breathless with exclamation, and the description abounds in adjectives like "dewy," "silvery," and "shadowy," intended to assure a tremulous sensuosity. Of all the literary influences, that of Byron is the most immediate and apparent. The vistas of sublime gloom are but extensions of the Byronic landscape. And the lonely plaints of exiled chieftains recall the proud lament of the Byronic hero. Nearly all the Eastern pieces are indebted to the *Hebrew Melodies;* and "The Expedition of Nadir Shah into Hindostan" in particular is clearly a direct imitation, in idea, stanza, and meter, of "The Destruction of Sennacherib." Again and again the volume testifies to the devotion that led the boy of fourteen, on hearing the news from Missolonghi, to carve the fact on the sandstone, as if on his own numbed brain, "Byron is dead."

Tennyson, like his great exemplars Virgil and Milton, was

always the artificial poet in the sense that he drew deliberately
upon the traditional artifices of his craft; and in *Poems by
Two Brothers* we may find ample evidence of his literary
loyalties and derivations. But there is little more in the volume
than in the translation from Claudian to suggest the peculiar
temper of his art. The melancholy of "I Wander in Darkness and Sorrow," "Memory," and "Remorse" may in part
have been the poet's own, but it is expressed by world-
weary shades, "unfriended, and cold, and alone," who be-
wail their lost hope and innocence in a language far too
facile to ring true. Likewise the descriptive detail of "Midnight" and "On Sublimity" may arise from a characteristic
regard for the mystery of glimmering light and the half-
tones of dark; but whatever may be fresh in the vision is
carefully concealed by the clichés of an attenuated roman-
ticism. The best and most original work of Tennyson's youth
at Somersby remained unpublished during his lifetime. It
was excluded by design from *Poems by Two Brothers* as
being "too much out of the common for the public taste." [17]

In the brown sheepskin notebook that contains rough
drafts of several of the pieces selected to "court notoriety,"
there is an unfinished blank-verse drama, written when the
poet was fourteen or fifteen years old and published by his
grandson more than a century later.[18] Like the other early
exercises, *The Devil and the Lady* is highly derivative in
substance; but it is uninhibited by any care for popular stereo-
types, and its language has the sound of the living voice behind it.[19] Essentially a Jonsonian comedy of humors developed with boyish exuberance, the play concerns the effort
of an aged necromancer to escape being cuckolded by his
young wife. Departing on a long journey, Magus summons up
the Devil to protect his lusty Amoret from her suitors. Once
he is out of earshot, the lady may bid him a fitting farewell:

> Go thy ways!
> Thou yellowest leaf on Autumn's wither'd tree!

Thou sickliest ear of all the sheaf! thou clod!
Thou fireless mixture of Earth's coldest clay!
Thou crazy dotard, crusted o'er with age
As thick as ice upon a standing pool!
Thou shrunken, sapless, wizen Grasshopper,
Consuming the green promise of my youth!
Go, get thee gone, and evil winds attend thee,
Thou antidote to love!

The Devil sends Amoret to bed and he himself, disguised, receives her would-be lovers: Antonio the lawyer, Pharmaceutus the apothecary, Stephanio the sailor, Angulo the mathematician, Campano the soldier, and Benedict the monk, each speaking with propulsive energy the jargon of his own profession. Then as the action — or rather the talk — reaches a brawling climax, Magus, deterred indeed by ill winds, unexpectedly returns. The lovers hide; Magus meditates on life's mutabilities; the Devil taunts his victims — and the manuscript stops with a final explosion of metaphor and pun.

Having upbraided Amoret for her inconstancy, the Devil early in the play reflects on his own shortcoming as a demon, his lack of the requisite diabolic passion:

I am in troth a moralising devil,
Quite out o' my element; my element, fire.

From the outset he is less the agent of evil than the voice of moral irony, disdainful of trumpery and superstition, yet half-respectful of an orthodox faith:

I value not your amulets and charms
The twentieth part of half a rotten murphy
Or a split pea, albeit I do confess me
I'm apt to turn tail on an Ave-Mary,
And quail a little at a Pater-Noster,
Except when it's said backwards.

Somewhat anachronistically (for the setting is medieval), he hits at the snobbish fribbles of Regency society, with all the colloquial directness of the satiric Byron; women, he says, will abandon their intrigues

When cold shall rarify and heat condense;
When Almacks shall become the rendezvous
Of burly citizens and citizens' wives,
And Lady J - - y wearied shall throw down
The reins of Fashion and — think better things;
When high soul'd man shall walk upon his head,
When Colonel B - - y shall shake hands with Decency
And read or write a sermon.

Like the mature Tennyson and like the boy who told his brother to consider the great star-patches, the Devil perceives the littleness of man in a cosmic perspective. "What have the worlds," he demands,

Of yon o'er arching Heaven — the ample spheres
Of never-ending space, to do with Man?
And some romantick visionaries have deem'd
This petty clod the centre of all worlds.

And in the humility of his own ignorance he raises the ultimate Tennysonian question, the problem of appearance and reality:

O suns and spheres and stars and belts and systems,
Are ye or are ye not?
Are ye realities or semblances
Of that which men call real?
Are ye true substance? are ye anything
Except delusive shows and physical points
Endow'd with some repulsive potency?

Thus the skeptical reason leads the honest Devil, as it would lead Tennyson himself, through the speculation of science toward a new epistemology and a troubling metaphysic.

The venerable Magus, who is the Devil's counterpart, represents the positive voice, the hard-won assent to "life in all its variations." A garrulous old Faust, he stands ready to affirm the worth of his manifold adventure. Though he suspects that his confidence in Amoret may be misplaced, he clings, as he feels all men must, to a belief in some final good, for

> When the keen Ether is condens'd with frost
> Who would not cleave to th' sunny side of the wall?

And his dim trust anticipates verbally by some sixty years the sanguine counsel of the Ancient Sage, who has found surer grounds for optimism:

> Wherefore be thou wise,
> Cleave ever to the sunnier side of doubt
> And cling to faith beyond the forms of Faith.

Magus lives by illusion in the necessary assumption that it is the true illusion. He has the artist's faith in his own experience and imagining, and he earns at last the sympathy of the young poet. When he returns at the end of the play, he describes the sea and the storm in a blank verse no longer gleefully imitated from the Elizabethan drama but marked now by the distinctive, serious, and somber accent of the *Idylls of the King:*

> Each hoar wave
> With crisped undulation arching rose,
> Thence falling in white ridge with sinuous slope
> Dash'd headlong to the shore and spread along
> The sands its tender fringe of creamy spray. . . .
>
> Thrice with bold prow I breasted the rough spume
> But thrice a vitreous wall of waves up sprung
> Ridging the level sea — so far'd it with me
> Foil'd of my purpose.

Wearing "the mask of age," Tennyson thus realizes his own idiom and frees himself to speak his own emotion. In the final soliloquy of Magus we may find not only the theme of *The Devil and the Lady* as a whole but also the adolescent's dread, both pathetic and amusing, of the adult world that forever corrupts the naive sensibility of youth or — to borrow the imagery of Keats — darkens the Chamber of Maiden-thought:

> We follow thro' a night of crime and care
> The voice of soft temptation, still it calls

> And still we follow onwards, till we find
> She is a Phantom and — we follow still.
> When couched in Boyhood's passionless tranquillity
> The natural mind of man is warm and yielding,
> Fit to receive its best impressions,
> But raise it to the atmosphere of manhood
> And the rude breath of dissipation
> Will harden it to stone.

The distinction between the pure sensations of boyhood and the complex emotions of maturity recalls Wordsworth's more assured description of the stages of growth in "Tintern Abbey" and may be related to the same empirical psychology, the associationism of Hartley, that governs the theory of the *Lyrical Ballads*. Yet we find also in the earliest Tennyson, as in the Wordsworth of *The Prelude* or the "Intimations" ode, a nonempirical concern, a questioning of sense and outward things, a mystical response to life itself and to the call of the "far — far — away" beyond the present experience. As a man of thirty, he told Emily Sellwood of his continuing "passion of the past" and his rather Wordsworthian feeling of oneness with nature:

Dim mystic sympathies with tree and hill reaching far back into childhood. A known landskip is to me an old friend, that continually talks to me of my own youth and half-forgotten things, and indeed does more for me than many an old friend I know.[20]

His "mystic sympathies," however, were less equivocal than Wordsworth's, and his mistrust of appearance was more persistent.[21] His first poetry of tree and hill accordingly suggests little real devotion to natural objects for their own sake. Nature in an early Somersby piece like the "Ode: O Bosky Brook" is already an atmosphere rather than a tangible entity: the moon haunts a Tennysonian landscape, "the screaming waste of desolate heath"; the pastures are stilled and plangent, "soft as dewy sleep"; [22] the woods are charged with indeterminate life, the "counterchang'd embroidery of light and darkness"; [23] and the sea itself, all mutability and all permanence, is the sum of private impressions,

> The lighthouse glowing from the secret rock,
> The seabird piping on the wild salt waste.

In nature the sensuous emotions, the yearning and the loneliness, find their correlative. But the soul's true awakening is outside nature; it demands the muting of all sensation; the night, "august obscure," is both symbol and setting, "the mother of all thought," the retreat from "the goodly show" of the visible world and the approach to some deeper vision:

> Not that the mind is edged,
> Not that the spirit of thought is freshlier fledged
> With stillness like the stillness of the tomb
> And grossest gloom,
> As it were of the inner sepulchre.
> Rare sound, spare light will best address
> The soul for awful muse and solemn watchfulness.

In the hushed moments of withdrawal from the society of Somersby and at lonely intervals throughout his later life, Tennyson knew "a kind of waking trance," induced by the repetition of his own name.[24] Such a state always brought with it a greatly heightened consciousness of individuality and then a sudden release, a dissolving of the limits of selfhood until the infinite alone seemed real and "the loss of personality (if so it were) [was] no extinction but the only true life." But once the ecstasy had passed, the ego would reassert its indestructible separateness; then, said the poet, "I am ready to fight for *mein liebes Ich,* and hold that it will last for aeons of aeons." To the conscious will annihilation was inconceivable; to the spirit it was a fact of experience. And since Tennyson was committed both to the knowledge of things seen or felt in sensuous terms and to the reality of his private intuitions, his central concern with the individual soul and the problem of immortality was strangely ambivalent, charged with the tension of opposites.

"The Mystic," an early piece suppressed after its appearance in 1830, attempts to describe the waking trance as the
necessary prelude to vision; isolated from all who cannot
"read the marvel in his eye," the mystic

> often lying broad awake, and yet
> Remaining from the body, and apart
> In intellect and power and will, hath heard
> Time flowing in the middle of the night
> And all things creeping to a day of doom.

But the effort to objectify the deeply personal emotion by
assigning it to a third person leads to an evasive diction
and renders the poem unduly cautious and remote. The unpublished "Armageddon" (written at about the same time
as *The Devil and the Lady*) is more explicit in its "mystical"
detail and correspondingly more convincing. This intense
though shapeless dream allegory, which was later to supply
the nucleus of "Timbuctoo," delineates both the exultant
increase in self-consciousness and the ultimate absorption of
the ego:

> I felt my soul grow godlike, and my spirit
> With supernatural excitation bound
> Within me, and my mental eye grew large
> With such a vast circumference of thought,
> That, in my vanity, I seem'd to stand
> Upon the outward verge and bound alone
> Of God's omniscience. Each failing sense,
> As with a momentary flash of light,
> Grew thrillingly distinct and keen. . . .
>
> I wondered with deep wonder at myself:
> My mind seem'd wing'd with knowledge and the strength
> Of holy musings and immense Ideas,
> Even to Infinitude. All sense of Time
> And Being and Place was swallowed up and lost
> Within a victory of boundless thought.
> I was a part of the Unchangeable,

A scintillation of Eternal Mind,
Remix'd and burning with its parent fire.
Yea! in that hour I could have fallen down
Before my own strong soul and worshipp'd it.

So fortified, the soul may accept with joy the terrible apoc-
alypse in "a great day/ Of wonderful revealings, and vast
sights/ And inconceivable visions"; for the mind, now pure
intellect, has attained the detachment of the clear stars shining out

> with keen but fix'd intensity,
> All-silence, looking steadfast consciousness
> Upon the dark and windy waste of Earth.

Tennyson's sense of dissociation from the darkened earth
may be compared to the loneliness, the *isolement*, of Berlioz,
who throughout his life suffered a recurrent nostalgia, a
feeling that he might never find the home or the destination
he had glimpsed.[25] To a friend Berlioz complained: "Space,
absence, forgetfulness, pain and rage assailed me. Despite all
my efforts, life escapes me. I only catch shreds of it." [26]
Tennyson likewise knew moods of melancholy frustration,
the obverse of his ecstasy, and he often felt the burden of
aloneness. But unlike Berlioz he cherished his passion of the
past as a positive emotion, and he regarded isolation not
merely as the source of despondency but also on occasion
as the prelude to vision. His actual experience anticipates the
isolement of John St. Loe Strachey — who borrowed the
term from Berlioz. In *The Adventure of Living* Strachey
strove to define the mystical state which he had known from
childhood, a state which, he supposed, must have been familiar to Wordsworth and to Tennyson:

I was literally "beside myself." I stood a naked soul in the sight of
what I must *now* . . . call . . . the All, the Only, the Whole, the
Everlasting. . . . It was the amplest exaltation and magnification of
the Ego which it is possible to conceive. I gained, not lost, by discarding the "lendings" of life. Something that was from one point

of view a void, and from another a rounded completeness, hemmed me in.[27]

Strachey was aware that the new psychology might account for this state as an outcropping of the unconscious self in a sort of day dream, neither wonderful nor mystic. But he himself attached the highest metaphysical significance to his vision. "Certainly," he insisted, "to me the feeling was essentially one of revelation, of being suddenly made to see and understand things which before had been dark or unknown. . . . My *Ego*, whatever it was or was to be, was, I perceived, a spirit and not a creature of flesh-and-blood, and also not a hypothesis, but a reality." [28]

Tennyson like Strachey came to value his mystical experience as evidence of man's intrinsic spirituality. When all other faith failed him and the sensuous world seemed but the product of a blind evolution, the intuition of meaning, the call of the inner life, remained. Such was to be the real solution to the conflicts of *In Memoriam*:

> If e'er when faith had fallen asleep,
>   I heard a voice, "believe no more,"
>   And heard an ever-breaking shore
> That tumbled in the Godless deep,
>
> A warmth within the breast would melt
>   The freezing reason's colder part,
>   And like a man in wrath the heart
> Stood up and answered, "I have felt."

Though essentially religious in effect, the intuition had no direct relation to any formal orthodoxy. It was individual and private and precarious, a faith beyond the forms of faith. Beside it, revealed religion seemed a necessary concealment, a humanizing of realities passing human comprehension. "Who knows," Tennyson asked, "whether revelation be not itself a veil to hide the glory of that Love which we could not look upon without marring our sight, and our onward progress?" [29] As a poet he felt himself always something of the seer, privileged on occasion to receive intimations of the "glory." But as a man among his fellows he felt the necessity of accepting the human condition, the circumscribed unmystical vision, and the weight of the onward struggle. And during his adolescence, particularly — though sustained by the personal intuition — he was sensitive to his own human limitations, fearful of misunderstanding, reluctant to face the outside world.

Tennyson approached his college career with less eagerness than foreboding, as if Cambridge were to mark the end of the life of wonder rather than the beginning of a new freedom. His last Somersby poems are elegies to the passing of youth, memorials to a lost innocence. The most oblique of them, "The Outcast," dated 1826,[30] depicts a man of "worn mind and fevered brain," nostalgic for his father's home but unable to return to a past wrecked by time:

> I will not seek my father's hall:
> There peers the day's unhallow'd glare,
> The wet moss crusts the parting wall,
> The wassail wind is reveller there.
> Along the weedy, chinky floors
> Wild knots of flowering rushes blow
> And through the sounding corridors
> The sere leaf rustles to and fro:
> And oh! what memory might recall
> If once I paced that voiceless Hall!

Less objective in tone, the fragment "Memory" describes recollection as "a conscience dropping tears of fire," tormenting an unhappy present in which Hope, the true daughter of Memory, has been supplanted by "the faery changeling wan Despair . . . / A frightful child with shrivelled cheeks." The heavily textured "Ode to Memory," [31] however, salutes Memory as the bringer of joy from the bright past "to glorify the present." Memory now is imagination itself, the creative force, selecting and sanctifying impressions, add-

ing strength to the desolation of Lincolnshire and ineffable
peace to the garden of Somersby:

> Artist-like,
> Ever retiring thou dost gaze
> On the prime labour of thine early days:
> No matter what the sketch might be:
> Whether the high field on the bushless Pike,
> Or even a sand-built ridge
> Of heaped hills that mound the sea,
> Overblown with murmurs harsh,
> Or even a lowly cottage whence we see
> Stretch'd wide and wild the waste enormous marsh,
> Where from the frequent bridge,
> Emblems or Glimpses of Eternity,
> The trenched waters run from sky to sky;
> Or a garden bower'd close
> With pleached alleys of the trailing rose,
> Long alleys falling down to twilight grots,
> Or opening upon level plots
> Of crowned lilies, standing near
> Purple-spiked lavender.

As the poet moved into a less sequestered society, Somersby
became in retrospect an Eden isolated from contamination
by miles of lonely moorland. In a doggerel rhyme, which
must have been written about the time of his departure
for Cambridge, he pledged himself to his first affections.
"What," he asked,

> shall sever me
> From the love of home? . . .
> Shall extreme distress,
> Shall unknown disgrace
> Make my love the less
> For my sweet birthplace? [32]

The griefs of his childhood, his misery at Louth, the fear
of his father and for him, receded into his buried life; and
the remembrance of the complete harmony that perhaps
never was, except in the rare moments of vision, alone re-

mained active. Gradually his own past coalesced with his intuition of a larger reality, the "far — far — away" which had called to his youth. In later years he grew greatly as an artist in the power of expression and in the awareness of human problems and public issues; but the strongest motifs of his poetry, the sadness, the yearning, and the wonder, were rooted in the sensibility of the child and nurtured by his personal and private experience.

❧ II ❧

THE REVEREND WALLS

Cambridge, 1827–1831

CHARLES Darwin, whose three years at Christ's College coincided almost exactly with Tennyson's at Trinity,[1] described his Cambridge career as a waste of time "as far as the academical studies were concerned."[2] Tennyson eventually recognized his residence at the university as the decisive period of his intellectual development, but like Darwin he received no great stimulus from formal academic training. Though Trinity would ultimately salute him as one of her greatest sons,[3] during his own Trinity days he saw little to admire in the cold, remote hierarchy of scholars presided over by Master Christopher Wordsworth. From the outset he was impatient with the inflexibility of a curriculum in which, he said, "none but dry-headed, calculating, angular little gentlemen" could take much delight.[4] He showed no interest in mathematics, the prerequisite discipline for all who aspired to Honours. He already suspected that the Newtonian science, to which Trinity owed its pre-eminence among the Cambridge colleges, might be too mechanistic to account for an organic evolving world. And he felt the Christian deism preached by Paley of Cambridge in the late eighteenth century, which he was still expected to endorse, to be inimical to all his intuitions of God and nature. Untroubled by such misgivings and willing to conform for the sake of convenience, Darwin soon found relief from the

22

academic routine in the boisterous company of high-spirited young men. Tennyson, on the other hand, was slow to win the sympathy and respect he required of his fellow students. Rustic in speech, careless of dress, abruptly forthright in manner, and almost morbidly shy, he seemed to the more conventional undergraduates an aloof and disdainful aesthete, an eccentric as outrageous as his erratic brother Frederick. In his solitude he sought refuge in desultory unprescribed reading and in his own verse.

During his first months at Trinity he almost certainly must have continued work on "The Lover's Tale," [5] a strange long narrative begun at Somersby and completed many years later by a sequel drawn from Boccaccio. If so, the lover's confession of an overpowering passion for his foster-sister, whom he has adored from their common cradle with a quite Freudian intensity, could be construed as a reflection of the poet's own acute dependence upon his family and his regard for the bonds of consanguinity as protection against alien forces of neglect and misjudgment. And the lover's madness on learning that his beloved has pledged herself to another might perhaps be interpreted as the correlative to the disturbing conviction that "there was a want of love in Cambridge." [6]

Tennyson's hope, or rather his wish, that poetry might yet "startle the dull ears of human kind" animates a sonnet of 1828 and its vision of a new society:

> Methinks I see the world's renewed youth
> A long day's dawn, when Poesy shall bind
> Falsehood beneath the altar of great Truth.[7]

But his own art seemed committed to less purposeful objects, to the sensuous seductions of escape from all social concern. "Sense and Conscience," an unfinished and somewhat contrived allegory of about the same date as the sonnet, laments the defeat of the "Giant Conscience" by the "Arch-Enemy Sense" and his aesthetic, fleshly retinue,

witching fantasies which won the heart,
Lovely with bright black eyes and long black hair
And lips which moved in silence, shaping words
With meaning all too sweet for sound.[8]

Tennyson clearly mistrusted his own sensuous endowment,
and he was troubled by the claims of his own conscience.
Cambridge forced upon him a reappraisal of his moral and
religious attitudes, but its official high, dry theology and its
austere rationalism gave him no reassurance. His uneasiness
is already apparent in the fragmentary "Perdidi Diem," which
measures a personal maladjustment against the great order
of creation:

I must needs pore upon the mysteries
Of my own infinite Nature and torment
My Spirit with a fruitless discontent.[9]

And the malaise is explored at length in his "Supposed Confessions of a Second-rate Sensitive Mind," [10] which describes
in loosely rhymed octosyllabics the vicissitudes of a "damned
vacillating state." Torn by doubt, the "confessor" yearns for
a lost community of faith, even for a return to the secure
beatitude of infancy and the quiet certainties of his mother,
who would have ascribed his present confusions to the sin
of pride. Yet pride, at least in self-identity and the free moral
will, is, he feels, necessary to the spiritual life; and now even
pride is dead. Time was, he remembers, when doubt seemed
the human prerogative:

"Yet," said I, in my morn of youth,
The unsunn'd freshness of my strength,
When I went forth in quest of truth,
"It is man's privilege to doubt,
If so be that from doubt at length
Truth may stand forth unmoved of change. . . .
Shall we not look into the laws
Of life and death, and things that seem,
And things that be, and analyze
Our double nature, and compare
All creeds till we have found the one,
If one there be?"

But now he sees that doubt is not availing to all: "every-where/ Some must clasp idols." For doubt is merely a philo-sophic method; and the idol, or the fixed ideal, is essential to the "sensitive mind," to the artist who must suspend disbelief if he is to achieve aesthetic coherence.

Unmoved by the orthodox Anglicanism that rooted its defense in the *Evidences* and the *Natural Theology* of Paley, Tennyson was nonetheless suspicious of a faith resting on narrow piety and unreasonable emotion. Yet he could not have been unaware of the active and vociferous Evangelical party which had deeply influenced the conduct of a whole new middle-class society and was making its impression even upon Cambridge. As a leader of the Evangelicals, Charles Simeon, Fellow of King's College and incumbent of Holy Trinity for fifty-three years until his death in 1836, had as large and dedicated a following as Newman — to whom he otherwise bore little resemblance — was shortly to have at Oxford.[11] Though he never ceased inveighing against the paganism of the university community, Simeon had succeeded long before Tennyson's time in making Cambridge the princi-pal training ground for the Evangelical clergy and the strong-est force in the procurement of church patronage for those of Evangelical views. His preaching like Wesley's made its appeal to the feelings of the individual, to the fear of eternal punishment and the hope for salvation; and his impact arose from the singular zeal of his own personality. In his house he kept a portrait of the missionary Henry Martyn whose sober gaze, he declared, constantly admonished him: "Be serious — be in earnest — don't trifle."[12] Throughout his life he accordingly viewed himself and his work with an unrelenting gravity; and on his deathbed, he solemnly described himself as "the chief of sinners and the greatest monument of God's mercy."[13] His conduct, self-conscious and perhaps self-righteous, inevitably excited ridicule as well as admiration. Tennyson's friend Monckton Milnes, shortly after his arrival at Trinity, wrote home on hearing a sermon by Simeon: "His action is absurd in the extreme. He brandishes his spectacles when he talks of the terrible, and smirks and smiles when he offers consolation." [14] The Simeonites, or "Sims," however, saw nothing ludicrous in their master's deportment. Continuing his work with a complacent godliness and no doubt exaggerating his mannerisms, they persisted well into the Victorian period. In the fifties they first attracted, then repelled the young Samuel Butler — and so inadvertently supplied the excuse for an impish parody of their tracts and the substance of an acid chapter in *The Way of All Flesh*.[15]

We have no direct evidence of Tennyson's reaction to the creed or practice of Simeon or the "Sims." [16] But we do have a fair gauge of his attitude toward religious "enthusiasm" and self-mortification in "Saint Simeon Stylites," a satiric monologue written not long after his Cambridge days were ended.[17] And we may, not too fancifully, suspect a parallel with Simeon not only in the saint's name but also to some degree in his manner of speech:

> Altho' I be the basest of mankind,
> From scalp to sole one slough and crust of sin,
> Unfit for earth, unfit for heaven, scarce meet
> For troops of devils, mad with blasphemy,
> I will not cease to grasp the hope I hold
> Of saintdom, and to clamor, mourn, and sob,
> Battering the gates of heaven with storms of prayer,
> Have mercy, Lord, and take away my sin!

Browningesque before Browning, "Saint Simeon" is the vigorous dramatic characterization of a self-satisfied martyr who has enjoyed his suffering in the faith, never as fixed as he has proclaimed it, that he has won salvation:

> 'T is gone; 't is here again; the crown! the crown!
> So now 't is fitted on and grows to me,
> And from it melt the dews of Paradise,
> Sweet! Sweet! spikenard, and balm, and frankincense.
> Ah! let me not be fool'd, sweet saints; I trust
> That I am whole, and clean, and meet for Heaven.

Simeon of Cambridge was hardly such a man, but there was enough of self-approval in his bearing and of ostentatious self-abasement among his disciples to provoke Tennyson's hostility. In the *Decline and Fall*, Gibbon, who may have been among the poet's sources of information concerning the Syrian saint,[18] had commented that "this voluntary martyrdom must gradually have destroyed the sensibility both of the mind and body; nor can it be presumed that the fanatics who torment themselves, are susceptible of any lively affection for the rest of mankind." [19] Tennyson, who could recall the morbid Calvinism of his Aunt Mary Bourne,[20] likewise believed fanaticism of any sort destructive of human understanding; and in the fanatical narrowness of the Simeonites he could have found neither a satisfactory guide to the moral life nor a worthy poetic "idol."

Fortunately for the poet, however, the Evangelicals commanded far less attention at Trinity than a small group of religious liberals impatient with the old rationalistic orthodoxy and receptive to the newer German idealism and the scholarship of the Higher Critics. Among the resident fellows, Connop Thirlwall [21] was the most eager to give the curriculum of study a fresh philosophic emphasis and the readiest to fight for general university reform, including the admission of Dissenters to degrees. Inevitably he incurred the displeasure of the conservative Christopher Wordsworth, who eventually forced his resignation. But his battle against outmoded restrictions, as much as his breadth of knowledge, assured his appeal to intelligent undergraduates dissatisfied, as Tennyson was, with the prevailing apathy of their lecturers.

The ablest of Thirlwall's students, indeed the most brilliant young men of the college, were all members of the Cambridge Conversazione Society, better known — though at first derisively — as the Apostles, a closed coterie of varied talents aggressively responsive to new ideas. Already much influenced by the broad theology of Frederick Denison Maurice, who a few years earlier had given the group its

intellectual stimulus and direction, the Apostles elected
Thirlwall an honorary member and warmly welcomed his
concern with modern literature and his spirited defense of
positions later to be taken by the Broad Church movement.
For his part, Thirlwall saw in the Society the potential
leaders of a new culture, each making his own contribution,
each learning from the others. John Kemble, whom Tennyson hailed as "a latter Luther and a soldier-priest" but who
chose instead to become a respectable philologist, remembered the Apostles as the great liberating force of his life.
"To my *education* given in that society," he wrote, "I feel
that I owe every power I possess, and the rescuing myself
from a ridiculous state of prejudice and prepossessions with
which I came armed to Cambridge. From the 'Apostles' I,
at least, learned to think as a *free man*." [22] Tennyson had
perhaps fewer prejudices to overcome; but it was from the
Apostles, rather than from any formal instruction, that he,
too, obtained his real Cambridge education.

Immersed in German metaphysics, Kemble once gleefully
told his friends, "The world is one great thought, and I am
thinking it." [23] Tennyson moved less happily in the realms
of abstruse speculation; but he followed the philosophical
debates of the Apostles with close attention. Their discussion
of the idealists may well have helped him define his own
concept of the three "Eternal Truths," [24] which coincide
precisely with the Kantian sanctions of the moral imperative:
the providence of God, the freedom of the will, and the
immortality of the soul. Though Tennyson disliked the in-
volutions of Coleridge's prose, the Apostles' regard for the
Coleridgean view of human history as an organic process
undoubtedly left its mark on his social thought. He endorsed their hostility to the Benthamite ethic of expediency
and self-interest. [25] And he shared their dislike of the apolo-
getics of natural theology, upon which the Cambridge examiners still insisted. He must have sympathized especially

with Kemble's repudiation of Paley as a "miserable sophist," an attack which very nearly cost Kemble his degree.[26] Tennyson himself denied that an intelligible First Cause was properly deducible from natural phenomena, and he had no respect for the sort of cosmic optimism that had once led Paley to exclaim: "It is a happy world after all. The air, the earth, the water teem with delighted existence." [27] His own observations, and perhaps also his basic dread of passion, had made him distrustful of nature's waste and violence. "The lavish profusion . . . in the natural world," he said, "appals me, from the growths of the tropical forest to the capacity of man to multiply, the torrent of babies." [28] He was, in effect if not in conscious intention, a convinced Malthusian; and his attitude toward the universal struggle for survival may, like Darwin's, have owed a good deal to the contentious *Essay on Population*.[29] More readily than the other Apostles, he looked to modern science for the rapid extension of knowledge; but when faith rather than fact was his concern, he found in the spiritual philosophies of his friends reasoned support for his own intuitions.

Tennyson's resolute dedication to his poetry, while it isolated him from the irresponsible raucous life of the typical undergraduate, assured him his place among the intense Apostles, likewise aloof from the "Philistines or Stumpfs" [30] of the university. Yet as a poet he had a limited tolerance of the abstract and the inhuman, and he could not for long have found pleasure in the company of the Apostles had they been arid pedants pharisaically devoted to their own moral and intellectual difference. They were in truth young men of wit and feeling, moody, ironic, volatile, hot-tempered, earnest, and skeptical, loyal to each other but distinct in personalities and attributes. Tennyson admired them first of all as individuals, and he remembered most vividly the manner of their talk, rather than the precise matter, when years later he revisited the "reverend walls" of Trinity.

> Where once we held debate, a band
> Of youthful friends, on mind and art,
> And labour, and the changing mart,
> And all the framework of the land;
>
> When one would aim an arrow fair,
> But send it slackly from the string;
> And one would pierce an outer ring,
> And one an inner, here and there;
>
> And last the master-bowman, he,
> Would cleave the mark.

The "master-bowman" was Arthur Henry Hallam, by all reports the most agile of the Apostles in debate and the most radiant in personal charm.[31] To the young Tennyson, impressed by such apparently effortless poise as he had never witnessed at Somersby, Hallam seemed the incarnation of mental vigor and "graceful tact"; in him were all the virtues of reason and understanding:

> Heart-affluence in discursive talk
> From household fountains never dry;
> The critic clearness of an eye
> That saw thro' all the Muses' walk;
>
> Seraphic intellect and force
> To seize and throw the doubts of man;
> Impassioned logic, which outran
> The hearer in its fiery course.

More completely than any of the other Apostles, he embodied the gentlemanly ideal, as the new middle-class culture of the nineteenth century strove to redefine it. His nobility was no mere accident of birth; his sympathy, no gracious pretense. He was all "the gentleness he seemed to be," a man who joined

> Each office of the social hour
> To noble manners, as the flower
> And native growth of noble mind.

And thus — according to a suggestive though sadly prosaic
stanza of the great elegy he inspired —

> he bore without abuse
> The grand old name of gentleman,
> Defam'd by every charlatan,
> And soil'd by all ignoble use.

The hero-worship which marked Tennyson's friendship
with Hallam was more than generously reciprocated; for the
type of the ideal gentleman was confident that he had found
the type of the perfect artist, the "yearner for all fair things,"
the poet of the age to come whom the Apostles were "before-
hand with the time/ In loving and revering." [32] But the respect of each for extraordinary qualities in the other could
not alone have established the intimacy that lasted until Hallam's death or the memory that animated the long after-
years of Tennyson's life. The outward circumstances of
Hallam's career at Eton, in London, and in Rome were
assuredly remote from Tennyson's Somersby experience. But
his habit of melancholy introspection, the uncertainty behind
his restlessness, and the essential bewilderment of spirit that
commingled with his ebullience, these were familiar enough
to the poet, and they made of Hallam the object, as well
as the giver, of sympathy. Tennyson accordingly found in
his friend a reflection of his own sensibility, a sharer of his
emotion and even his mystical intuition,[33] a confidant whom
he could address as one he had always known:

> So, friend, when first I look'd upon your face,
> Our thought gave answer each to each, so true —
> Opposed mirrors each reflecting each —
> Altho' I knew not in what time or place,
> Methought that I had often met with you,
> And each had lived in the other's mind and speech.[34]

His actual meeting with Hallam early in 1829 and his
election to the Apostles in May of that year ended for
Tennyson a period of despondent loneliness and brought him

new confidence both as man and as poet. Trinity, which at first had seemed bleakly indifferent to him, became a source of encouragement and affection. Even the omniscient Whewell, his tutor, was content to countenance his lamentable neglect of mathematics for the pleasures of poetry.[35] He, in turn, grew a little less hostile to the conventions and disciplines of the university. At his father's urging he joined Hallam, Monckton Milnes, and others in the competition for the Chancellor's Medal to be awarded a poem on the assigned subject of Timbuctoo. Having no real interest in the theme, he sent home for the manuscript of "Armageddon" and freely adapted whole paragraphs therefrom, including the climactic mystical vision, to meet the needs of a new and not altogether congenial setting. So composed, "Timbuctoo" has no clear poetic logic or cogency. But the newly added warning of the Spirit of Fable, the mythic imagination, that Discovery, which is the temper of scientific rationalism, threatens to darken and destroy the fair city of the ideal remains a significant reflection of Tennyson's Cambridge experience and foreshadows a major concern of his later work. And the blank verse generally, an innovation at a time when prize poems were still written in heroic couplets, reaches its own sonority and force. At all events, the poem as a whole, despite its obscurity, struck the examiners as sufficiently imaginative to merit the award.[36] Tennyson, who knew the limitations of the piece, was reluctant to see it printed; it was, he felt, "much inferior to the unsuccessful Ode submitted by Hallam," [37] and prize poems, in any case, even the best ones, were not, "properly speaking, Poems at all." [38] But the Apostles thought such self-deprecation quite unnecessary. Charles Merivale, who had won the medal the year before, was proud to read the poem at Commencement when the poet was too diffident to appear. Hallam, writing to Gladstone, whom he had known at Eton, cited it as testimony that Tennyson promised "fair to be the greatest poet of our generation, perhaps of our century." [39] And on its publication Milnes reviewed it for the *Athenaeum* as the product of a "really first-rate poetical genius." [40]

Though other critics may have questioned their judgment, the Apostles were as devoted to literature as to philosophy, and the success of "Timbuctoo" made Tennyson at once their literary idol. They must therefore have looked forward with high hopes to the first paper he was to read at a formal Saturday session of the club. Tennyson struggled to meet his obligation, but after writing the better part of an essay on ghosts, he destroyed most of his attempt. Only the opening paragraphs remain in his notebook, and these suggest that the tone of the prose from the outset was either too factitiously Gothic or else too ironic for serious presentation. The teller of "deep, horrible agreeable ghost stories," he began,

will feel himself in possession of Power greater than that of the Caesars — a Power over the inmost recesses of the human mind, a despotism voluntarily submitted to with shuddering and with delight: every cheek is blenched, every eye fixed upon the narrator: he speaks in a simple manner of a high matter: . . . he unlocks with a golden key the iron grated gates of the charnel-house; he throws them wide open and forth issue from the inmost gloom the colossal Presences of the Past *majores humano*, some as they lived, seemingly pale with exhaustion and faintly smiling; some as they died in a still agony, like the dumb rage of the Glaciers of Chamouny, a fearful convulsion suddenly frozen by the chill of Death and some as they were buried, with dropped eyelids, in their cerements and their winding sheets.[41]

Such verbal conjuring was profitless; Tennyson could not continue, for he could not believe in his materials; the mystic of "Timbuctoo" could have no real commerce with black magic. He was accordingly forced to resign from the club, but was immediately made an honorary member, and as such his prestige seemed only the greater.

The reverence of the Apostles was of immeasurable stimulus to Tennyson as poet, though their excessive adulation made him more sensitive than ever to adverse criticism. But their specific influence on his work has frequently been overestimated. Their belief that poetry was in essence prophecy and that art should instruct as it delights coincided with his own most sanguine hopes and, besides, had ample precedent in the classical aesthetic theories he had already learned to respect. He himself made a sharper distinction than the Apostles Trench and Alford between poetic teaching and didacticism in verse. And he resisted the efforts of James Spedding and others to lead him into a poetry of direct social significance. Yet for a time he responded, as they did, to the moral energy of Shelley and the concept of poetry as the rouser of unawakened earth. Thoroughly Shelleyan in idea and imagery, "The Poet" sketched, perhaps for Apostolic edification, the myth of the ideal singer, born "in a golden clime" and blest with vision:

> He saw through life and death, through good and ill,
> He saw through his own soul.
> The marvel of the everlasting will,
> An open scroll,
>
> Before him lay; with echoing feet he threaded
> The secretest walks of fame:
> The viewless arrows of his thoughts were headed
> And wing'd with flame. . . .

The bringer of a new dawn, the seer prepared the way for the militant Freedom, whose weapon was poetry:

> Her words did gather thunder as they ran,
> And as the lightning to the thunder
> Which follows it, riving the spirit of man,
> Making earth wonder,
>
> So was their meaning to her words. No sword
> Of wrath her right arm hurled,
> But one poor poet's scroll, and with *his* word
> She shook the world.

"The Poet," however, remained a description of one poetic ideal rather than a program of action. Whatever courses he might be urged to pursue, Tennyson would make his own decisions, and he had no present desire to shake the world with thunderous revelation. In "The Poet's Mind" he defended a commitment to the aesthetic vision from the taunts of Blakesley, whose rationalism might wither the whole garden of fancy; half in earnest, half in jest, he drove off the cynic:

> Dark-brow'd sophist, come not anear;
> The poet's mind is holy ground;
> Hollow smile and frozen sneer
> Come not here.

But in yet another mood he could hail Blakesley as his

> Clear-headed friend, whose joyful scorn,
> Edged with sharp laughter, cuts atwain
> The knotted lies of human creeds,
> The wounding cords which bind and strain
> The heart until it bleeds.[42]

From the Apostles he learned the importance of being truly earnest, but also the role of sharp laughter or the calmer comic spirit in destroying pretense and complacency. In "A Character" he drew the portrait of Sunderland, the ablest of the Cambridge orators but a self-satisfied dandy, "quiet, dispassionate and cold":

> Most delicately hour by hour
> He canvass'd human mysteries,
> And trod on silk, as if the winds
> Blew his own praises in his eyes,
> And stood aloof from other minds
> In impotence of fancied power.

Actually a "character" in the Theophrastian sense, the satire carried a general truth for the poet himself, a reminder that the complete aesthete must always invite ridicule and that no mind, not even a poetic one, could thrive wholly apart from the rough world of men.

As his reputation grew at Trinity, Tennyson joined with less constraint in the social life of his college. To the Apostles and sometimes to less esoteric groups he would recite old ballads or read from manuscript his own verses in a rolling incantation, "mouthing out his hollow oes and aes." As a reader, in the manner perhaps of Dylan Thomas, he intoned his "deep-chested music" with so strong an awareness of assonance that the mere prose meaning of his words often receded beneath the surge of melody.[43] Some of his Cambridge poems like the exotic "Anacaona," which celebrates in lush rhymes "the golden flower of Hayti," or the mournful "Oriana," which in refrain and décor anticipates the Pre-Raphaelite ballads, seem to have been written solely for the purpose of sonorous declamation. In reading such pieces he lost his self-consciousness altogether and abandoned himself entirely to the enchantments of language.

He found release, too, in amateur theatricals, and his interpretation of Malvolio, starched and solemn, won warm applause. He amused the Apostles with his burlesque of the rotund and panting George IV and his impersonation of Milton's Satan as a toad at the ear of Eve.[44] He told earthy anecdotes of Lincolnshire in a broad native dialect. He improvised verse sketches of Cambridge notables and eccentrics. He fenced, he rowed, he took long walks with good companions. He began, in short, to display the genius for friendship and the intense magnetism of personality that in the years ahead would earn him intimacy with the greatest of the Victorians, a respectful affection quite independent of his almost incredible popularity as poet. Cambridge came to recognize his tall athletic figure, his darkly handsome features, his physical prowess. "It is not fair," his friend Brookfield complained, "that you should be Hercules as well as Apollo." [45] For the moment life seemed good, and the future a challenge and an appetite:

For I could burst into a psalm of praise,
Seeing the heart so wondrous in her ways,
E'en scorn looks beautiful on human lips!
Would I could pile fresh life on life, and dull
The sharp desire of knowledge still with knowing!
Art, Science, Nature, everything is full,
As my own soul is full, to overflowing. . . .
I thank thee, God, that thou hast made me live.[46]

There are, however, few psalms of praise in the volume
entitled *Poems, Chiefly Lyrical*, which Tennyson published,
with Hallam's encouragement, in June of 1830. Nor, apart
from the breezy chauvinism of "English War Song" and
the truer cavalier notes of "National Song" ("There is no
land like England"),[47] is there much exuberance of life.
Except in the early "Ode to Memory," personal emotion
is present only by implication. "The Mystic" purports to
be an objective character study. "Isabel," a highly idealized
tribute to the poet's mother (though the subject is not identified as such), touches only with the utmost tact and obliquity
on the domestic strife of Somersby, the good woman's
"courage to endure" and her quiet victories over "all the
outworks of suspicious pride." Even the intimate "Confessions" is made a matter of supposition and assigned ironically
to "a second-rate sensitive mind." The best of the pure
lyrics, "A Spirit Haunts the Year's Last Hours," transfers
a characteristic melancholy to the soul of a dying garden.
Death indeed broods over many of the poems; [48] but it is
an easeful death, without horror or self-involvement, a death
which is the surrogate of art. As in "The Sleeping Beauty,"
the stopping of motion makes possible an aesthetic arrangement:

Her constant beauty doth inform
Stillness with love, and day with light. . . .
She sleeps, nor dreams, but ever dwells
A perfect form in perfect rest.

And though Tennyson's own sense of perfect form remains
as yet largely undeveloped, his effort throughout the volume
is aimed at the sublimation of a still troubled sensibility and
the achievement of an autonomous aesthetic order.

Among the poems concerned directly or indirectly with
art, "The Poet" and "The Poet's Mind," as we have seen,
present diverse views of the artist's proper function and attitude. "The Sea Fairies" anticipates "The Lotos-Eaters" in
both theme and imagery as a dramatic rendering of the
seductions of a sensuous art, the temptations to escape from
reason and responsibility. And "The Dying Swan" suggests
that poetry, though achieved by lonely sacrifice, may bring
beauty and joy to the human wasteland, even as the wild
swan's death-hymn floods the barren plains and desolate creeks
"with eddying song." More elaborately wrought, often Keatsian in texture,[49] "Recollections of the Arabian Nights" may
be read as a narrative of the poetic quest rather than merely
as an exercise in orientalism. Recalling his childhood delight
in the exotic world of Haroun Alraschid, the narrator recounts the night journey of his boyish dreams, "adown the
Tigris," through a lush landscape, under overarching palms
dark as "another night in night," until his shallop emerges on
a broad level lake and touches the shore of an enchanted
garden, the epitome of a still and perfect art, where

> The living airs of middle night
> Died round the bulbul as he sung;
> Not he, but something which possess'd
> The darkness of the world, delight,
> Life, anguish, death, immortal love,
> Ceasing not, mingled, unrepress'd,
>   Apart from place, withholding time.

There he disembarks, sinks entranced upon the bank, as if
dying unto an old life, then arises reborn and enters a great
pavilion, where "with dazed vision" he beholds the lovely
Persian girl and at last the caliph himself, the patron of all

the arts, presiding over the wondrous creations he has inspired. Though hardly designed as consistent allegory, the
poem thus has definite overtones of aesthetic meaning, and
the progress of its action through what seems to be a partial
death into a rarefied and timeless life clearly invites some symbolic interpretation. Like ideal Byzantium to the mature and
highly disciplined Yeats, Haroun's Bagdad to the young
Tennyson is essentially the city of eternal artifice, in a realm
of self-subsistent reality beyond all movement and desire.

The ladies of the 1830 volume are the shadowy muses of
society verse: "airy, fairy" Lilian, fickle, amorous Madeline,
dream-smitten, "spiritual" Adeline.[50] Each is fashioned as if
for illustration in the style of the popular annuals of the
period, the Christmas gift books. None has a trace of true
vitality or passion. Adeline's reverie serves only to evoke
a series of balanced rhetorical questions and discreetly erotic
images. Madeline's moodiness provides the poet exercise in
varying his stanzaic tempo. And Lilian's flitting affords practice in the manipulation of light vowels and trochaic rhythms,
while her inane giggle merely exasperates:

> If prayers will not hush thee,
> Airy Lilian,
> Like a rose-leaf I will crush thee,
> Fairy Lilian.

Not to be confused with any of these is the intense Mariana,
who is not described at all but must be deduced from the
decaying house she lives in and its dreary setting in "the level
waste, the rounding gray." The one token of life in Mariana's
desolate world is a single poplar, "All silver-green with
gnarled bark," as tall and masculine as the lover who has
deserted her. Mocking and deluding, the tree becomes a
fixed obsession; its shadow sways constantly outside her cur-
tain and falls "Upon her bed, across her brow"; and its
rustling answer "to the wooing wind" joins nightmarish
creaks and ghostly voices wholly to confound her sense.

A study in frustration, which may have had its counterpart in the loneliness of Tennyson's first term at Cambridge, "Mariana" is more carefully shaped than any other poem in the volume. Its precise detail, its controlled assonance, its clear sensuous diction, and its consistency of tone and atmosphere, these qualities stamp it as a worthy product of the school of Keats. But the mode of rendering the emotion in lyric form through expressionistic description of setting is characteristically the poet's own.

Measured against "Mariana" and "Recollections of the Arabian Nights," most of the other pieces seem tentative in execution, far too completely given over to stylistic experiment. Many of them, breaking without apparent cause from fixed stanza patterns, fall shapelessly into irregular verse paragraphs, modeled perhaps on the units of the Coleridgean "ode." Tennyson's father had once advised him to "break [his] lines occasionally for the sake of variety";[51] and the broken meters of 1830 are ample evidence that the advice was taken to heart. Few of the poems establish the normative rhythm that is essential if departures from it are to have significant effect. The language, moreover, is frequently open to the charge of affectation; the archaism of the songs is strained and self-consciously poetic; and the free use of unnatural compounds, printed without hyphenation, like "summerpride," "diamondeyed," "blosmwhite," and "fountainpregnant," is almost always an impediment to the movement and an annoyance to the reader. Besides, though several of the lyrics succeed in the depiction of passing moods, there is nowhere in the volume an assured style for intellectual discourse; the "Supposed Confessions" loses much of its real poignancy in the diffuseness of its imagery and argument; and a rhyme like "The 'How' and the 'Why,' " which raises the serious problem of identity, sinks beneath the weight of its questioning into a foolish bathos. But the Apostles, who had heard many of the verses read from manuscript,

thought the beauties of the book far more considerable than
its shortcomings; their poet now belonged to the whole age,
and they would do what they could to advance his public
reputation.

For the present, however, Tennyson was concerned less
with the fortunes of *Poems, Chiefly Lyrical* than with the fate
of the Spanish liberals, whose conspiracy to overthrow a
reactionary government had enlisted the support of his
friends. Within a month of the volume's appearance, he was
off with Hallam across France to deliver "apostolic" funds
and code messages to the sinister Ojeda.[52] The secret rendezvous in the Pyrenees was without doubt the most fantastic
adventure of his life, and he was never to forget its wild
and rugged setting,

> Beside the river's wooded reach,
> The fortress, and the mountain ridge,
> The cataract flashing from the bridge,
> The breaker breaking on the beach.

But the rebel cause, doomed to failure from the first, merely
brought disillusion to the Apostles and a deep distrust of
political violence.

Back at Trinity in the autumn, Tennyson shared in the
excitement that presaged the first Reform Bill and in the
conservative fears of mass demonstrations, which threatened
an attack on the university itself. But before long he was to
have much more immediate cause for alarm, compared to
which his political anxieties seemed unmotivated and unreal.
Late in February of 1831 he was summoned home to attend
his father in his last illness. The gloom of Somersby closed
around him, and Cambridge, where his experience had been
mixed, became an image all of vitality and light.

❧ III ❧

THE MUSES' WALK

Arthur Hallam and the 1832 Poems

IN July of 1831 Hallam addressed an anxious inquiry to Tennyson's eldest brother: "Poor Alfred has written to me a very melancholy letter. What can be done for him? Do you think he is really very ill *in body*? His mind certainly is in a distressing state." [1] Tennyson had indeed been close to nervous collapse ever since his father's death in March. His sense of bereavement, greater than he could have anticipated, had led him into a not unfamiliar hypochondria. For a while in the spring he had tormented himself with an unnecessary fear of blindness, and for several months he had submitted to the rigors of an unpalatable diet. A real source of his misery was no doubt the burden of responsibility which had been thrust upon him in his new position as virtual head of the whole uneasy establishment at Somersby. He still wished to return to Cambridge and, in order to do so, was almost willing to satisfy his grandfather's requirement that he plan to enter holy orders. But he knew that he had no "call" to the Church; he felt his own religion at best still unsettled, and he questioned his capacities for moral action. He considered himself essentially the artist, but, despite the counsel of the Apostles, he was not at all sure how art might sustain society or even give him a means of self-support. Hallam, who alone understood his problems, strove to fortify in him the sense of dedication. Mingling healthy admonition with sympathy, he

42

wrote: "You say pathetically, 'Alas for me! I have more of the Beautiful than the Good!' Remember to your comfort that God has given you to see the difference. Many a poet has gone on blindly in his artist pride." [2]

If artist pride attended withdrawal from the public eye, Hallam resolved to correct the fault without delay. He quietly took upon himself the offices of amateur literary agent. Having failed to extract from Tennyson any of his more attractive manuscripts for periodical publication, he "placed" a competent, if rather unoriginal, sonnet, without the poet's consent, in the August issue of the *Englishman's Magazine* recently acquired by Edward Moxon, whom he had met in London. And to the same number he contributed his own essay "On Some of the Characteristics of Modern Poetry, and on the Lyrical Poems of Alfred Tennyson," a belated review of the 1830 volume which, though somewhat too indulgent, rightly linked his friend to the poets of sensation in the "aesthetic" school of Keats and boldly appraised his mastery of lyric moods and forms and his implicit resistance to the sort of didacticism demanded by most of the other Apostles. After a tour of the west country he met Tennyson at Sheffield to encourage his plans for new work and was much pleased to find him now "brimful of subjects and artist thoughts" [3] and eager at last to go forward. The appearance, in October, of two thin and dimly Keatsian sonnets in literary annuals was an event of no poetic importance but at least was a hopeful sign of recovery. By the end of 1831 Tennyson had fully responded to Hallam's stimulus. He was once again in close touch with his Cambridge friends and was already thinking of a new volume worthy of their approval.

In the early months of 1832, however, the Apostles found their central concern often more political than poetic. The Reform Bill, designed to widen the middle-class franchise, continued to excite their anxieties out of all proportion to the changes that the measure would actually effect. Tennyson

shared enough of their conservative fears to denounce privately

> the shallow fret and frothy fume
> Of brass-mouthed demagogues, O'Connell, Hume,
> And the others whom the sacred Muse of rhyme
> Disdains to name.[4]

But he was clearly less alarmed than Hallam or Spedding, and
when the bill at last became law, he felt so little dismay that
he rushed out in the "dead waste" of the Somersby night
to ring the church bells in public jubilation. As yet he had in
truth no very firm political conviction. If the Apostles suggested that he turn the disdainful muse toward social prophecy or analysis, he could render such counsels with an amused
irony as in the dissonant hammer-beat lines of "What Thor
said to the Bard before Dinner":

> On squire and parson, broker and banker,
> Down let fall thine iron spanker,
> Spare not king or duke or critic,
> Dealing out cross-buttock and flanker
> With thy clanging analytic.[5]

In the *Poems, Chiefly Lyrical* there had been no obvious
political bias, or at least none apparent to W. J. Fox, who
had praised the volume at length in the Radical *Westminster
Review*,[6] or to Leigh Hunt, who had mentioned it favorably
in the *Tatler*. But the mere presence of a liberal's admiration
was, at that politically sensitive time, in itself sufficient reason for a Tory's disparagement. Christopher North's notorious critique in *Blackwood's* for May of 1832 owed much
of its bitterness to the fact that kinder estimates had come
from less conservative periodicals.

North began his review with a virulent attack on the
critics, including Hallam, who had overstated the marks of
genius in the 1830 volume, and then with his own brand of
mocking overstatement he proceeded to demolish the "distinguished silliness" of a group of poems too slight to deserve

such invidious attention. He granted, however, the high
merit of "Mariana" and "Recollections of the Arabian Nights"
and admitted in summary that Alfred Tennyson was, after
all, "a poet." More diverted than annoyed by the article,
Hallam felt that it would serve to advance Tennyson's reputation, for North's attack, almost as much as his final concession, was evidence that the values of the poetry could not
be ignored even by an influential journalist known to be a
harsh judge of literature. The poet, on the other hand, thoroughly resented the flagrant mistreatment of Hallam and the
skittish petulance with which he himself had been censured as
an "owl," an author of "dismal drivel," and an affected,
often less than sane, aesthete. Unable as always to accept
adverse criticism with equanimity, he penned the testy squib
"To Christopher North":

> You did late review my lays,
>   Crusty Christopher;
> You did mingle blame and praise,
>   Rusty Christopher.
> When I learnt from whom it came,
> I forgave you all the blame,
>   Musty Christopher;
> I could *not* forgive the praise,
>   Fusty Christopher.

Dread of further attack undoubtedly delayed for a while
the publication of a new volume. But Tennyson was too
confident in the spring and summer of 1832 to experience
the pains of a wounded sensibility as acutely as he would in
the years that lay immediately ahead. His friends were
drawing him back from solitary self-absorption into a half-
forgotten conviviality. For five weeks at Somersby he played
host to Hallam, fresh from the "brawling courts / And dusty
purlieus of the law." In June he met Hallam, Kemble, and
Spedding in London and discovered for himself the life of a
great city, where in another mood he had once been oppressed

by the morbid thought that before long "all its inhabitants would be lying horizontal, stark and stiff in their coffins." [7] And in July he and Hallam made a tour of the Rhine valley, visited Cologne and Bonn, and climbed the Drachenfels — a holiday remembered in the doggerel of "O Darling Room," probably written for Hallam's amusement. [8]

> For I the Nonnenwerth have seen
> And Oberwinter's vineyards green,
> Musical Lurlei; and between
> The hills to Bingen have I been,
> Bingen in Darmstadt, where the Rhene
> Curves toward Mentz, a woody scene.

After Germany came an idyllic interlude at Somersby: Hallam's courtship of Emily Tennyson, his readings in the Tuscan poets, the ballads flung to the moon, the threading of "some Socratic dream," the woodland rambles, and the "wine-flask lying couch'd in moss." At such a time the castigations of a reviewer must have seemed of little meaning or consequence. But Tennyson, readying his manuscripts for the printer, insisted nonetheless, against Hallam's wiser judgment, that the epigram to North remain among them.

After various delays the volume finally appeared under Moxon's imprint in December, titled simply *Poems* and dated — no doubt to extend its currency — "1833." No longer "chiefly lyrical," most of the pieces were conceived as dramatic units and developed at some length in terms of allegorical narrative and symbolic description. Though some would be suppressed altogether and many would undergo strenuous revision before reissue ten years later, the best of them already revealed a considerable advance in craftsmanship over the 1830 verses and a far firmer control of theme. To any reader who valued the poetic imagination as such, "The Hesperides," "The Lotos-Eaters," "Oenone," "The Palace of Art," and "The Lady of Shalott" should have been ample evidence of a new and vital force in English poetry.

Hallam and the Apostles were understandably sanguine. Yet the volume was even less cordially received by the press than its predecessor; with few exceptions, the reviewers [9] found it affected and "metaphysical," alien to their own literary prejudices and remote from the problems of their time. Three somewhat contrived sonnets did approach political issues; but the "Buonaparte" insisting that the lust for power was self-defeating seemed irrelevant to the England of 1832; and the two self-consciously Miltonic pieces on Poland's resistance to tsarist terrorism attracted little attention. As a whole the book was indeed by design neither topical nor timely. Its real concern was with the essence of art itself and the function of the artist in a more or less misapprehending society.

Of all Tennyson's poems, "The Hesperides" is his most eloquent defense of a pure poetry isolated from the rude touch of men. In its self-subsistent mythology, the sacred tree of the golden apples is the counterpart of the aesthetic ideal, and the daughters of Hesperus who guard the tree, with the help of their father and an inexorable dragon, are the correlatives of the artist or, more generally, of the mind devoutly dedicated to the imaginative life.[10] Hercules, one of whose labors in ancient legend is to slay the dragon and to steal the fruit, has yet to invade the garden of the West; but a premonition of the danger he will present fires the song of the sisters, forever fearful that "one from the East" may discover their secret. The East is the common day of human action; the West is the evening of a consecrated half-light, of mystery and quiet contemplation and "hoarded wisdom." "All good things," sing the Hesperides, "are in the west"; and their incantation rises magically to celebrate the harmony, the aesthetic oneness, of their western world:

> But when the fullfaced sunset yellowly
> Stays on the flowering arch of the bough,
> The luscious fruitage clustereth mellowly,

Goldenkernelled, goldencored,
Sunset-ripened, above on the tree.
The world is wasted with fire and sword,
But the apple of gold hangs over the sea.
Five links, a golden chain, are we,
Hesper, the dragon, and sisters three,
Daughters three,
Bound about
All round about
The gnarléd bole of the charméd tree,
The golden apple, the golden apple, the hallowed fruit,
Guard it well, guard it warily,
Watch it warily,
Singing airily,
Standing about the charméd root.

Drawing in part on similar imagery, "The Lotos-Eaters"
associates a sensuous intoxication, and, implicitly, one sort of
aesthetic experience, with release from the active struggle in a
"long rest or death, dark death, or dreamful ease." Rolled
wearily shoreward, Ulysses and his men come upon a land of
perpetual afternoon, bathed in a mellow amber light, a still
land where "the charmed sunset" lingers "in the red West."
But the mariners, unlike the Hesperides, serve no hieratic
function. Drugged by the lotos bloom, they gain no quickened
awareness of the beauty about them. Languorously they
seek to lose themselves in a "half-dream" of quietude. They
envy the natural spontaneity with which, carefree and un-
questioning, "the folded leaf is wooed from out the bud."
Yet they themselves cannot attain the serene thoughtlessness
of earth. The memory of old responsibilities shadows their
peace. And an ill-concealed sense of guilt lurks behind their
resolution to war no more with evil. Thus, though they hymn
the enchanted landscape with the richest assonance and in the
most Keatsian detail of which the poet is capable, they remain,
in spite of themselves, too desperately eager for the beautiful
illusion to achieve its calm. By indirection the argument itself
suggests that an easeful escape from life into an inhuman

passivity, an amoral art for art's sake, is neither entirely possible nor humanly desirable.

More explicitly and with a greater measure of self-identification, "The Lady of Shalott" explores the maladjustment of the aesthetic spirit to the conditions of ordinary living. Though the lady, in this first of Tennyson's Arthurian poems,[11] will reappear as Elaine of the *Idylls of the King*, she is here a grander and more elusive figure than the pathetic, love-smitten ingenue, "the lily maid of Astolat." She is the dedicated artist, the complement or antitype of the poet, perhaps properly to be understood in Jungian terms as the anima, the unconscious self.[12] And the curse upon her is the endowment of sensibility that commits her to a vicarious life. Confined to her island and her high tower, she must perceive actuality always at two removes, at a sanctifying distance and then only in the mirror that catches the pictures framed by her narrow casement; and, though sometimes disconsolate and "half sick of shadows," she must continue to weave her sublimated impressions of the world below into "a charméd web." When the image of the bold Lancelot, who represents all the vitality she has been denied, flashes before her, she can no longer endure the burden of isolation; she turns to confront experience directly, and the magic web at once disintegrates. Released from the spell but herself destroyed, she floats, like the dying swan "chanting her death song," down by night to Camelot, where her beauty inspires awe but no real understanding:

> They crossed themselves, their stars they blest,
> Knight, minstrel, abbot, squire and guest.
> There lay a parchment on her breast,
> That puzzled more than all the rest,
>   The well-fed wits at Camelot.
> *"The web was woven curiously,*
> *The charm is broken utterly,*
> *Draw near and fear not — this is I,*
>   *The Lady of Shalott."*

In the last stanza of the 1842 version, the fine irony of Lancelot's tribute to the lady's "lovely face" supplants the perplexity of the comfortable townsmeñ. Yet the mere presence in the 1832 poem of the "well-fed wits" (who are judged by the epithet) underscores Tennyson's mistrust of the philistines and at the same time affirms his essential sympathy with the artistic temper which is both blessed and cursed by its difference.

Though far less tightly unified than "The Lady of Shalott," two insubstantial pieces in the mode of the gift books likewise portray the feminine soul, the anima, in esoteric withdrawal from life, a retreat represented, as in "The Hesperides," by the symbol of evening light. Margaret is seen in the context of the remote transfiguring West:

> You are the evening star, alway
> Remaining betwixt dark and bright:
> Lull'd echoes of laborious day
> Come to you, gleams of mellow light
> Float by you on the verge of night.[13]

And Eleänor, born "far off from human neighbourhood, "is placed against "the steady sunset glow" and given the aesthetic capacity to neutralize all strident natural emotion:

> In thee all passion becomes passionless,
> Touch'd by thy spirit's mellowness,
> Losing his fire and active might
> In a silent meditation,
> Falling into a still delight,
> And luxury of contemplation.

Neither of these "fancy portraits," however, approaches true roundness as a depiction of the aesthetic soul. Neither compares in depth or cogency with "The Palace of Art," which explores with mixed feeling the moral consequence of devotion to an isolated beauty.

At Cambridge Richard Trench, the most solemn of the Apostles, once severely reminded the poet, "Tennyson, we cannot live in art." [14] And as late as 1832 Trench still apparently required reassurance, for Hallam felt it necessary to explain to him somewhat apologetically, lest Tennyson be mistaken for the complete aesthete, that "Alfred's . . . nervous temperament and habits of solitude give an appearance of affectation to his manner, which is no interpreter of the man, and wears off on further knowledge." [15] But by the spring of that year the Apostles had clear evidence of Alfred's higher intentions. "The Palace of Art," circulating in manuscript, had won the strong approval of Merivale and Spedding, and both were vocal in declaring the soundness of its sentiment. Described as "a sort of allegory," the poem in its first published version was addressed to an unidentified "Friend" who as "an artist" would "understand / Its many lesser meanings." The dedication made the moral purpose of the whole abundantly clear; selfish absorption in the beautiful was "sinful,"

> And he that shuts Love out, in turn shall be
> Shut out from Love, and on her threshold lie
> Howling in outer darkness.

The lesser meanings were not so obvious; they might be deduced only from the texture of the verse, from the care with which the dangerous seductions of art were described, and from the sureness of the imagery with which the psychological experience of the artist was traced.

A pastiche of impressions rather than a single organic unit, "The Palace of Art" moves by delays toward its preconceived solution. The over-all proportions are arbitrarily ordered; and Tennyson in revising the poem for later editions was able to add, subtract, and transpose without in any way disturbing his argument. Yet he was unwilling in 1832 to sacrifice details for which he could find no place; and he introduced footnotes to carry rejected stanzas on sculpture and astronomy which he might have included in the text if he had been sure that the lines had "succeeded" or "the poem were not already too long." The strength of the piece until near the end lies indeed in an accumulation of disparate passages, sharp vignettes, and sudden insights. Built as a perfect square on a lofty crag-platform, misted off from the life of the valley below by four high-vaulting fountains, the palace itself with its gilded gallery and its statues tossing incense from golden cups is pretentiously ornate in its décor; but its spacious apartments contain tapestries and paintings of a purer beauty, portraits of austere poets and philosophers, religious and mythic icons, landscapes dramatically lit or serene as a canvas by Constable:

> One showed an English home — gray twilight pour'd
> On dewy pastures, dewy trees,
> Softer than sleep — all things in order stored,
> A haunt of ancient Peace.

The "vain-glorious, gorgeous soul" for whom the "lordly pleasure-house" has been devised beholds all its furniture with pride and lives vicariously — without commitment — through all its records of human struggle and triumph:

> "I take possession of men's minds and deeds.
> I live in all things great and small,
> I dwell apart holding no forms of creeds,
> But contemplating all."

And like Vathek before her or Dorian Gray long after, she savors all sensations of taste and "deep or vivid colour, smell and sound" until at the end of three years she meets the nemesis of the decadent: satiation and ennui. Then, lest she be destroyed, God, who knows "the abysmal deeps of Personality," [16] plagues her with a despair which kills all remnants of self-assurance within her. Forthwith her mind becomes an arena of conflicting emotion, of terror and defiance and protective irony:

> Deep dread and loathing of her solitude
> Fell on her, from which mood was born
> Scorn of herself; again, from out that mood
> Laughter at her self-scorn.

Uncertain shapes and Dantean phantoms with "hearts of flame" close in upon her as her very palace walls mirror back the living death of the spirit, a decay which reduces the soul to "a spot of dull stagnation,"

> A still salt pool, lock'd in with bars of sand,
>   Left on the shore, that hears all night
>   The plunging seas draw backward from the land
>   Their moon-led waters white.

Lost, "exiled from eternal God" and "all alone in crime," she reaches at last an awareness of her "sin" and in atonement discards her royal robes and descends to the human valley. But, compared to the residence she has abandoned, the "cottage in the vale" she now seeks seems but a vague objective; and her final desire to return with others to the palace when she has purged her guilt leaves quite uncertain the extent to which she will ever recognize the claims of society. Meanwhile, even the cottage life may prove another hedonistic adventure, an exploitation of simplicity as relief from excessive ornament.

Nevertheless, though "The Palace of Art" supplies no very convincing alternative to the aesthetic retreat, it delineates with some clarity the artist's confused state of mind, his isolating endowment and the burden of communication that he may feel forced upon him. No other poem of the 1832 volume registers so directly or didactically the poet's reluctant sense of social responsibility. But several dramatize closely related themes: the loneliness of the sensitive soul and the unhappy impact of self-indulgent passion. "Mariana in the South," like the earlier "Mariana," treats of unfulfilled love in terms of a setting which images frustration; but the actual house of the deserted girl is now of less importance than the sterile landscape beyond, the "burning sand" and "dry salt-marshes," and the cruel delusive dream of a walk in fertile fields beside full-fed brooks, among "the spikéd maize." The lyric later to be called "Fatima" presents, with a quite uncharacteristic abandon, a fiercer lust of the flesh, likened

to the pulsing heat of the sun that leaves the spirit "parch'd
and wither'd" in the vain desire for absolute possession. And
"The Sisters," which in style and situation foreshadows the
ballads of William Morris, tells the tale of an amoral lady
who, deranged by sexual jealousy, makes a comely artifact of
the man she has murdered. Similar motifs, handled with
greater restraint, combine to produce "Oenone," which describes the judgment of Paris through the lament of his forsaken first love. The spurning of Pallas, who has offered the
young sensualist the wisdom born of "self-reverence, self-
knowledge, self-control," for Aphrodite, who promises him
"the fairest and most loving wife in Greece," marks the victory of beauty for beauty's sake, almost of art for art's sake,
which will bring disaster to the whole ancient culture. But
Oenone herself is not guiltless; in yielding desperately to passion, she must suffer its torment. Her will not to die alone and
her "far-off doubtful purpose" of revenge relate her to a larger
tragedy than she can know, for the fire that burns her heart already prefigures the flames of Troy.

Helen, who is the immediate object of Oenone's hate,
leads the train of fateful ladies in "A Dream of Fair Women,"
each the symbol of "Beauty and anguish walking hand in
hand/ The downward slope to death." The cold bewildered
victim of desire, Helen regrets her life; "Where'er I came,"
she sighs, "I brought calamity." Iphigenia, who stands beside her, recalls the nightmare of her sacrifice, the ships and
temples flickering in the intense light of Aulis and the "stern
black-bearded kings with wolfish eyes," immovable in
their dark resolve. Cleopatra, on the other hand, cherishes
defiant memories of her life in Egypt, of Antony and his
passionate embraces, wit, and extravagance, "realm-drain-
ing revels," and the final courage to die. Jephtha's daughter
mingles nostalgia and exultation as she relives her eager
girlhood in the gardens of Israel and its high fulfillment in
submission to the divine purpose. But the fair Rosamond

remembers only a sad betrayal and "the dragon eyes of anger'd Eleanor." Meanwhile, the poet before whom the vision unrolls remains perplexed by the problem of evil and powerless, as a dreamer must be, to avert the defeat of gentleness, when

> All those sharp fancies, by down-lapsing thought
> Stream'd onward, lost their edges, and did creep
> Roll'd on each other, rounded, smooth'd and brought
> Into the gulfs of sleep.

In the forest of the dead past, where he meets the lost ladies, he finds tokens of his own youth; and the smell of violets pours back into his "empty soul" the recollection of a time when he himself was "joyful and free from blame," an innocent in a world of pure sensations unclouded by moral misgiving or social demand.[17]

The original introduction to "A Dream of Fair Women," which likened the ideal poet to a balloonist sailing above the "solid, shining ground," seeing all in a broad new perspective, and waving signal flags to an earth-bound audience, was deleted from later editions of the poem. But the simile, though awkwardly topical, nevertheless helps suggest the mood of all that is best in the 1832 volume. The dream-vision itself has the dreamlike blend of participation and detachment that Tennyson still associated with the aesthetic act, the imaginative acceptance of diverse emotions and the careful maintenance of distance and necessary disinterest. If the poem shows a personal concern with the fate of all beauty that must die, it also reveals a power of objective portrayal, a skill at dramatizing temperament through the deft use of symbolic setting. In drawing on the historical or mythic past, it escapes the pressures of modern "realism." The fair women, especially Cleopatra and her antithesis, Jephtha's daughter, transcend the accidents of a particular time, for the detail that sharpens their portraits is psychologically rather than literally accurate. Like Oenone, the Lady of Shalott, and the daughters of Hesperus, they move across a literary landscape which requires no concession to any specific local color.

On the other hand, the May Queen and the Miller's Daughter, who also find places in the volume, are set against an explicitly English backdrop drawn with close regard for homely circumstance. Each stands in effect at the center of a genre study contrived and sentimental but nonetheless recognizably "real" in its properties. The mawkish "New Year's Eve" strives to render pathetic the death of "little Alice," the May Queen, by calling attention to the domestic delights she must leave behind, her garden tools upon the granary floor and the rosebush trained about the parlor window. And "The Miller's Daughter," redeemed in part by a playful irony, unfolds its tale of wedded love in a series of staged vignettes of the miller and his chair, the long and listless boy trout-fishing beside the chestnut boughs "that hung / Thick-studded over with white cones," and the reflection in the mill-pond of "a full fair form" leaning across "a long green box of mignonette." Neither piece engages the poetic imagination; the pictorial detail in each, applied rather than felt, delineates a familiar scene but carries no overtone of larger meaning or suggestion. Yet the reviewers of the *Poems*, who in general had small praise for "The Hesperides" or "A Dream of Fair Women," found the domestic idyls simple and unaffected, "very sweet and natural," [18] evidence presumably that the poet could on occasion descend from his balloon to record the surfaces of English life in the early nineteenth century. And Moxon must have shared something of their taste, for when he first saw the manuscript, he was, according to Hallam's report, "in ecstasies with the 'May Queen.'" [19] Under such stimulus Tennyson was to yield frequently in later years to the popular vogue of actualism, the rendering in idyllic terms of sharply visualized fact and gesture; and the concern with tenderly graphic sentiment, to which he could never have felt deeply committed, would often serve merely to furnish escape from his own doubt and passion.

On glancing at the 1832 *Poems*, Coleridge, less responsive than he once had been to new work, complained that Tennyson had begun "to write verses without very well understanding what metre" was.[20] A century later, however, T. S. Eliot, impressed by the high technical competence of the volume as a whole, remarked of "The Hesperides" in particular that "a young man who can write like that has not much to learn about metric."[21] Yet even Coleridge, who was clearly disturbed by certain real irregularities of rhythm and stanza pattern, confessed to finding "some things of a good deal of beauty" among the pieces he had examined. And indeed it is difficult to believe that any impartial critic could have failed to find at least some token of a serious and dedicated talent. But few reviewers of the 1830s practiced or even professed critical disinterest; and the most influential of all who dissected the volume was openly hostile and flagrantly abusive. In the *Quarterly* for April 1833, John Wilson Croker, remembering his old antipathy to Keats, sought to demolish Tennyson as the latest and feeblest member of the "Cockney School" by exposing every possible blemish of image or diction and by heaping ridicule upon the defenseless "Darling Room" and the unfortunate squib "To Christopher North." If it could not kill, the assault nonetheless left deep scars upon the poet's sensibility. Tennyson remembered Croker's vituperation all his life; and especially during his long productive "silence," when he revised and reshaped most of the condemned poems, he returned repeatedly to Croker's specific strictures.

Convinced that the political bias of the *Quarterly* was common knowledge, Hallam tried to persuade him that the review had in any case called attention to the poetry and so, in spite of itself, might eventually do more good than harm. Though reluctant to be consoled, Tennyson must have drawn some amused satisfaction from Hallam's report that the Cambridge Union, ignoring the attack or else defying it, was about to debate the solemn question: "Tennyson or Milton, which

the greater poet?" [22] And however much his "artist pride"
had been wounded by public obloquy, he could not betray
the confidence of Hallam himself, whose loyalty had known
no bounds. Fearful of a latent self-pity he more and more
yielded to his friend's irresistible faith that "poems are good
things but flesh and blood is better." [23] Throughout the
summer of 1833 he continued his writing with a renewed
assurance, probably derived in large measure from the personal happiness he found in the lives of those about him,
above all in Hallam's engagement to Emily and the resultant
joy at Somersby. Whatever its source, an unusual contentment animated "The Gardener's Daughter," the new long
idyl of domestic romance that he read aloud at a farewell
supper in his London lodgings given for Hallam early in
August just before the latter's departure on a holiday tour of
the Continent.

In September he must have shared vicariously in Hallam's
excitement over the galleries of Vienna as described in an
ecstatic letter, the final sentences of which would always
remain fresh in his memory:

and oh Alfred such Titians! by Heaven, that man could paint! I
wish you could see his Danaë. Do you just write as perfect a Danaë!
Also there are two fine rooms of Rubens, but I know you are an
exclusive, and care little for Rubens, in which you are wrong: al-
though no doubt Titian's imagination and style are more analogous
to your own than those of Rubens or of any other school. [24]

It was fitting that the letter should conclude with so generous
a compliment; for it was to be the last word to Tennyson
from the one who had best understood his character as man
and as poet and who had most warmly encouraged his gifts
of imagination and style. In less than a fortnight Hallam was
dead; and Tennyson was left with an abrupt sense of un-
deserved life and a sudden need to question the meaning
of all flesh and blood and the ultimate worth of any art.

❧ IV ❧

A USE IN MEASURED LANGUAGE

The Silent Years, 1833–1842

THREE months after his son's death, Henry Hallam, mastering his grief with stoic reason, told Tennyson that he himself had found "occupation and conversation . . . very serviceable" and that he feared the poet's "solitary life . . . in the country" must be "sadly unpropitious."¹ But his solicitude, though well intentioned and generous, showed little understanding of the emotional needs of a young man as introspective by temperament as Arthur himself had been, and far less responsive to outward stimulus. In an almost suicidal gloom, Tennyson was still unprepared to turn for solace to social conversation. He had first to face the specters of his own doubt and bewilderment. Yet insofar as his poetry was concerned, his solitary self-communing was in no way unpropitious.

Though he must often have brimmed "with sorrow drowning song," in the dark autumn of 1833 he also knew frequent moods of less acute anguish when he might discover "a use in measured language," a mode of sublimating or at least ordering his despair in words that would "half-reveal and half-conceal" his troubled feelings. He had already made a number of scattered entries in what was in effect the intense private diary later to be reshaped into *In Memoriam*.² He had come to see the role that the dead Hallam was to play as an influence on his future:

59

Whatever way my days decline,
I felt and feel, tho' left alone,
His being working in mine own,
The footsteps of his life in mine.[3]

And in less elegiac verses he had begun to argue with himself the counter claims of dying and living, denial and assent.

Deliberately conceived to express "the need of going forward," [4] "Ulysses" is clearly the most vigorously assertive
of the poems occasioned by Hallam's death. Drawing from
Dante rather than Homer the suggestion of the hero's last
voyage, Tennyson invokes the image of travel as the symbol
of a continuum, a restless aspiration coincident with life
itself. The resolve of Ulysses to find fulfillment in action
parallels and indeed echoes, as Professor Bush has noted,
Hamlet's awareness that a man is less than human

If his chief good and market of his time
Be but to sleep and feed

and if he allow his "capability and god-like reason / To fust
in [him] unused." [5] But while Hamlet is concerned to execute
a reasoned purpose, Ulysses is driven, Faust-like, to follow endlessly unsatisfied desire as a good in itself. His challenge to heroic hearts assumes hope only where there is
movement, and life where there remains the will "To
strive, to seek, to find, and not to yield."

As it appears in the rough first draft in Tennyson's notebook, the monologue develops this yearning in a vein more
lyrical than dramatic. Ulysses is absorbed exclusively in his
own inability to pause, to make an end. He has nothing to say
of Telemachus, and he shows no condescension to the
blameless round of common duties he must abandon. The
past that he remembers is largely painful:

Much have I suffered [6]

stands austerely in place of the final

All times I have enjoyed
Greatly, have suffered greatly, both with those
That loved me, and alone.

And the future holds the possibility of noble toil, but not as yet the conviction that "Though much is taken, much abides," nor the promise of the evening sea:

> The lights begin to twinkle from the rocks;
> The long day wanes; the slow moon climbs; the deep
> Moans round with many voices. Come, my friends,
> 'Tis not too late to seek a newer world.

The first version, made before the end of 1833, is, in short, still too close to a personal description of what the poet felt — or at least determined to feel — to achieve either the full sense of character or the fine balance of rhetoric that make memorable the published poem. Yet it already seeks objectivity in that it masks the sorrow of uncertain youth in the experience of nostalgic but resolute age. And already it evinces a characteristic and original control of the blank-verse medium: deft manipulation of the caesural pause; considerable metrical variety from the iambic norm, obtained in large part by the free use of the initial trochee and the sudden gravity of the medial spondee; and, above all, ability to evoke setting and mood through assonance, consonance, and telling epithet — all, for example, in the one spacious line that recalls the delight of battle

> Far on the ringing plains of windy Troy.

"Tithonus," which again calls upon an aged protagonist, was designed as the counterpart of "Ulysses" and was written in its original form at about the same time,[7] though it was not published until many years later when it had been re-shaped into a superb tone poem, the saddest and perhaps the most beautiful of all the excursions into Greek mythology:

> The woods decay, the woods decay and fall,
> The vapors weep their burthen to the ground;
> Man comes and tills the field and lies beneath,
> And after many a summer dies the swan.

In "The Grasshopper," a coyly labored piece in the 1830 volume, Tennyson had cast a disparaging glance at the legend of the mortal to whom Eos had granted eternal life without eternal youth. There he had described the "insect lithe and strong" as suffering "no withered immortality" and thus clearly "no Tithon as poets feign." In "Tithonus," however, he accepted the integrity of the myth and, with his usual sympathetic insight into classical materials, revitalized it as the embodiment of his own sense of life's intolerable burden. Here the decay that offers ultimate release in death to all natural objects brings Tithonus only an endless attrition of vital power. Bound pathetically to the goddess, whose beauty, now almost an offense to him, is renewed with each returning day, he sees in her a perpetual reminder of the passion that he as "a white-haired shadow" can no longer reciprocate. Though the situation and the symbolism are essentially sexual, Eos stands in effect as the correlative not of sexual love but of the more general life-principle, to which Tennyson himself in more sanguine mood had once dedicated energies too abundant even to consider possible depletion. Tithonus, conversely, yearning for escape from a cruel immortality, represents the despair of continuing an existence now void of purpose. In spirit he is the antithesis of Ulysses. Whereas the latter responds to the gleam of the untraveled world and the challenge of the Western stars, Tithonus finds frustration in "the gleaming halls of morn," the "empty courts" and "ever-silent spaces of the East." Ulysses believes it "dull to pause"; Tithonus feels it tragic that any man should desire to pass "beyond the goal of ordinance / Where all should pause, as is most meet for all." Verbally the one answers the other; together they are the two voices of a divided sensibility.

Without the aid of dramatic myth or character, the conflict of life and death is developed directly in "The Two Voices," an extended debate which translates the opposed moods of the classical idyls into the advancing and receding rhythms of an intellectual dialectic. Here, as in some of the great medieval dialogues, the argument proceeds through the long night of the soul in a darkness which is the very image of despair. The voice of denial, relentless in its logic, rationalizes Tithonus' will to die as the only reasonable response to "A life of nothings, nothing worth," while the self, struggling for survival, recalls its lost sense of purpose, its resolve — in the spirit of Ulysses —

> "to strive a happy strife,
> To war with falsehood to the knife,
> And not to lose the good of life."

Yet at the outset the protagonist, no longer sure of true or false, is no match for the adversary. Nor should we expect equal combat if we consider the original title of the poem, "The Thoughts of a Suicide," or Tennyson's own comment on the state of mind that produced it: "I was so utterly miserable, a burden to myself and to my family, that I said, 'Is life worth anything?' " [8]

The first voice, reverting like Ulysses (though with contrary intent) to the language of Hamlet, begins by asking the same question:

> "Thou art so full of misery,
> Were it not better not to be?"

And during the course of the debate both the voice and the hard-pressed ego draw upon Hamlet's arguments for and against self-slaughter: whether it is more cowardly to flee pain than to face it, whether man may indeed ever make an end or something after death be not more terrible than the ills of life.

> I said: "I toil beneath the curse,
> But, knowing not the universe,
> I fear to slide from bad to worse."

The self cannot forget what a piece of work a man is or what place — ideally at least — he holds in the scheme of creation. Man is "so wonderfully made," nature's highest work:

> "She gave him mind, the lordliest
> Proportion, and, above the rest,
> Dominion in the head and breast."

But the voice, deriding the ideal as illusion born of empty pride, insists on a universal relativism; neither the best nor the worst of creatures, man is simply insignificant, and "Because the scale is infinite," the will of a Ulysses to seek and to find is, like every human dream of progress and power, futile and contemptible:

> " 'Twere better not to breathe or speak,
> Than cry for strength, remaining weak,
> And seem to find, but still to seek."

The self, nonetheless, can still warm to "the heat of inward evidence," its own intuitions that engender an honest doubt, a questioning of sense and outward things; for man retains "That type of Perfect in his mind" which has no counterpart in nature; and, however the cynic may scoff, some men have known moments of particular insight when they have been touched "with mystic gleams"

> "Of something felt, like something here;
> Of something done, I know not where;
> Such as no language may declare."

So, after long disputation, the debate transcends the grounds of discourse altogether, and the soul, persuaded by its own reasons beyond reason, realizes its one essential longing for life, "More life, and fuller." As the darkness lifts, the defeated voice turns its last irony against the new day: "Behold, it is the Sabbath morn." But the self, now above the reach of derision, is ready to cherish the Sabbath for its symbolic worth and even to bless a grave father, mother, and child on their way to early church. It is perhaps regrettable aesthetically that this group, framed by the window casement, is so stiff and stylized a metaphor of social harmony. Yet the blessing of life, even in such conventional terms, effectively banishes the counsel of despair and admits at last a second

voice, the quiet affirmation of joy. Feeling, "altho' no tongue
can prove," that love is the animating principle of all creation,
the self may finally move out from the narrow chamber of
debate into the great world of acceptance, represented not
indeed by the family chapel but by an animated and quite
Wordsworthian landscape:

> "And forth into the fields I went,
> And Nature's living motion lent
> The pulse of hope to discontent."

In the passage from suicidal despair to intuitive assent,
"The Two Voices" foreshadows the basic intellectual pattern of *In Memoriam*. But the debate, though it arose from
the gloom of bereavement, is in nowise elegiac; the sense
of death lends weight to the denials of the bitter voice, but
the memory of the dead Hallam nowhere directly enters the
argument. The "Morte d'Arthur," on the other hand, which
likewise dates at least in part from the winter of 1833–34,[9]
presents the theme of death through the holy dying of King
Arthur, a figure of mythic nobility and now an idealization,
we may suppose, of the other and more immediate Arthur.
And if the King indeed reflects the heroic aspect of Hallam
and the old order of friendship and shared values which
Hallam seemingly once held together, Sir Bedivere, left
alone in a broken land, almost certainly speaks for the
nostalgic Tennyson:

> "But now the whole Round Table is dissolved
> Which was an image of the mighty world;
> And I, the last, go forth companionless,
> And the days darken round me, and the years,
> Among new men, strange faces, other minds."

Though scarcely to be read as an allegory of his friend's
passing, the tale adapted from Malory thus furnishes some
clear correlative to the poet's emotion. The tone of the whole
is Tennyson's own; and even the incidental imagery which
embellishes the narrative is charged with a Tennysonian terror

and a characteristic recoil from deserts of lonely vastness: Arthur labors for breath "Like one that feels a nightmare on his bed / When all the house is mute," and the keening queens raise a cry of lamentation

> like a wind that shrills
> All night in a waste land, where no one comes,
> Or hath come, since the making of the world.

Yet the larger merit of the "Morte d'Arthur" lies in its independence as a poem, its achievement of an objectivity apart from any private or personal suggestion. The modulated blank verse attains its own aesthetic self-sufficiency. The diction is precise, concrete, and heavily monosyllabic, so that each word receives due stress, and the tempo throughout is deliberate and slow. The assonance and alliteration are carefully calculated, and sound and sense frequently merge in imitative harmony, as in the description of Bedivere's painful progress across the rock ridges:

> Dry clash'd his harness in the icy caves
> And barren chasms, and all to left and right
> The bare black cliff clang'd round him, as he based
> His feet on juts of slippery crag that rang
> Sharp-smitten with the dint of armed heels —
> And on a sudden, lo! the level lake,
> And the long glories of the winter moon.

The landscape and the figures against it — the King, Bedivere, the three queens, the arm clothed in white samite rising from the lake — are all realized in graphic detail; and Arthur in particular looks about him "wistfully with wide blue eyes / As in a picture." For the poem is designed quite literally as an epic "idyl," a "little picture" of heroic character and gesture at a moment of crisis or illumination. Arthur is revealed, above all, by his final composure, his last words of gnomic wisdom spoken from the funeral barge, from beyond life altogether:

> "The old order changeth, yielding place to new
> And God fulfills himself in many ways,
> Lest one good custom should corrupt the world."

Change is thus divinely ordained, lest men stagnate in human satisfactions; change and the desire to reach the Changeless prompt prayer, and prayer distinguishes men from the beasts of the field "That nourish a blind life within the brain." Of an ultimate release and rest, Arthur is not entirely sure, for all his "mind is clouded with a doubt"; but he hopes nonetheless to find healing and renewal in return to the island-valley of Avilion, a first and last security, as it were, in the far-off womb of time. He has achieved the essential acceptance: life with all its mutability has been a discipline worth the living; death is its necessary and perhaps sanctifying complement.

Through the measured language of the "Morte d'Arthur" Tennyson was thus able to attain aesthetically the ideal serenity still denied him in his own life. As a craftsman he could act with assurance; but as a young man faced with practical decisions he was scarcely less bewildered than the bereft Bedivere alone on the shore yearning after the king's receding barge. In the months following Hallam's death he talked frequently, though vaguely, of emigrating to a more congenial climate and, then, found himself forced to rationalize his failure to do so, as in the verses directed to James Spedding: [10]

> You ask me, why, tho' ill at ease,
> Within this region I subsist,
> Whose spirits falter in the mist,
> And languish for the purple seas.

He could expect Spedding, who now became his closest confidant, to understand his need for a place in a social context and his preference for the old order of British stability and "settled government," which he hoped to see preserved despite the movement of the "banded unions," the more or less organized reformers of the thirties, intent, he feared, upon radical innovation. In a number of lyrics, all mildly Burkean in their nostalgic conservatism, he sought to persuade himself that he could find his own peace of mind only within a tradition of quiet reason, where freedom, slowly broadening down, scorned all the falsehood of extremes. He continued to work on "Hail, Briton," a long political sequence, probably begun two or three years earlier,[11] written like "You Ask Me Why" in the *In Memoriam* stanza, and expressing like the other poems a philosophy of deliberate gradualism and a hatred of windy demagoguery. And in isolated quatrains he assailed the new "tyranny" of the masses, the petulant haste of a too-eager democracy, as a threat to the well-being of an organic and somewhat mystically conceived State, which would in due course admit every necessary modification in its own structure, for

> The State within herself contains
> A vital strength as in the seed
> The model of her future form
> And liberty indeed.[12]

As social commentary such verses were informed by fear rather than by fact and marked less by a prophetic insight than by a fundamental distaste for political action. Yet they reveal, clearly enough, a significant regard for the storied past and a characteristic mistrust of every precipitant emotion.

As if to escape the anarchy of his own moods, Tennyson sometime in 1834 drew up an elaborate day-by-day program [13] of systematic study, reading, and review. The mornings he planned to devote to history and the sciences — chemistry, botany, electricity, animal physiology, and mechanics; the afternoons, to the languages — German, Italian, and Greek; the evenings, to poetry; Sundays, to theology. It is unlikely that he followed very closely so exacting a schedule; but he did, at all events, try by self-discipline to give his life some semblance of order and to place his thinking about man and society in some general perspective. Moreover, he was turning in other directions from his private sorrows; he was increasingly preoccupied by the domestic problems of Somersby, and he was beginning to respond more positively to the demands and enthusiasms of his Cambridge friends. By the summer, when he visited John Heath at Kitlands near Dorking, he seemed capable once again of sharp observation and amused detachment. Such elements, at any rate, underlie his comical salute to the village innkeeper, "fat and gray and wise," mellow as an old cucumber, "mine host," whose "tavern is our chief resort." [14] The following spring, having sold his "Timbuctoo" medal to raise funds for travel, he spent two months with Spedding and Edward FitzGerald at Mirehouse and Ambleside in the Lake Country; and, though still at times phlegmatic and despondent, he found frequent release in animated literary conversation.

When his grandfather, the old squire of Bayons Manor, died in July of 1835, he was prepared to understand and at the same time to moderate the conduct of his mother and his erratic brothers, who fancied themselves wholly "dispossessed" by the dead man's will. Yet he must have beheld with a quiet irony the pretensions of his favored uncle, now known as Tennyson d'Eyncourt, bending every effort to acquire a pedigree and to establish a fantastic feudal estate, the moated mansion that might one day, perhaps, suggest the "gewgaw castle" of *Maud*, "New as his title, built last year." As the months passed he himself reluctantly assumed responsibility for the management of practical affairs at Somersby. And in 1837 when the family was at last forced to leave the vicarage, it was his task to find a new home and to move the whole indecisive household. That he chose to settle at High Beech conveniently near London suggests that he no longer wished to live in complete isolation from the busy world of professional letters.

Meanwhile, during the last years at Somersby and then at intervals up to 1842, he was carefully revising such of his published poems as he cared to see preserved. Hearing early in 1835 that John Stuart Mill was preparing a belated review, he regretted that there should be even a favorable notice of his old work. "I do not wish," he told Spedding, "to be dragged forward again in any shape before the reading public at present." [15] More than once in the long decade of "silence," he refused Moxon permission to reprint any part of the early volumes.[16] Some of the pieces he had already modified almost beyond recognition; with others he was still dissatisfied. He was, he claimed later, "nearer thirty than twenty before [he] was anything of an artist," [17] and he wanted to bring the full resources of a mature art to bear upon all his verse before considering any new edition. Since the artist, he believed, was to be "known by his self-limitation" [18] and since "only the concise and perfect work" could last,[19] he sought to curb his own excesses by removing needlessly replete descriptions, reducing the number of fulsome epithets, and regularizing his meters and stanza patterns. Sometimes by the mere transposition of phrase or by slight shift in focus he could obtain new and memorable effects. One of the quatrains, for example, describing the tapestries in the Palace of Art had originally been evocative and sad:

> Some were all dark and red, a glimmering land
> Lit with a low round moon,
> Among brown rocks a man upon the sand
> Went weeping all alone.

Reordered and simplified, it acquired the strange terror of a surrealist landscape, the sense of infinite desolation beyond tears:

> One seem'd all dark and red — a tract of sand,
> And some one pacing there alone,
> Who paced for ever in a glimmering land,
> Lit with a low large moon.

Frequently, however, revision demanded more drastic alteration, even the rewriting or rethinking of the whole poem. "The Lady of Shalott," for instance, reworked from beginning to end, was made much less ornate, less strained in diction, and clearer in narrative outline. "Oenone," in turn, lost much of its swooning sensuosity as its blank verse assumed a greater economy of statement and a new, somewhat Miltonic dignity of movement. Both "The Palace of Art" and "The Lotos-Eaters" gained thematically from substantive changes. The addition to the allegory of several stanzas on democracy, anarchy, and revolution ascribed part of the guilt of the aesthetic soul to the studied disregard of such political realities. And the substitution in the idyl of a new Lucretian ending for the earlier lush catalogue of the delights of lotos-land demonstrated the philosophic consequence of lotos-eating, the readiness of the escapist to find sanction for his own indolent passivity in the behavior of the remote indifferent gods. Though quite as deliberately contrived, the new "Conclusion" to "The May Queen" was far less successful in poetic effect; it served merely to revive poor volatile Alice so that she might sententiously resign herself to righteous dying. On the other hand, the introduction in "The Miller's Daughter" of a passage describing the meeting of the other Alice and her suitor's mother, won over in spite of herself by the girl's sweet shyness, added a little dramatic tension to the otherwise loose sequence of sentimental vignettes.

The extent to which Tennyson was influenced by the reviewers in making all such revisions remains debatable.[20] Assuredly sensitive as always to hostile criticism, he did indeed alter or suppress certain specific phrases or sometimes even whole poems which had been subjected to merciless ridicule. Yet he steadfastly refused to change any single line with which he himself was still well pleased. The journalists who called attention to his faults might remind him of the currents of popular taste, but as far as his own art was concerned they had very little to teach him. He himself was quite conscious of his own defects and fully aware of the aesthetic directions that his verse ideally should follow.

And far better than anyone else he understood the past and present intentions of each particular poem. There was, therefore, much in the revisions that the critics could neither have dictated nor foreseen, and the ultimate arbiter of all change was his own sharpened discrimination as craftsman. Nor was the deeper concern — both in the revised pieces and in the new work — for the function of the artist in society forced upon him against his will. It was, rather, an important part of his personal development, of his discovery during the 1830s that to live at all he must live among men, must find a means of becoming "one with [his] kind" without compromising his individual talent.

And as he came to feel a deepened social responsibility, he began to suspect that an indulgence in merely private sentiment might also represent a betrayal of his own most compelling intuition. Escape into an art of sensations, beautiful or melancholy, might demand the sacrifice of beauty itself, the denial of that ultimate order of being, the far-far-away to which in moments of vision he had from the beginning committed his whole poetic and "mystical" imagination. "To me," he wrote in 1839, "often the far-off world seems nearer than the present, for in the present is always something unreal and indistinct, but the other seems a good solid planet, rolling round its green hills and paradises to the harmony of more steadfast laws. There steam up from about me mists of weakness, or sin, or despondency, and roll between me and the far planet, but it is there still." [21]

The fixed far planet appears as the "awful rose of dawn," the objective order of beauty in "The Vision of Sin," wherein the "sin" is the mist or shadow that comes between the artist and the true objects of his art. The sinner of this dream-allegory is seen first as a young poet who rides an earth-bound Pegasus toward a palace of sensation, perhaps a little like the "purple-lined palace of sweet sin" in Keats's "Lamia." Once inside the palace gate, the youth is caught up by a rout

of abandoned dancers reeling to a voluptuous "nerve-dis-
solving" music. Then before the dreamer can intervene to
warn him, the dream itself is interrupted by a new dream, in
which the poet, now a "gray and gap-toothed" specter,
alights at a ruined tavern in a dreary wasteland. There to
wrinkled ostler and "bitter barmaid, waning fast," he sings a
last sardonic song of disillusion, which with grim wit reduces
all the fair ideals of man, Friendship, Virtue, and Freedom,
to masked hypocrisies and discerns in the sensual dance of all
life only the fearful *danse macabre:*

> "Trooping from their mouldy dens
>   The chap-fallen circle spreads:
> Welcome, fellow-citizens,
>   Hollow hearts and empty heads!
>
> "You are bones, and what of that?
>   Every face, however full,
> Padded round with flesh and fat,
>   Is but modell'd on a skull.
>
> "Death is king, and Vivat Rex!
>   Tread a measure on the stones,
> Madam — if I know your sex,
>   From the fashion of your bones."

The bitter song is undoubtedly the more intense for Tennyson's own experience of bitter moods. But it is nonetheless incisive and dramatic, and without moralizing it carries its
own implicit moral: a merely sensual art or artist is self-
defeating. The poet of the dream is destroyed by seeking
to live in the world of his narrowed sensibilities. But the far
planet, the larger ideal, remains untouched; above the dead
landscape of the heath rises "the mystic mountain range,"

> And on the glimmering limit far withdrawn
> God made Himself an awful rose of dawn.

In later years the physicist Tyndall asked the meaning of
the metaphysical rose. But Tennyson, exercising the evasive-

ness with which he learned to silence his questioners, simply
replied that "the power of explaining such concentrated expressions of the imagination was very different from that of
writing them." [22] He wished his verse to communicate
poetically or not at all; if his metaphors seemed unclear, he
had but little inclination to translate them into prose. Perhaps
only with Hallam had he ever been able fully and directly
to discuss his aesthetic intentions. Yet the letter of 1839 concerning the mists of self and the reality beyond stands, in
effect if not by design, as a gloss on "The Vision of Sin."
And it remains in itself evidence that Tennyson in the years
of silence following Hallam's death could still at times confess his inmost feelings, his aloneness and his fear of his own
melancholia, to an understanding correspondent. His con-
fidante in this instance was Emily Sellwood, who, at length
after almost inordinate delay, would become his wife and the
patient sharer in all his variable moods. Toward other young
women [23] to whom he was decorously attracted he behaved
with a discreet chivalry, gallant as the occasion or the occasional love lyric demanded, but always rather aloof and
defensively enigmatic. To Emily, on the other hand, he could
speak in his own voice without pretense or constraint. Even
the "idyllic" sonnet describing the silent vows they first ex-
changed at the wedding of his brother Charles in 1836
breathes a measure of personal intensity into the little genre
picture it presents:

> For while the tender service made thee weep,
> I loved thee for the tear thou could'st not hide,
> And prest thy hand, and knew the press return'd,
> And thought, "My life is sick of single sleep:
> O happy bridesmaid, make a happy bride!"

And the few fragments of his early correspondence with
Emily that his son thought it proper to preserve reveal something of the influence of love on his general attitude toward
life and even a little of his specific emotions as a lover, for-

ever by his own reckoning unworthy of the beloved's affection.[24]

Almost from the beginning he may have suspected that his romance might be frustrated, at least temporarily, by the force of outward circumstance, especially his own lack of money and the opposition of Emily's father to a poet far too bohemian in his manners, too slovenly in his dress, and too liberal in his religious views. But his conviction that he had at all events gained from his love some fresh insight into life's possibilities apparently carried him through his disappointment at the forced breaking of his engagement in 1840. Though we have no direct record of his reaction, we may fairly gauge his response from the odd catechism called "Love and Duty," [25] which begins by asking the consequence of a frustrate love:

> Of love that never found his earthly close,
> What sequel? Streaming eyes and breaking hearts?
> Or all the same as if he had not been?

The questions themselves, mocking the language of a rebuffed romantic sentimentalism, dictate the answers: there must be no prolonged "brooding in the ruins of a life," no "long mechanic pacings to and fro" nor any "apathetic end," for love has educated the lover's soul, has taught it patience and given it an abiding ideal, a faith "large in Time / And that which shapes it to some perfect end." Lest selfish passion destroy peace, love counsels renunciation:

> For Love himself took part against himself
> To warn us off, and Duty loved of Love
> O, this world's curse — beloved but hated — came
> Like Death betwixt thy dear embrace and mine,
> And crying, "Who is this? behold thy bride,"
> She push'd me from thee.

Then the lovers, uttering "the whole of love" in one brief eternal summer night, part presumably forever. But duty, which is both life and death-in-life, bids them continue living in the Tennysonian consolation that a lost love is assuredly better, "nobler," than no love at all.

"Locksley Hall" — if it can rightly be assigned to a time near the end of the nine years' "silence" [26] — may also arise in part from the poet's personal experience of sundered love. It seems unlikely, to be sure, that the faithless Amy of the poem, "Puppet to a father's threat, and servile to a shrewish tongue," could in any respect represent Emily Sellwood, who in any case was not forced into a marriage of convenience with a drunken clown. But, despite his ranting rhetoric, the Byronic hero who denounces Amy quite possibly reflects Tennyson's milder resentment of parental interference and almost certainly registers his deep dissatisfaction with his own economic status and "the social wants that sin against the strength of youth," the crass materialism of a society where "Every door is barr'd with gold, and opens but to golden keys." "Locksley Hall" was, of course, designed as a dramatic recital and not as a thinly disguised subjective complaint. And with its overstatements, its violence of passion, its staged declamations, and its interludes of conscious grace, it is actually an experiment in a new form, more operatic than strictly lyrical, striving deliberately rather for variety and contrast of tone and gesture than for unity of effect or definition of mood. Yet its movement from defeat toward a reaffirmation of life follows the direction of "The Two Voices" and reproduces with almost excessive heightening the general process of Tennyson's emotional development. Both the denial and the assent, however, are localized in early-Victorian terms so that they seem to relate to the struggle of a whole generation rather than to the psychological conflict of one poet. As if illustrating the pattern of *Sartor Resartus*, which may indeed have suggested some details of story and imagery, the hero turns from an Everlasting No, born of self-absorption and romantic malaise, of which blighted affection is but one aspect, to the Everlasting Yea of activity in a self-confident and energetic "Mother-Age." "I myself," he resolves, "must mix with action lest I wither by despair." Yet determined escape into merely physical adventure will offer no solution; he must repudiate his wild dream of uninhibited passion beneath an oriental sun and awaken to the wonder of the European "march of mind" and the immediate miracle of the steamship and the railway. In the idea of progress, the faith in unlimited advance on the most obvious plane, he finds a new substitute religion, wholly naive in its exuberance yet satisfactory enough for the moment and far more comprehensible and acceptable to the first Victorians than either Carlyle's transcendentalism or Tennyson's own intuitions of metaphysical purpose:[27]

> Not in vain the distance beacons. Forward, forward let
> us range,
> Let the peoples spin for ever down the ringing grooves of
> change.[28]

Raising such a cry, he speaks as a practical man at one with his kind, if not "the heir of all the ages, in the foremost files of time," at least the child of a still sanguine and enormously inventive nineteenth century, the energy of which promised to sweep away the dead past just as the final seaward-roaring wind threatens to overwhelm Locksley Hall itself. But in his representative role, he loses any identity he might have attained as an individual recovering from an emotional crisis. Though he suspects that his better poised comrades may scorn his "foolish passion," his self-consciousness never extends to self-awareness. To the end he remains untouched by the comic spirit that would have made credible his rejection of Byronism and assured his genuine conversion.

Unlike his anonymous hero, Tennyson himself throughout the thirties grew steadily in the power of ironic detachment. In his own family circle he learned to check the

frequent tearfulness of his mother, to whom he was always most seriously devoted; with affectionate mock-severity
he would rebuke her, "Dam your eyes, mother, dam your
eyes." [29] And in the world of letters he came to see the
inanity of the sentimental Annuals and the impropriety of
his continued presence among the contributors, "a barnyard
fowl among peacocks." Accordingly he declined Monckton
Milnes' invitation to submit a poem to the 1837 *Tribute*,
edited by Lord Northampton; for, as he explained, "To write
for people with prefixes to their names is to milk he-goats;
there is neither honour nor profit." [30] But when his friend
took offense, he not only hastened to apologize but agreed
to send the editor some "Stanzas" ("O that 'twere possible"), the great lyric that would one day serve as the inspiration of *Maud*. A man of affairs like Milnes, he insisted, must
not misinterpret the "unhappy badinage" of "a nervous,
morbidly-irritable man, down in the world, stark-spoiled with
the staggers of a mis-managed imagination and quite opprest
by fortune and by the reviews." [31] If there was much truth
in such a self-portrait, there was also behind it a genial
sense of humor and a salutary self-deprecation. These same
elements animate "Will Waterproof's Lyrical Monologue,"
an amiable exercise in irony and easy colloquialism, "made
at the Cock," celebrating one of Tennyson's favorite haunts
in the late thirties, the London chophouse where he could
retreat from his own earnestness and all the gnawing
hypochondria of his home into a realm of relaxed contemplation and cheering pint-pots where

> High over roaring Temple-bar,
>   And, set in Heaven's third story,
> I look at all things as they are,
>   But thro' a kind of glory.

In the city also he found new friends, Thackeray and Carlyle,
Landor, Forster and Macready, men of wit, irony, and experience, each more familiar than he with the temper of a

robust literary society. And in frequent excursions into the English countryside, to the sea coasts, and as far afield as Aberystwyth in Wales, he made fresh observations of lives unlike his own and rural scenes bathed in a quiet local color which he attempted to record in his new and now distinctly "English" idyls.

Apart from "Will Waterproof," few of the poems first published in 1842 made more than passing reference to London, which by that time had become Tennyson's chief source of intellectual stimulus. Like "The May Queen" of the earlier volume, the "English Idyls" [32] as such turned nostalgically to a semipastoral setting not yet seriously disturbed by the railways and still at a slight remove from the troubling "march of mind." In "The Gardener's Daughter" of 1833, the earliest and most elaborate of the series, the poet had carefully marked out the appropriate idyllic landscape:

> Not wholly in the busy world, nor quite
> Beyond it, blooms the garden that I love.
> News from the humming city comes to it
> In sound of funeral or of marriage bells;
> And, sitting muffled in dark leaves, you hear
> The windy clanging of the minster clock;
> Although between it and the garden lies
> A league of grass, wash'd by a slow broad stream,
> That, stirr'd with languid pulses of the oar,
> Waves all its lazy lilies, and creeps on,
> Barge-laden, to three arches of a bridge
> Crown'd with the minster-towers.

And against this highly civilized backdrop he had arranged his "little picture" — the gardener's daughter herself, "gown'd in pure white, that fitted to the shape," her arm lifted to fasten back a rose vine, the sunlight in her hair, and the shadow of the flowers trembling on her waist. Tennyson eventually came to feel the poem "full and rich . . . to a fault," but he saw no way of avoiding an ornate description of the girl since the lover who beholds her

"is an artist." [33] Nevertheless, though consciously simpler
in style, the idyls written later in the thirties are likewise
contrived exercises in objectivity, each in its way an escape
from personal commitment and the burden of the self.
"Dora," which much impressed Wordsworth, tells its tale of
saintly endurance with a too laborious reduction of language
and emotion, virtually without adjectives, in simple assertive
sentences intended perhaps to achieve the elemental effect
of a Biblical parable.[34] And "Walking to the Mail" experiments with dialogue as a means of disclosing, half in amusement, half in sympathy, the marital difficulties and the political alarms of a Tory squire. In "Audley Court" a colloquial
idiom mingles pleasantly with a somewhat mock-heroic style,
a verbal heightening, which lends the simple country picnic
an almost Homeric dignity:

> There, on a slope of orchard, Francis laid
> A damask napkin wrought with horse and hound,
> Brought out a dusky loaf that smelt of home,
> And, half-cut-down, a pasty costly made,
> Where quail and pigeon, lark and leveret lay,
> Like fossils of the rock, with golden yolks
> Imbedded and injellied.

Happily singing songs like shepherds in an idyl of Theocritus,
both Francis, the farmer's son, and the "I," the narrator of
the poem, "in the fallow leisure of [his] life," speak for
Tennyson as he tried to see himself in calm detachment — the
one, wittily disillusioned, eager to live free of dutiful entangle-
ments, the other musing idly on dreams of sweet romance.
The objective tone of such pieces might thus serve a
personal need. Through imagined characters presented as
"normal" healthy human beings, the poet strove to convince
his new public and perhaps himself that he was at one with
his age, capable of popular speech, and by no means willfully
eccentric even in his more "poetic" flights of fancy. "The
Epic," accordingly, written about 1838 [35] as a modern frame

for the heroic "Morte d'Arthur," offers both an apology for
the use of ancient materials and an ironic self-portrait. Ever-
ard Hall, the "epic" poet, convinced that "a truth / Looks
freshest in the fashion of the day," is embarrassed to be
caught remodeling models; yet no more than Tennyson
himself does he require much urging before declaiming
his work, "mouthing out his hollow oes and aes / Deep-
chested music." And the epic fragment that he reads, the
narrative of Arthur, is, we are told, made more acceptable by
its possible relevance to the nineteenth century:

> Perhaps some modern touches here and there
> Redeem'd it from the charge of nothingness.

The same desire to add the redeeming modern touch appears even in some of the 1842 poems which have no necessary concern with the present and none of the local color
we associate with the "English Idyls." A prosaic four-line
introduction to "Godiva" explains that the piece was inspired
by a wait between trains at Coventry, and the tale itself,
heavily overwritten and never quite serious in its sobriety,
insists that the past which "we, the latest seed of Time," cry
down may yet remind us of virtue tried and triumphant.
"The Day Dream," which completes the story of the sleeping
beauty begun in the 1830 volume, passes off its narrative as a
trifle designed for the amusement of a modern and apparently
humorless maiden, Lady Flora, who appears in a prologue and
epilogue; and, though the "Moral" denies the necessity of any
moral at all, the "Envoi" suggests that, if the poem must have
an "application," then the wonders of the tale may at least
lead to speculation on time, progress, and the miracle of a new
science "As wild as aught of fairy lore." Behind the facetious
whimsy of "The Goose" may also lurk a "modern" message —
in this instance, a warning, perhaps, to the Tories that their
Corn Laws are killing commerce on which the prosperity of
England must depend.[36] "The Talking Oak" has no such

ulterior motive; but the loquacious tree, remembering a long past, does make it clear that a simple early-Victorian lass has charms beyond those of her more calculating predecessors and sweetness enough to stir an aged oaken sap. "Amphion," on the other hand, a much more successful attempt at fantasy, turns an ironic glance toward the dreary present. Time was when old Amphion could sway the whole woodland with his song, but the modern poet, alas, finds no sympathy in nature:

> 'T is vain! in such a brassy age
>   I could not move a thistle;
> The very sparrows in the hedge
>   Scarce answer to my whistle;
> Or at the most, when three-parts sick
>   With strumming and with scraping,
> A jackass heehaws from the rick,
>   The passive oxen gaping.

The "modern Muses" are but "wither'd Misses," well read in horticultural treatises, yet quite unable to elicit from their gardens the response of a happy green abundance. The poet, therefore, resolves patiently to cultivate his own "proper patch of soil" without the aid of Amphion's magic but certainly also without undue regard for the sterile fashion of a prosy time.

FitzGerald clearly overvalued the colloquial rhymes and the contemporary idyls, which Tennyson had written with no very full engagement of his poetic personality. But he was altogether just in his general estimate of the manuscripts which he saw readied at last for the printer toward the end of 1841. "Alfred," he announced, "will publish such a volume as has not been published since the time of Keats, and which once published, will never be suffered to die." [37] The volumes issued by Moxon in May of 1842 (there were actually two, the first consisting largely of revised or re-printed poems, the second devoted to new ones) established

Tennyson beyond question as the foremost poet of his time and made a substantial bid for long survival. Yet the most memorable pieces, those ultimately least to be suffered to die, were scarcely those which catered to the vogue for the actualistic genre study and the self-consciously applied "modern touches" of homely sentiment or current idiom. Nor were they the immensely popular short ballads "Lady Clara Vere de Vere," "Lady Clare," and "The Lord of Burleigh," each of which weighed the claims of simple faith against the pretensions of noble blood. As time passed and literary manners changed, readers would return instead to the best of the early poems, as they had been reshaped during the long and active "silence," and more insistently still to the new pieces in which the poet had found a correlative for his own moods: "Ulysses," "The Two Voices," "Morte d'Arthur" (without its modern frame), "The Vision of Sin," and perhaps "Locksley Hall." In all of these Tennyson still speaks in his own controlled poetic voice, sensitive to new modes but without straining after a determined modernity. In none does he appear as the overtly subjective artist confessing his own passion; yet all reflect in some degree the developing sensibility that was all the while expressing its moods and perceptions in the scattered lyrics of In Memoriam, which still seemed much too private for publication.

Two highly personal lyrics, however, did find their way into the second volume of the 1842 Poems, and each remains as a witness both to Tennyson's intensity of feeling throughout the silent years and to his greatly increased command of lyric form. The less concentrated of the two, "A Farewell," occasioned (we may assume) by the departure from Somersby, poignantly describes a death-in-life, a separation from the past "for ever and for ever," as eternal as the self-renewing present of the cold rivulet. The firmer "Break, Break, Break," a miracle of verbal purity and rightness, marks the yearning and regret never fully to be uttered yet here perfectly suggested by sharp contrast and clear image. Against the measured rhythm of the breakers rings out the call of life — the happy shout of childhood and the confident song of youth; but the cry of joy serves simply as a reminder of "the sound of a voice that is still." Likewise, the stately ships, tokens of a resolute maturity, move on toward their haven of fulfillment; yet their motion must recall "the touch of a vanish'd hand" and so evoke the sense of immutably broken purpose. The sea itself, symbol of all sound and movement, encompasses the three ages of man in an endless cycle of energy; but no return in all of time can restore to the individual his lost experience:

> Break, break, break,
>   At the foot of thy crags, O Sea!
> But the tender grace of a day that is dead
>   Will never come back to me.

No other of the 1842 pieces quite attains the bold simplicity of this; no other registers so directly Tennyson's own deep nostalgia or indicates more clearly how his grief without denying itself could achieve beauty through the discipline of art.

✎§ V §✎

A STRANGE DIAGONAL

1843–1850

SIR Robert Peel was apparently too preoccupied as Prime Minister to concern himself much with literature. Yet it seems odd that, when preparing the civil list of pensions in 1845, he knew nothing at all of Tennyson until a prescribed reading of "Ulysses" convinced him of the poet's high merit.[1] For by 1845 Tennyson had already acquired a considerable reputation and even some small degree of popularity. Already he was receiving for his approval — though to his great annoyance — books and manuscripts of second-rate verse from British scribblers and far-off hopeful Americans. The sales of his own poetry had begun to justify Moxon's confidence. And the reviewers, though still admonitory and often captious, were growing year by year more receptive and more respectful. Cambridge, which had been loyal almost from the beginning, was shortly to honor him by requesting a formal ode for the installation of Prince Albert as chancellor of the university.[2] Meanwhile, Oxford, which had been largely indifferent to the earlier volumes, was responding warmly to the 1842 *Poems,* and in 1844 the Decade, the debating club to which Arthur Clough belonged, had discussed with due earnestness "the relative merits of Wordsworth and Tennyson." [3] Wordsworth for his part, well pleased to recognize in Tennyson a sincere admirer and perhaps even a disciple, declared him "decidedly the first of our living poets." [4]

Carlyle, who cared little for any living poet as such, rather wished that Tennyson would turn his talents to prose. Nonetheless he confessed to feeling in such pieces as "Dora" and "The Two Voices" the "pulse of a real man's heart. . . . A right valiant, true fighting, victorious heart; strong as a lion's, yet gentle, loving and full of music." [5] And it was clearly the man, not the poet, who attracted and held Carlyle's attention — a singularly unconventional man, a "large-featured, dim-eyed, bronze-coloured, shaggy-headed man, . . . dusty, smoky, free and easy; who swims, outwardly and inwardly, with great composure in an articulate element as of tranquil chaos and tobacco-smoke." [6] Jane Carlyle, who esteemed both the man and his work, agreed that there was indeed "something of the gypsy in his appearance, which for me is perfectly charming." [7] Without necessarily exploiting his charm, Tennyson all through the 1840's maintained an air of mild bohemianism, partly because the pose was natural and congenial to him and partly also because it offered a defense against encroachments on his private life. Accordingly, the aged Samuel Rogers, stiff in joints and morals, suspected him of "many infirmities"; [8] whereas the still exuberant Savage Landor beseeched his companionship:

I entreat you, Alfred Tennyson,
Come and share my haunch of venison,
I have too a bin of claret,
Good, but better when you share it.
Tho' 'tis only a small bin,
There's a stock of it within.
And as sure as I'm a rhymer,
Half a butt of Rudesheimer.
Come; among the sons of men is one
Welcomer than Alfred Tennyson? [9]

Though less irregular and less hearty than his friends supposed, Tennyson's course of "genteel vagrancy," as George Darley aptly called it,[10] was at all events far removed from the sober domesticity of his most popular verses. But it was the expression less of a gypsy nonchalance than of a refusal to make too intense or personal a commitment; it was not unlike the self-consciousness of the narrator in his own new idyl, "Edwin Morris":

> It is my shyness, or my self-distrust,
> Or something of a wayward modern mind
> Dissecting passion. Time will set me right.

As befitted a genteel vagrant, Tennyson found relief from the burdens of home and self in long walks, country visits, and constant holiday travels. With Carlyle he paced the streets of London for hours by night discussing the precarious condition of England. Alone he journeyed to "the monument of poor Burns" at Kirk Alloway, to the Highland lochs, and over the sea to Skye.[11] In Cornwall on a search for Arthurian materials he was delighted to hear high praise of Tennyson from his fellow-poet Hawker of Morwenstowe, from whom he had carefully concealed his identity. And in Ireland he was amused to be regarded as a subversive swarthy foreigner, perhaps a French spy preparing for a French invasion of Erin. From his 1846 trip to Switzerland with Moxon a fragmentary journal, as yet published only in part, remains an intimate witness to his humor and excitability; a few scattered jottings, for example, like an exercise in the technique of the interior monologue, directly reproduce a crowded day's experiences:

we bought Keller's map — off by 2 o cl: steamer to Weggis — dined on veal and jambon — hired a horse — up the Righi — looked over and saw the little coves and wooded shores and villages under vast red ribs of rock — very fine — dismiss my horse at the Bains where we entered with an Englishman and found peasants waltzing — gave 2 franks to boy who had ordered beds, summit — crowd of people — very feeble sunset — tea — infernal chatter as of innumerous apes — M. and I to bed in one room — fleabitten — rush out at four — sunrise, strange look of clouds packed on the lake of Egeri — far off Jungfrau looking as if delicately pencilled — Rossberg, Küssnacht, breakfast, began to descend at 9 — strange aspect of hill cloud and snow as if the mountains were on fire — infamous Swiss boy — we watch the clouds opening and shutting as we go down, . . . long hot descent — dine at Weggis — landlady takes me out to select live fish for dinner — I am too tenderhearted so we go without fish — boat touches — off to Fluelen — very sleepy — carriages — road to Italy — Tell's chapel — bad beer — sour ill-looking maid — go into church — two rouged harridans in flounce and furbelow . . . return to Sweizer Hof — other rooms.[12]

Such a chaos of free association may, oddly enough, stand as a remote gloss on the exquisitely ordered art of "Come Down, O Maid," the Jungfrau idyl that was certainly the most memorable product of the Swiss journey. Though the noisy "chatter as of innumerous apes" could hardly have inspired the euphonious "murmuring of innumerable bees," the whole passage nonetheless indicates the vividness with which every raw impression, every sound and sight, registered itself on an open consciousness and so became the potential substance of a refined and concentrated imagery.

As his wanderings increased the objectivity of his work, so his tentatively gypsy conduct allowed him a calmer and more detached perspective on his own life. And detachment was essential throughout the forties when private miseries threatened to overwhelm him. In September of 1842 he described his family circle to Edmund Lushington (who within a few weeks was to become his brother-in-law): "What with ruin in the distance and hypochondriacs in the foreground, God help all." [13] The hypochondriacs were his brothers, Arthur, Edward, Charles, Septimus, and Horatio, in their several states of debility. The ruin was the imminent failure of Dr. Matthew Allen's "pyroglyphic" enterprise, a project for the machine production of ornamental woodcarvings, in which the poet rashly had invested the whole of his small inheritance together with a legacy from Arthur

Hallam's aunt. By the time that the ruin was definite and final Tennyson himself was so close to complete nervous collapse that he retreated for the winter of 1843–44 to a hydropathic hospital at Cheltenham. Though recovered by the spring and never again quite so depleted in spirit, he was still subject to periodic attacks of neurasthenia; and three years later he took another "water cure," this time at an establishment in Malvern operated (appropriately enough) by a Dr. Gully.[14]

By the end of 1845 his financial condition had improved; the death of the speculative Allen restored a large part of his lost investment, and the pension granted by Peel assured him a steady if small income. Yet he still felt much too insolvent and unsettled to declare once more his love for Emily Sellwood. And he was reluctant to inflict his personal problems even upon his most intimate friends. Above all, he was firm in his refusal to expose his private life to the idle chit-chat and scandalmongering of that large anonymous "literary" public which was, he suspected, growing year by year more interested in every aspect of his character and conduct. His attitude is apparent from a lyric addressed vaguely "To —," printed in the *Examiner* in 1849 and later subtitled "After Reading a Life and Letters." [15] Here the unnamed friend, perhaps his brother Charles, has wisely rejected the pursuit of poetry and the possibility of public fame for "a deedful life, a silent voice":

> And you have miss'd the irreverent doom
> Of those that wear the Poet's crown:
> Hereafter, neither knave nor clown
> Shall hold their orgies at your tomb.

The practicing Poet, on the other hand, who has given the people his best and withheld the worst, must eventually fall prey to "the many-headed beast" and its resolve to seek out all private infirmities and so "keep nothing sacred."

Moving slowly but surely toward his place as a popular

literary idol, Tennyson thus felt at odds with his public, uncertain of the temper of his new audience, and profoundly distrustful of the censorious race of "Grundyites." But despite his reticence he himself showed no disposition to desert the way of poetry for a less conspicuous though possibly more "deedful" career. He continued to shape and reshape the elegies to be published at long last as *In Memoriam*. He meticulously labored on at his newest and as yet longest narrative, *The Princess*. And he continued to polish some of the already heavily revised 1842 pieces; in "A Dream of Fair Women," for example, he heightened Cleopatra's memory of Antony until in two new stanzas it reached the intensity and terror of heroic passion:

> "The man, my lover, with whom I rode sublime
> On Fortune's neck: we sat as God by God:
> The Nilus would have risen before his time
> And flooded at our nod.

> "We drank the Libyan Sun to sleep, and lit
> Lamps which outburn'd Canopus. O my life
> In Egypt! O the dalliance and the wit,
> The flattery and the strife."

He read widely in new books, especially in those related to his own poetic concerns; and he often pondered the strength of his favorite older poets. Beside the achievements of the past, his own work struck him as thin and ineffectual. He regretted "the foolish facility of Tennysonian verse" and yet envied "the exquisite lightness of touch in Keats." All of his poems together, he told Aubrey de Vere, were scarcely worth Lovelace's "Althea," and by no artifice could he match any one of Burns's natural songs, each of which had "in shape . . . the perfection of the berry; in light the radiance of the dewdrop." [16] Still he was challenged rather than rebuffed by such high performance, and he persisted in his desire for a reputation that would outlast the taste of his own time.

To the extravagant praise that a few of his admirers were heaping upon him he remained quite indifferent; but to unfair abuse he was always aggressively sensitive. When Bulwer, outraged at the pension from Peel, attacked him in *The New Timon* of 1846 as "School-Miss Alfred," "outbabying Wordsworth and outglittering Keates [*sic*]," he retaliated in "The New Timon and The Poets," which John Forster without his consent passed on to *Punch*.[17] What license, he asked, had Bulwer, the fop, the dandy, "the padded man — that wears the stays," to pose as the champion of virility, the scourge of weakness? The real Timon would have dismissed the impostor, and true poets everywhere must do likewise, for

> . . . men of long-enduring hopes,
> And careless what this hour may bring
> Can pardon little would-be *Popes*
> And *Brummels*, when they try to sting. . . .

> What profits now to understand
> The merits of a spotless shirt —
> A dapper boot — a little hand —
> If half the little soul is dirt? . . .

> A *Timon* you! Nay, nay, for shame:
> It looks too arrogant a jest —
> The fierce old man — to take his name,
> You bandbox. Off, and let him rest.

The very act of writing stanzas of such sharp satiric bite meant, of course, that Tennyson had neither ignored nor pardoned. And unpublished drafts of other replies testify — with an even greater sense of personal injury, though with far less dramatic skill — to the impact of Bulwer's attack.[18] Yet in the midst of his agitation Tennyson was admonished by his old awareness of time and the vanity of rancorous self-assertion; ultimately both slandered and slanderer would dwindle to insignificance,

> For as to Fame who strides the earth
>   With that long horn she loves to blow,
> I know a little of her worth,
>   And I will tell you what I know.
> This London once was middle sea,
>   Those hills were plains within the past,
> They will be plains again — and we,
>   Poor devils, babble, "we shall last." [19]

Such was the mood of a retraction entitled "The Next Morning" (revised and published in *Punch* as "After-Thought" a week after "The New Timon and the Poets" and reprinted many years later as "Literary Squabbles"):

> Too harsh! I loathe it and retract:
>   Yet see, Sir, spite of spite is born,
> And men turn vermin in the fact
>   Of paying aught of scorn with scorn.
>
> Ah God! we petty fools of rhyme
>   That shriek and sweat in pigmy wars
> Before the stony face of Time,
>   And look'd at by the silent stars; . . .
>
> And strain to make an inch of room
>   For our sweet selves, and cannot hear
> The sullen Lethe rolling doom
>   On us and ours and all things here.[20]

Thus at the height of the fray, the most public since his quarrel with Christopher North, Tennyson was moved by a feeling of its fundamental unreality, just as the Prince of *The Princess* suffers a "weird seizure" at the very moment of battle, an isolating sense of illusion which disengages his concern.

The conflicting motives of detachment and self-justification are apparent also in "Edwin Morris" and "The Golden Year," two new idyls written some months before the Bulwer affair.[21] Edwin Morris is the wholly aesthetic poet, all too accomplished, "All perfect, finish'd to the finger-nail,"

"A full-cell'd honeycomb of eloquence." His rhymes are overcalculated, "elaborately good," and his speech is clearly enough a parody of Tennyson's own most elaborate manner (as in "The Gardener's Daughter"), with its assured rhetoric and cadenced repetition — he arranges, for example, his memory of first love as an artful harmony in nature:

> "To some full music rose and sank the sun,
> And some full music seem'd to move and change
> With all the varied changes of the dark,
> And either twilight and the day between;
> For daily hope fulfill'd, to rise again
> Revolving toward fulfilment, made it sweet
> To walk, to sit, to sleep, to wake, to breathe."

The narrator of the idyl, who (as we have seen) reflects a measure of Tennyson's "self-distrust," finds a jarring note in Morris' elegant periphrases, "A touch of something false, some self-conceit, / Or over-smoothness"; and to all such artifice he himself prefers the more direct idiom of Tennyson's middle style.

In "The Golden Year" Leonard the poet affects a genteel vagrancy perhaps, but certainly no precious language. He has been accused of withdrawal from the turmoil of his time:

> They said he lived shut up within himself,
> A tongue-tied Poet in the feverous days.

But he is actually less eager to escape social problems than to view them in the perspective of a political gradualism. He foresees the slow sure coming, as if by evolutionary process, of the golden year when "wealth no more shall rest in mounded heaps" but all shall share in the world's goods and a free trade and an enlightened press shall carry peace and Christian principle from land to land. Yet though his sanguine vision of the future seems characteristically Tennysonian, Leonard is not allowed to go unchallenged. Old James, a testy Carlylean, dismissing him as an idle dreamer, insists that the only possible golden year lies in good hard practical work here and now in the teeming present. Tennyson hardly endorsed such a philosophy even in this idyl, but simply by presenting it he was able to detach himself a little from Leonard, the character with whom he must have felt most sympathy.

As originally planned, the framework of *The Princess* was also to provide room for a gently ironic self-portrait, which would satisfy the peculiar need for participation without full commitment. A very early draft [22] describes at some length an Arthur Clive who as the "one central star" of a college set called The Shakespeare occupies a place perhaps similar to that of the other Arthur among the Cambridge Apostles. But despite his given name, Clive is not Hallam; his physical attributes — rough soft hair, swarthy tender skin, prematurely lined face, large hands — all suggest none other than the young Tennyson as the more mature Tennyson wished to picture him. A later manuscript repeats most of this detail but renames the character Arthur Arundel "the Poet" and assigns to him a marked though diffident Tennysonian talent:

> Small were his themes — low builds the nightingale —
> But promised more: and mellow was his voice,
> He pitch'd it like a pipe to all he would;
> And thus he brought our story back to life.[23]

Eventually the frame was reshaped; and Clive, or Arundel, was omitted altogether. Yet Tennyson found other and less obvious ways of speaking for himself from a dramatic context. In the published poem the chief narrator appears in the first person and, in accord with the advice to be his own hero if he will, assumes the role of the Prince as he begins the chain-story. Then when the tale has ended, the "I" returns as the composing poet to explain the difficulties of unifying the several narratives, burlesque and solemn, mock-heroic and true-heroic, and so of reconciling "the mockers and the realists":

> And I, betwixt them both, to please them both,
> And yet to give the story as it rose,
> I moved as in a strange diagonal,
> And maybe neither pleased myself nor them.

During the forties, sometimes to the dismay of his friends, often to the perplexity of his reviewers, Tennyson himself as man and artist moved in much the same fashion toward some remote fulfillment.

The Princess, begun as "The New University" at least eight years earlier,[24] appeared after much decision and indecision on Christmas day of 1847. Soon afterwards Tennyson, anticipating objections, wrote to FitzGerald, "My book is out and I hate it, and so no doubt will you." [25] Yet however real may have been his dissatisfaction with his accomplishment, he had no thought of abandoning or suppressing the work over which he had labored so long. Within a few weeks he prepared a reissue of the poem with some slight changes; in 1850 he revised it rather heavily and intercalated the rhymed songs and the "Interlude" between Parts IV and V; and in 1851 he introduced into the fourth edition the curious descriptions of the Prince's "weird seizures." Over the years thereafter innumerable minor alterations bore witness less to his sense of having in some sort failed than to his lasting interest in the rich elaboration of his text. Ultimately he would admit, though still half-apologetically, his warm regard for certain single passages of the medley; he declared "some of the blank verse" here and there throughout the poem "among the best I ever wrote," and he came to feel the highly contrived "Come Down, O Maid" one of his "most successful" essays in "simple rhythm and vowel music." [26]

Convinced, as he must have been from the beginning, of the stylistic brilliance of his performance, Tennyson strove to clarify the thematic intention of *The Princess* and to justify, if possible, the complications of his method. Accordingly, in each successive edition from 1848 to 1853 he enlarged the frame of the fantasy. "It may be remarked," he said, long after the changes were complete, "that there is scarcely anything in the story which is not prophetically glanced at in the prologue," [27] or — he might have added — accounted for in the "Conclusion." As virtually another "English idyl," the "Prologue" juxtaposes old and new in a picture of summer contentment: seven leisured young men fresh from college, devoted to the pleasant traditions of their class and culture, picnic with friends by a Gothic ruin on Sir Walter Vivian's estate, while all about them throngs of workers and country girls gather on the sloping lawns to enjoy the wonders of a Mechanics' Institute, patient lectures on the latest miracles of industry and practical experiments with electric circuits, telegraphs, and clock-work engines, novel sport going "hand in hand with science." Since all in some way are concerned with education, Lilia, the spirited daughter of Sir Walter, may appropriately ponder the sort of instruction for women she might sponsor, were she "some great princess"; and the collegians, mingling banter and affection, may fulfill her dream by making her the heroine, "six feet high, / Grand, epic, homicidal," of a chain-story in which each in turn may play the hero, "Seven and yet one, like shadows in a dream." Though the men are determined to speak with a light protective masculine irony, Lilia and the women, who desire that the theme be treated earnestly, are invited to sing songs, as serious as need be, between the narratives. Thus the tale is to be

> something made to suit with time and place,
> A Gothic ruin and a Grecian house,
> A talk of college and of ladies' rights,
> A feudal knight in silken masquerade,
> And, yonder, shrieks and strange experiments. . .
> This *were* a medley!

As the story proceeds, the "medley" extends from the materials to the shadings and tones of the verse itself. In the "Interlude" Lilia protests against the "raillery, or grotesque, or false sublime," and her song, intoned with conviction, helps impose a new sobriety upon the narrators. The style henceforth loses most of its satiric edge, and the plot moves toward a grave denouement. In the "Conclusion" the poet of the party, ever aware of his divided audience, considers the problems of editing the tale and dressing it up "poetically":

> What style could suit?
> The men required that I should give throughout
> The sort of mock-heroic gigantesque,
> With which we banter'd little Lilia first:
> The women — and perhaps they felt their power,
> For something in the ballads which they sang,
> Or in their silent influence as they sat,
> Had ever seem'd to wrestle with burlesque,
> And drove us, last, to quite a solemn close —
> They hated banter, wish'd for something real.

Then, at the end of the picnic, the "Tory member's elder son," viewed with some irony, passes a very insular judgment on the "mock heroics" of radical France and incidentally achieves a very fair estimate of the diluted mock heroics of *The Princess,*

> Too comic for the solemn things they are,
> Too solemn for the comic touches in them.

Had Tennyson chosen to sustain the satiric mode without the admixture of solemnity, he might readily have succeeded in producing one of the most distinguished artificial comedies in English verse. Few of his critics recognized what should have been immediately apparent: his remarkable talent for burlesque, his frank delight in the humor of concentrated language, his ability to find the ridiculous in a misplaced epical sublime.[28] If *The Princess* is never precisely a mock-epic, it draws freely for comic purposes — at least in its first cantos — on the conventions of a classical heroic style.

Here are epic catalogues of female genius, formal epic addresses, Homeric turns of syntax, devices of Virgilian rhetoric. Princess Ida is first seen in epic posture:

> There at a board by tome and paper sat,
> With two tame leopards couch'd beside her throne,
> All beauty compass'd in a female form,
> The Princess; liker to the inhabitant
> Of some clear planet close upon the sun,
> Than our man's earth.

The father of the Prince vents an epic rage upon the letter and the gift from the father of Ida, as if he were thereby destroying the whole cause of feminism:

> Now, while they spake, I saw my father's face
> Grow long and troubled like a rising moon,
> Inflamed with wrath. He started on his feet,
> Tore the king's letter, snow'd it down, and rent
> The wonder of the loom thro' warp and woof
> From skirt to skirt; and at the last he sware
> That he would send a hundred thousand men,
> And bring her in a whirlwind; then he chew'd
> The thrice-turn'd cud of wrath, and cook'd his spleen,
> Communing with his captains of the war.

An epic momentousness attends the rout of the women when they discover male interlopers in their midst:

> There rose a shriek as of a city sack'd;
> Melissa clamor'd, "Flee the death;" "To horse!"
> Said Ida, "home! to horse!" and fled, as flies
> A troop of snowy doves athward the dusk
> When some one batters at the dovecote doors,
> Disorderly the women.

And a calculated inflation or formality of statement again and again lends epical dignity to the amusement and irony, as, for example, in the simile describing feminine script:

> In such a hand as when a field of corn
> Bows all its ears before the roaring East,

or the depiction of:

A classic lecture, rich in sentiment,
With scraps of thunderous epic lilted out
By violet-hooded Doctors, elegies
And quoted odes, and jewels five-words-long
That on the stretch'd forefinger of all Time
Sparkle forever.

With such resources of language at his disposal and with so
sure a command of parody, Tennyson, we may feel, should
have given his comic gifts free rein in a consistent mock-
heroic. That he did not, suggests that, as the composition
of the poem advanced, he found his subject essentially incompatible with the satiric method, too close in fact to his
own needs to be developed with full ironic detachment.

   The apparent subject of *The Princess* is of course the
higher education of women, an issue of immediate importance
in early-Victorian England. Tennyson, who considered it
one of the "great social questions" [29] of his time, was more
prepared to understand than to mock. Though impatient
with the intellectual aspirations of genteel literary bluestock-
ings, he remembered affectionately the circle of his sisters
and their friends, known as the "Husks," [30] who in the last
days at Somersby had studied and written poetry — and
cultivated "husky" epithets as the mark of their liberation.
He made himself familiar with the current literature of
feminism, its reasonable demands no less than its extravagant
proposals. And he may even have discussed with F. D.
Maurice the plans for a "female academy," which led to the
founding in 1848 of Queen's College, London.[31] *The
Princess*, then, must not be read as a mere burlesque of the
feminist cause. Though Ida's university seems an ill-conceived
and at times altogether ludicrous experiment, Ida herself is
far less an object of ridicule than is the Prince's father, who
sees woman simply as the helpless, fair-skinned prey of the
bold male animal. "The best interpreters of the poem," said
Tennyson, are the songs between the parts, and these are

uniformly serious. Yet, concerned as they are with the equal
love of man and woman and the role of the child as token
of that love, the songs actually have little direct bearing on
the problem of female education. If they do indeed interpret
the action, they must indicate a real theme beyond the apparent occasion of the poem, a meaning apart from all
contemporary sympathies.

Though ambivalent in his reactions to militant feminism,
the Prince, from whose point of view the whole plot is
presented, is steadfast in his quest for the true Ida. A most
unheroic hero, highly sensitive, to a degree effeminate, "with
lengths of yellow ringlet, like a girl," the Prince can become assertively masculine only when the Princess discovers
and accepts her suppressed womanhood. Until then, he
must endure the curse of his house, the "weird seizures"
which prevent him from knowing "the shadow from the
substance" and so from engaging his whole self in the world
of appearances. Yet as long as others mistake the insubstantial
for the real, the curse may also prove a blessing, indeed
may stand as correlative to the isolating poetic sensibility by
which the artist achieves aesthetic distance from his materials.
Thus, observing Ida in all her false pride, a self-appointed
goddess, majestic amid her tame leopards, the Prince suffers
a familiar disorientation and at the same time senses the essential unreality of the scene before him:

> I drew near;
> I gazed. On a sudden my strange seizure came
> Upon me, the weird vision of our house:
> The Princess Ida seem'd a hollow show,
> Her gay-furr'd cats a painted fantasy,
> Her college and her maidens, empty masks,
> And I myself the shadow of a dream,
> For all things were and were not.

And again as he looks back upon the university gardens
from which he has just been expelled, he feels himself a

ghost among ghosts; yet he perceives what those committed
to aggressive action fail to see, the cross-purposes of mis-
guided emotion and the disparity between motive and situation, for

> The Princess with her monstrous woman-guard,
> The jest and earnest working side by side,
> The cataract and the tumult and the kings
> Were shadows; and the long fantastic night
> With all its doings had and had not been,
> And all things were and were not.

Later, at the moment of battle, when he can bring himself
neither to attack Ida's perversity nor to defend his father's
naive antifeminism, a final "seizure" divorces him in spirit
altogether from the hostilities. Consequently dazed and
dreaming, he falls wounded on the field, lapses into a long
trance "as in some mystic middle state," and eventually experiences a kind of death-in-life, "Quite sunder'd from the moving Universe." In delirium he rejects the false Princess;
then, conscious once more, he finds Ida herself ready to
repudiate her own falsity. Now at last the appearance and
the reality coincide; and the Princess, become an embodiment of self-reverent truth, may release him from his curse
and banish forever his "haunting sense of hollow shows."

Far from being an unnecessary intrusion in the medley,
the "weird seizures" thus reinforce its deepest theme, the
clash between shadow and substance, illusion and truth, the
ultimate relation of art and life. Princess Ida in the final
analysis is more than the Prince's alter ego and complement; like the Lady of Shalott or the soul in "The Palace of
Art," she is at her most intense the poet's anima, the projection of Tennyson's own aesthetic vision and conflict. In her
absence she is represented at the court of the Prince by an
artifact, "a great labour of the loom," reminiscent perhaps of
the magic web woven in Shalott. Behind the high walls
of her academic retreat, in her temples of artifice, she culti-

vates all knowledge, including art, with the inhuman abandon of the soul in the Palace, who likewise occupies an "intellectual throne." Her father warns the Prince that she has written "awful odes . . . Too awful, sure for what they treated of"; and the Prince indeed soon finds her a "strange poet-princess," the author of "solemn psalms and silver litanies" celebrating her cultural achievements. August and terrible, when she speaks she is "A Memnon smitten with the morning sun." She surrounds herself with heroic statues, ideal images of Amazonian women, so that she may altogether transcend

> Convention, since to look on noble forms
> Makes noble thro' the sensuous organism
> That which is higher.

But her concept of the noble makes no allowance for sympathetic feeling; her art recognizes no human frailty. Though not herself exempt from a fierce imperious rage, she aspires to be like "the placid marble Muses, looking peace" upon the aloof aesthetic of her university. Persuaded that she must remain above all debilitating natural emotion, she dismisses the affective poetry of longing or regret. The nostalgic "Tears, Idle Tears," sung on the geological field-trip, she greets "with some disdain" as the product of a weakness, which merely "moans about the retrospect." And the Prince's lyric "O Swallow, Swallow," she contemptuously brands "a mere love-poem." For her own part, she values a poetry beyond and far above such sentiment; indeed, she confesses,

> ourself have often tried
> Valkyrian hymns, or into rhythm have dash'd
> The passion of the prophetess.

As the soul in "The Palace of Art" strives for a "godlike isolation," so the Princess, while still able to resist love and nature, chooses to remain "orb'd in [her] isolation." Seeking an absolute intellectual and aesthetic self-sufficiency, both are guilty of a deathful pride, and both must suffer the burden of the self; the soul, as we have seen, comes to know "scorn of herself" mingled with "laughter at her self-scorn," and the Princess, before her descent to the level of common humanity, experiences a similar desperate uncertainty:

> But sadness on the soul of Ida fell,
> And hatred of her weakness, blent with shame.
> Old studies failed; . . .
>   so fared she gazing there;
> So blacken'd all her world in secret, blank
> And waste it seem'd and vain, till down she came.

Ida's coming down is marked by her achievement of an unwonted compassion, and with it an understanding of the sort of poetry she has rejected She may therefore read the exquisite love lyric "Now Sleeps the Crimson Petal" with the proper tenderness, and she may recognize in the mountain idyl "Come Down, O Maid" the appropriate image of her own recovery:

> And come, for Love is of the valley, come,
> For love is of the valley, come thou down
> And find him.

Then, once more like the aesthetic soul (who also expects to find renewal in the valley), she confesses her sin against life, her failure "in sweet humility," her search "far less for truth than power / In knowledge," until a saving intuition, "A greater than all knowledge, beat her down." So humbled yet exalted by love, she ends her posturing as "queen of farce" and begins her true role as a vital human being, strong still in intellect but responsive now to the logic of the heart.

    With the spiritual rebirth of Ida, the medley approaches its ending, wherein no trace of the mock-heroic remains. Though the equal partnership, the marriage of true minds, that the Prince now gravely proposes, evades rather than resolves the problem of female education (which in any case has receded far into the background), it is clearly relevant to the implicit aesthetic theme; as man the Prince has attained the object of his quest, and as artist he has succeeded in bringing his ideal of beauty out of the shadow world and into harmony with his own sharpened sense of the substance of living. That the human reality is somehow to be equated with wedded love is suggested throughout *The Princess* by the ballads sung by the ladies, which, according to the "Conclusion," make inevitable the "solemn close." Written late in the forties and added to the poem shortly before the renewal of Tennyson's engagement to Emily Sellwood,[32] these songs may quite possibly reflect something of the poet's yearning for the long-postponed stability of marriage. But as poetry, though much admired and frequently anthologized, they are in themselves quite uneven; and only two of the six, the least explicitly domestic of the group, achieve high distinction. "Thy voice is heard thro' rolling drums" scarcely deserves the "warbling fury" with which Lilia sings it. "As thro' the land at eve we went," which describes the reconciliation of a quarreling husband and wife at the grave of their lost child, is far more mawkish than moving. And the less sentimental short idyl "Home they brought her warrior dead" is too contrived to be pathetic. "Sweet and Low" as a softly crooned lullaby better realizes its intention, though its unruffled simplicity barely escapes coyness.[33] On the other hand, the bugle song "The splendour falls on castle walls" perfectly fuses form and content in a ringing harmony where the horns of Elfland, likened to fully respondent souls, echo forever through the verse itself. And "Ask Me No More," shaped with the conscious artistry of a Ben Jonson, achieves the strength of a great love lyric — its formal grace, clarity of diction, wit of argument, and tenderness of feeling.

Though introduced expressly to prepare the way for the

sober finale of *The Princess*, these rhymed ballads seemed
delightful in themselves to readers who had thought the
earlier editions of the medley quite deficient in the poet's
characteristic lyrical power. Yet it is actually in the blank-
verse lyrics imbedded in the original narrative, rather than
in the intercalary songs, that Tennyson's lyric genius reaches
its fullest expression. "Now Sleeps the Crimson Petal" fuses
a succession of ornate and rather exotic images with such
economy and grace that its delicate artifice imposes a natural
restraint upon the tide of its sentiment. "Come Down, O
Maid" likewise, singing without rhyme, is as "artificial" —
as calculated in cadence, assonance, and alliteration — as the
poet, here heavily indebted to Theocritus, cared to make it:

> So waste not thou, but come; for all the vales
> Await thee; azure pillars of the hearth
> Arise to thee; the children call, and I
> Thy shepherd pipe, and sweet is every sound,
> Sweeter thy voice, but every sound is sweet;
> Myriads of rivulets hurrying thro' the lawn,
> The moan of doves in immemorial elms,
> And murmuring of innumerable bees.

But the finest and most assured of all is "Tears, Idle Tears,"
which, scorned though it is by the restless forward-looking
Ida, gives firm embodiment to Tennyson's own brooding
passion of the past, his abiding concern for "the days that
are no more."

Written, as we are told, "in the yellowing autumn-tide at
Tintern Abbey," "Tears, Idle Tears" may have been inspired in part by Wordsworth's great meditation on the role
of memory, which Tennyson must have associated with the
setting.[34] But whereas Wordsworth's "Lines" cherished the
past as a necessary stage in present development, Tennyson's
lyric is nostalgic for a time sad and lost yet forever fresh
and new, the "far — far — away" of his childhood yearning,
the closeness of which brings the poignancy of death to the

lesser life of the present. It communicates what he himself called a "sort of mystic *dämonisch* feeling," a deep sense of "some divine despair," the ultimate oxymoron of the universal "Death in Life." Each image or impression accordingly involves its antithesis: [35] the autumn-fields are stricken but happy; the ship of arrival is the ship of departure; the song of waking birds reaches failing ears; and the casement at dawn brightens as the dying eyes fixed upon it grow darker. An absolute control of language and of movement disciplines all frustration and vain misgiving, until the past remains serene and imperishable in its beauty,

> Dear as remember'd kisses after death,
> And sweet as those by hopeless fancy feign'd
> On lips that are for others; deep as love,
> Deep as first love, and wild with all regret;
> O Death in Life, the days that are no more!

If in *The Princess* as a whole Tennyson moved along a strange diagonal, in "Tears, Idle Tears" he traveled the far stranger oblique path that joins life to art and by the same token marks the distance of each from the other.

IN MEMORIAM

"The Way of the Soul," *1833–1850*

IF the Prince in marriage to Ida achieved a final release from his "weird seizures," Tennyson himself was never so completely to escape his own recurrent sense of dissociation. Nor had he a real desire to do so, for in his moments of detachment, reverie, and withdrawing self-consciousness he found the sanction of his imaginative life. His marriage to Emily Sellwood, which had taken place at long last in June of 1850, brought him a happiness and fulfillment deferred for over ten years. Yet even on his quite idyllic wedding trip to the Lake Country he felt at times the necessity of isolation, and he would then, it is said, wander alone and silently so far afield and in such abstraction that the gateway of the honeymoon house at Coniston had to be painted a dazzling white lest he altogether lose his way.[1] Emily, however, respected and defended his solitude. She had accepted him not in deference to his growing popular reputation but in sincere regard for the qualities of mind and soul she saw revealed in the verses addressed to Hallam, lyrics which Tennyson had long considered too personal for public scrutiny. Privately printed in March as *Fragments of an Elegy* and published less than a fortnight before their marriage, at her urging and under the title she herself had suggested, *In Memoriam*, as she must have felt, was first of all a memorial to Tennyson's own past and an earnest of

107

the conviction that would sustain him in the years to come.

Though it was to serve a whole generation as a sort of Victorian *Essay on Man*, *In Memoriam* drew its primary strength from the poet's most intimate subjective experience. It is much more, of course, than a chapter in autobiography, and Tennyson did not wish it to be read as such. The "I," the self of the poem, he explained, "is not always the author speaking of himself, but the voice of the human race speaking through him." [2] But such universality as the "I" attains is incidental to the deeply personal analysis; the self is representative only insofar as it must learn to accept the conditions of a general humanity and the circumstances of a particular culture. Whatever its public overtone, *In Memoriam* was written to satisfy a private need, and as a whole it occupies a place in Tennyson's own development comparable to that of *The Prelude* in the career of Wordsworth. Like *The Prelude*, which appeared posthumously in the same year,[3] it describes the loss of hope and the recovery of assent, the reassertion of the dedicated spirit; it grounds a new faith on the persistence of the remembered past; and it freely reorders literal facts to achieve its psychological pattern, to illustrate "the growth of a poet's mind" or, as Tennyson called it, "the way of the soul." Yet, despite the calculated arrangement of its parts, *In Memoriam* is far less systematic a chronicle than *The Prelude*, and far less epical in formal intention. Of its many critics, T. S. Eliot has been, I think, the most acute in perceiving the mode of its composition and the novelty of its design. "*In Memoriam*," he writes, "is the whole poem. It is unique: it is a long poem made by putting together lyrics, which have only the unity and continuity of a diary, the concentrated diary of a man confessing himself. It is a diary of which we have to read every word." [4]

Throughout the diary the poet keeps apologizing for the brevity and inconclusiveness of the individual entries. The lyrics, he fears, are but "wild and wandering cries, / Confusions of a wasted youth," "brief lays, of Sorrow born," "short swallow-flights of song," "mournful rhymes," "echoes out of weaker times, / . . . half but idle brawling rhymes"; they may seem to be "private sorrow's barren song"; they utter only "the lesser griefs"; they "are only words, and moved / Upon the topmost froth of thought." Such deprecation, to be sure, was partly conventional; yet much of it sprang from the diarist's real diffidence, which carried over to the tentative title, *Fragments of an Elegy*, and probably influenced a rather cavalier treatment of the manuscript itself, which Tennyson constantly mislaid and, just before the trial printing, left behind on the shelf of a cupboard in the London lodgings he had vacated.[5] Yet the elegies were from the beginning a part of his being, the very body of his changing emotion — as indeed an image early in the sequence intimates:

> In words, like weeds, I'll wrap me o'er,
> Like coarsest clothes against the cold.

Before determining the stanza form that was best to serve his purpose, he may possibly have experimented with other lyric measures. In one of his notebooks, at any rate, we find three quatrains rhyming *a b a b*, the first of which reads:

> A cloud was drawn across the sky,
> The stars their courses blindly run.
> Out of waste places came a cry
> And murmurs from the dying Sun.[6]

These lines he reshaped as part of the third section of the finished poem, where in a brief dramatic myth they are spoken by the lying lips of Sorrow:

> "The stars," she whispers, "blindly run;
> A web is woven across the sky;
> From out waste places comes a cry,
> And murmurs from the dying sun."

But most of the poetic diary, we may assume, was written

directly in the *In Memoriam* stanza, *a b b a*, which he rapidly brought to perfection. Whenever (at intervals over the years after the first shock of Hallam's death) the need of concentrated confession or self-colloquy bore heavily upon him, he turned naturally to his chosen form as the inevitable mold of his sentiments. If careless of the physical condition of his manuscript and even at times skeptical as to its over-all intellectual coherence, he nonetheless worked and reworked its individual lyrics with slow deliberation and infinite concern. His finished poem accordingly escapes the monotony that the one fixed pattern might have imposed upon it. The rhythm is enlivened by studied metrical inversions. The stanzaic movement is wonderfully varied: a line may stand alone as an end-stopped unit; or the period may be a couplet or a self-contained quatrain or indeed several run-on stanzas; or, again, the whole lyric (section LXXXVI), intricately linked, may form a single sentence. The texture, moreover, shifts, as the emotion dictates, from a bareness of expository statement to the richest descriptive sensuousness. And the tone ranges without strain from the frightened cry of "Be near me when my light is low" to the confident assertion of "Ring out, wild bells."

Hallam is the one recurrent "object" of *In Memoriam* as a whole, the single entity to which the diverse moods directly or indirectly relate, and ultimately even the "objective," or at least part of it, toward which the spirit aspires. But the composing poet himself is the real "subject," and the quality of his changing sensibility, rather than the affirmed fact of Hallam's merit, constitutes the central interest of the poem. Hallam is the symbol of life — life which the final faith believes indestructible but which the first grief sees only to have been suddenly and inexplicably removed from its human context. Hallam's passing brings death into the poet's world, and death in its many connotations,[7] as the survivor must learn to accept or transcend it, becomes at the outset Tennyson's essential theme. It is not, of course, unusual that an elegist should concern himself primarily with his own sense of loss. But the peculiar intensity with which Tennyson transfers attention from the object to the subject may be illustrated by a comparison of a great lyric of *In Memoriam* with a far less distinguished expression of a similar sentiment. Richard Monckton Milnes, also moved by the death of Hallam, attempted to describe his bewilderment on hearing the sad news:

> I thought, how should I see him first,
> How should our hands first meet,
> Within his room, upon the stairs, —
> At the corner of the street?
>
> I thought, where should I hear him first,
> How catch his greeting tone, —
> And thus I went up to his door,
> And they told me he was gone! [8]

In setting and even in some details these prosy lines seem remarkably close to the poignant seventh section of Tennyson's poem:

> Dark house, by which once more I stand
> Here in the long unlovely street,
> Doors, where my heart was used to beat
> So quickly, waiting for a hand,
>
> A hand that can be clasp'd no more —
> Behold me, for I cannot sleep,
> And like a guilty thing I creep
> At earliest morning to the door.
>
> He is not here; but far away
> The noise of life begins again,
> And ghastly thro' the drizzling rain
> On the bald street breaks the blank day. [9]

But the difference is more significant than the similarity. Milnes merely records a feeling of disappointment. Tennyson succeeds not only in dramatizing situation and mood but in effecting a complete reversal of subject and object: at the door of the death house the mourner stands like a restless ghost — the "guilty thing" of *Hamlet;* and he himself partakes of death, which the dead man, paradoxically, has escaped. Elsewhere throughout the sequence, until he has found the way to life and to faith in the continuity of Hallam's afterlife, the subject must reiterate his commitment to death or to the more perplexing death-in-life. He is tempted "To dance with Death, to beat the ground." Could he call back his friend, he would gladly yield up "The life that almost dies in me." He is morbidly aware that "somewhere in the waste / The Shadow sits and waits for me." He finds sleep, to which he surrenders his whole will, a "kinsman . . . to death and trance / And madness." And as he considers the vastness of space and the littleness of man, he feels himself already "half-dead to know that I shall die." Diary-like, the virtually formless structure of *In Memoriam* gives it one particular advantage over other major elegies; the poet may explore at leisure the idea of death and all the contradictory emotions it engenders in him; he may contemplate his grief in time and make due allowance for his slow psychological recovery.

Since the way of the soul is neither direct nor entirely consistent but beset by waverings and alternatives, the unity of the poem as a whole derives less from its large loose argument than from the intensity and often the confusion of its single subject. Stylistic rather than architectonic, it depends above all on the recurrence of an imagery to which Tennyson's sensibility both consciously and unconsciously attaches particular meaning. Though admirable in itself, the "Dark house" lyric gains added strength from its context in the sequence, for it brings together four basic images which have already acquired a certain resonance: the dark (or night), the day (or light), the rain (or water), and the hand. Throughout the poem "dark" appears as the most frequent connotative epithet; and the light-dark antithesis again and again provides a ready though still compelling tension of opposites — which are the correlatives of life and death, assent and denial — until at last, as in the climactic ninety-fifth lyric, the polarities may be reconciled in a mystic half-light, where

> . . . East and West, without a breath,
> Mixt their dim lights, like life and death,
> To broaden into boundless day.

Water — in the neo-Platonic tradition a common image of the one and the many — is Tennyson's perpetual and ambiguous symbol of changeless change. As ocean, sea, "dead lake," "Godless deep," "Lethean springs," river, brook, wave, flood, "greening gleam," cloud, frost, "spires of ice," possessive snow, killing or revitalizing rain,[10] water is everywhere the token both of man's mutability and of the infinite amorphous oneness of nature which mocks the transient human being. Eventually it is the water of life that must "rise in the spiritual rock" bringing regeneration; but in much of the poem it is the ominous "stillness of the central sea" or the tide that wears away "the solid lands," and it holds for the individual the terror of death by drowning and the menace of a "vast and wandering grave." Thus the poet is fearful at the outset that the ship bearing the dead man for burial in consecrated earth may founder and the body be lost where

> . . . the roaring wells
> Should gulf him fathom-deep in brine,
> And hands so often clasp'd in mine,
> Should toss with tangle and with shells.

Here, as in "Dark house," the water is associated with the forces of death and destruction, and the hands are a synecdoche for the whole vanished life, for the physicality that once contained the living object.

The image of the hand, found also in "Break, Break, Break,"
is charged with unusual significance throughout *In Memoriam*.[11] Having grasped the hand of the living Hallam, the
poet now knows himself to have touched death, and in his
own deathful bereavement he remains eager that the same
hand should recall him to life. If Hallam could come back,
he would, in proof of his essential vitality, "strike a sudden
hand in mine." Since he cannot return in the flesh, his example may yet "Reach out dead hands to comfort me."
At the climax of the poem, where the "I" briefly transcends
time, Hallam reappears in an eternal present, and then "The
dead man touch'd me from the past." Finally revisiting the
dark house no longer dark, the poet can imagine the familiar
gesture of friendship and sympathy:

> And in my thoughts with scarce a sigh
> I take the pressure of thine hand.

Elsewhere the hand is the symbol of aspiration — "I reach
lame hands of faith" — or of agency — "the dark hand
[death] struck down thro' time," or "Out of darkness came
the hands / That reach thro' nature, moulding men," or again,
in an image reversing Michelangelo's view of the Creation,
"God's finger touch'd him, and he slept." Touch is the
first and most basic sensation and soon the means by which
the infant discovers his own identity:

> The baby new to earth and sky,
>   What time his tender palm is prest
>   Against the circle of the breast,
> Has never thought that "this is I:"
>
> But as he grows he gathers much,
>   And learns the use of "I," and "me,"
>   And finds "I am not what I see,
> And other than the things I touch."

The hand accordingly comes to represent the material body
that defines and isolates the individual and pulses with the
only sort of life he can immediately understand.

Though neither private nor esoteric, these images may be accepted as natural components of the poet's language, the characteristic idiom of the particular diarist. But beside them are poetic figures and other devices, freely drawn from the pastoral convention, which have struck some readers as disturbingly artificial. Unlike Eliot, who hears the voice of "a man confessing himself," Yeats complained that *In Memoriam* "is neither song nor any man's speech when moved." [12] Tennyson, however, was not inhibited by the post-Victorian fear of artifice or convinced that all verse must necessarily approximate the rhythms of speech. Despite Yeats's objection, much of *In Memoriam* does achieve the directness of the dramatic spoken word. Yet those parts of it which aspire to other levels of style likewise often attain their own power and intensity. A deliberate use of pastoral motifs helps relate the poem to a long cultural tradition, the values of which have been called into question both by the poet's loss and by the new doubts of the nineteenth century. And departures from the convention serve to emphasize what is far from pastoral in Tennyson's world.

As in other pastoral elegies, the poet, at least by implication in several of the early sections, appears in the guise of a mourning shepherd:

> I sing to him that rests below,
>   And, since the grasses round me wave,
>   I take the grasses of the grave,
> And make them pipes whereon to blow.

He repeatedly pictures the course of living as a path or way or track,[13] across the fields of a once shared but now lonely experience. He remembers a goodly past,

> where not a leaf was dumb;
> But all the lavish hills would hum
> The murmur of a happy Pan. . . .

> And round us all the thicket rang
> To many a flute of Arcady.

He appeals to the classical muses, the high Urania, whom
Shelley invoked in *Adonais,* and the humbler elegiac
Melpomene. Like Shelley, too, he regards the hour of death
as selected from all time, and he imagines the sudden sympathetic decline of nature on that "disastrous day,"

> Day, when my crown'd estate begun
> To pine in that reverse of doom,
> Which sickened every living bloom,
> And blurr'd the splendour of the sun.

And like Milton in *Lycidas,* he considers in some detail the
tragedy of blighted fame and finds in nature an appropriate
analogue for untimely death: "Thy leaf has perish'd in the
green." Though he substitutes the movement of the death
ship for the conventional progress of the bier, he is concerned, as were his great predecessors, with the proper
disposition of the body and the appropriate "ritual of the
dead." Like Theocritus, who concludes with an epithalamium
his idyl celebrating the feast of the resurrection of Adonis,
he ends his entire sequence, rather unexpectedly, with a marriage hymn. And like many elegists, he draws — or seems to
draw — on the Adonis myth itself; as from the grave of the
god sprang a red or purple flower, so may grow a token of
the life that was Hallam's:

> 'Tis well; 'tis something; we may stand
> Where he in English earth is laid,
> And from his ashes may be made
> The violet of his native land.

But the earth is, after all, English earth, and the violet
will blow in the English springtime. As *In Memoriam*
develops, the conventions of the artificial pastoral fuse more
and more with the elements of a real pastoral. The "meadows
breathing of the past / And woodlands holy to the dead"
assume definite outlines, and each tree or flower is drawn
from observation with a careful and literal truth to nature.

Though recalled with deep nostalgia, the old life at Somersby
is presented in concrete sensuous detail; the witch-elms
checker the flat lawn in sharp patterns of light and shade;
the air is cool in "the ambrosial dark," and the distant landscape winks through the heat; in the morning comes the
sound of the scythe against the damp grass, and at evening

> We heard behind the woodbine veil
> The milk that bubbled in the pail,
> And buzzings of the honeyed hours.

The idyllic mode, which dictates the pastoral artifices, helps
shape these fond sad recollections of a life in harmony with
its natural setting. Yet the poet is not to be deceived either
by his selective memory or by his conscious control of
"measured language." There is very little of the pathetic
fallacy in the elegies. The nature that seems to die on the
fateful September day of Hallam's death must in any case
suffer decay with the coming of autumn. For nature, seen
in her vast impersonality, cares nothing for man. If on a
small scale she has provided the genial background of a
pastoral idyl, as the agent of evolutionary change she is
uncompromisingly "red in tooth and claw" and quite indifferent to every human yearning for beauty, order, and permanence. With affection and characteristic precision, Tennyson
perceives the burning red maple and the spiced carnation
and the night moths "with ermine capes / and woolly breasts
and beaded eyes"; but all the while his imagination and intellect are haunted by the concepts of a science too large and
too abstract to engage his personal sympathies.

In the postulates of the new knowledge, the "I" finds no
reassurance of the value of either life or art. He has followed
with concern the nebular hypothesis of the astronomers,
and he has been early in his acceptance of the doctrine of
uniformitarian change propounded by Lyell and the advanced geologists; but he is unable to discover evidence of
purpose in the dark "worlds of space" or human value in

the "Aeonian hills." He dreams of an ordered pastoral nature, a lost Eden, or of a far-off future time when the complete design of creation may again stand revealed; but he at once recognizes his dream as the projection of subjective desire, which may indeed have no correspondence with reality:

> So runs my dream: but what am I?
> An infant crying in the night:
> An infant crying for the light:
> And with no language but a cry.

The naked "cry" that rings through the bleakest of the elegies is so poignant that many readers have felt it the most compelling voice in the poem. Tennyson, however, whose aesthetic judgment always demands pattern and control, cannot but repudiate the confusion that, in destroying his perspective, has

> made me that delirious man
> Whose fancy fuses old and new,
> And flashes into false and true,
> And mingles all without a plan.

If the universe itself, he insists, lacks planned continuity, then the macrocosm must be simply the product of an aesthetic madness, a chaos of

> Fantastic beauty; such as lurks
> In some wild Poet, when he works
> Without a conscience or an aim.

Ultimately, in the final lyrics, he comes to regard "knowledge" itself, if "cut from love and faith," as the expression of a similar delirium, "some wild Pallas from the brain / Of demons." But by then the "reverence" he has acquired protects him from the menace of such knowledge; and faith, transcending disorder and denial, allows him at least an intimation of aesthetic wholeness:

> I see in part
> That all, as in some piece of art
> Is toil coöperant to an end.

In Memoriam itself, as a finished "piece of art," is designed so that its many parts may subserve a single meaningful "end," a distinct if rather diffuse pattern of movement from death to life, from dark to light. The prologue, written last, when Tennyson had determined a suitable arrangement, suggests the course of the central argument and at the same time attempts to anticipate possible objection to what may seem "wild" — that is, morally and poetically undisciplined — in the separate lyrics. The three Christmas poems (sections XXX, LXXVIII, and CV) somewhat mechanically mark the passage of the years, and the parallel lines indicate by a shift of adverb the stages of the changing emotion:

> And sadly fell our Christmas-eve. . . .
> And calmly fell our Christmas-eve. . . .
> And strangely falls our Christmas-eve. . . .

Numerous phrases from the earlier sections, carefully repeated in a new setting toward the conclusion, are likewise expected to reinforce the impression of unity.[14] And the epithalamium, which some critics have thought a most inappropriate epilogue, is consciously intended to dramatize in a joyful ritual the poet's final assent to life's purposes. Whatever the disorder of its original composition, *In Memoriam* is thus meant to escape the error of wildness, delirium, and mere subjective rhapsody; it is even, according to Tennyson's own rather ponderous description of its total design, to be read as "a kind of *Divina Commedia*, ending with happiness."[15]

But the happy ending is not, as in Dante, foreseen with certainty. The intellectual commitment of the early lyrics is to science rather than to theology. The poet assumes, perhaps too readily, that all real knowledge is scientific or at least empirical;[16] of the "larger hope" which seems essential to his will to live, he is quite persuaded that he "cannot know," since "knowledge is of things we see." He is driven, therefore, to ask whether the unseen God, to whom he lifts his lame hands of faith, can coexist with an amoral nature, the "scientific" view of which he endorses as proven and obviously accurate:

> Are God and Nature then at strife,
>   That Nature lends such evil dreams?
>   So careful of the type she seems,
> So careless of the single life?

The question, which could not have arisen in quite the same terms before Tennyson's time, foreshadows the precise problem that was to confront John Stuart Mill in "Nature," the first of his *Three Essays on Religion*. But Tennyson saw more clearly than Mill the ineffectuality of any attempt at a logical answer. The question merely prompts a more fearful one; if the testimony of "scarped cliff and quarried stone" proves Nature careless even of the type (she cries, "I care for nothing, all shall go"), must man, too, with all his bright illusions and high idealisms, perish as no more than another trial and error of the evolutionary process?

> And he, shall he,

> Man, her last work, who seem'd so fair,
>   Such splendid purpose in his eyes,
>   Who roll'd the psalm to wintry skies,
> Who built him fanes of fruitless prayer,

> Who trusted God was love indeed
>   And love Creation's final law —
>   Tho' Nature, red in tooth and claw
> With ravine, shriek'd against his creed —

> Who loved, who suffer'd countless ills,
>   Who battled for the True, the Just,
>   Be blown about the desert dust,
> Or seal'd within the iron hills?

It is irrelevant to object that *In Memoriam*, published nine years before *The Origin of Species* and more than twenty before *The Descent of Man*, is not proto-Darwinian insofar

as it does not present the doctrine of natural selection and
transmutation. For the elegist is concerned with the purpose
and quality of human life rather than the means by which
mankind reached its present state. His great question arises
out of the precise intellectual atmosphere in which the Darwinian hypothesis was to be born, and it anticipates the serious
debate that Darwinism in particular and Victorian science
in general would provoke. Man, "who *seemed* so fair" under
the older idealistic dispensation, now seems debased by a mo-
nistic naturalism which denies the soul and insists, with a
dogged literalness, that "The spirit does but mean the breath."
The fundamental conflict of the poem thus turns on an epistemological problem: the extent to which the old appearance
did correspond with the reality, or to which the new "knowledge" (or "science") does give an adequate account of the
human condition. The poet professes a deep devotion to
knowledge and looks forward to its wide extension:

> Who loves not Knowledge? Who shall rail
> Against her beauty? May she mix
> With men and prosper! Who shall fix
> Her pillars? Let her work prevail.

But he demands that knowledge "know her place," submit to
the guidance of wisdom, learn that "reverence" must interpret
and supplement the known and the knowable:

> Let knowledge grow from more to more,
> But more of reverence in us dwell;
> That mind and soul according well,
> May make one music as before.

When it lacks due reverence for the claims of the soul, knowledge forfeits its right to command the allegiance or respect
of mankind; having regained his assent, the poet rather truc-
ulently declares suicide preferable to life in a world of
"magnetic mockeries":

> Let Science prove we are, and then
> What matters Science unto men,
> At least to me? I would not stay.

He does not, of course, at the last believe knowledge capable of such proof; for he has once again warmed to the same "heat of inward evidence" that conquered the cold reason in "The Two Voices"; he has found life's necessary sanction quite beyond the things we see, altogether beyond knowing.

Concern with the mode of perception and the reality of the perceiving self turns the essential "action" of *In Memoriam* toward the inner experience. As in Tennyson's earliest verse, the dream and the vision are called upon to explore and at last to validate the wavering personality. In the night of despair, "Nature lends such evil dreams" to the frail ego; and in hours of hope "So runs my dream, but what am I?" Dreaming, the poet wanders across a wasteland and through a dark city, where all men scoff at his sorrow, until "an angel of the night" reaches out a reassuring hand. Half-waking, he tries to recall the features of the dead Hallam, but these "mix with hollow masks of night" and the nightmare images of Dante's hell:

> Cloud-towers by ghostly masons wrought,
>   A gulf that ever shuts and gapes,
>   A hand that points, and palled shapes
> In shadowy thoroughfares of thought;
>
> And crowds that stream from yawning doors,
>   And shoals of pucker'd faces drive;
>   Dark bulks that tumble half alive,
> And lazy lengths on boundless shores.

Only when "the nerve of sense is numb" and the self yields to the calm of the hushed summer night does the moment of full apprehension come, the "epiphany" that reveals the continuous life for which his whole heart hungers; as he reads Hallam's letters, the past suddenly asserts its persistence and its infinite extension:

> And strangely on the silence broke
> The silent-speaking words, and strange

Was love's dumb cry defying change
To test his worth; and strangely spoke

The faith, the vigour, bold to dwell
On doubts that drive the coward back,
And keen thro' wordy snares to track
Suggestion to her inmost cell.

So word by word, and line by line,
The dead man touch'd me from the past,
And all at once it seem'd at last
His living soul was flash'd on mine,

And mine in his was wound, and whirl'd
About empyreal heights of thought,
And came on that which is, and caught
The deep pulsations of the world,

Aeonian music measuring out
The steps of Time — the shocks of Chance —
The blows of Death. . . .[17]

Eventually the trance is "stricken thro' with doubt"; the appearances of the world in all its "doubtful dusk" obscure the vision, and the poet returns to awareness of simple physical sensation. Yet he brings with him renewed purpose and composure; his experience has given him the certitude that "science" could not establish and therefore cannot destroy.

Though unable to sustain his vision, the "I" of the poem finds in his mystical insight the surest warrant for spiritual recovery. Tennyson, as we have seen, had been familiar with such "spots of time" from his childhood, and there was, of course, ample literary precedent for his use of "mystical" materials. In the Confessions of St. Augustine — to cite but one striking example — he might have found a remarkably similar passage recounting the ascent of the mind by degrees from the physical and transitory to the unchangeable until "with the flash of a trembling glance, it arrived at *that which is.*" [18] Yet he was perplexed as always by the difficulty of communicating what was essentially private and, in sensuous terms, incommunicable. The poet accordingly, having described his trance, at once recognizes an inadequacy in the description:

> Vague words! but ah, how hard to frame
> In matter-moulded forms of speech,
> Or ev'n for intellect to reach
> Thro' memory that which I became.

The mystical vision is assuredly the sanction of his faith, but he does not choose to seek fulfillment in a sustained and conscious pursuit of the mystic's isolation. Having found faith, he must assume his place in society and "take what fruit may be / Of sorrow under human skies." And as poet, aware of his mission, he must work in his fallible yet inexhaustible medium, the "matter-moulded forms of speech."

But whether or not it defies translation into poetic language, the trance has for the poet a profound religious implication. Lifted through and beyond self-consciousness, his individual spirit attains a brief communion with universal Spirit; "what I am" for the moment beholds "What is." Yet Tennyson at no time insists that his private vision is representative or even that some way of "mysticism" is open to all others. He assumes only that each man will feel the necessity of believing where he cannot prove; and only insofar as he makes this assumption does he think of his voice in the poem as "the voice of the human race speaking through him." For his own part, he rejects the standard "proofs" of God's existence, especially Paley's argument from design, which the Cambridge Apostles had attacked and which a later evolutionary science seemed further to discredit:

> That which we dare invoke to bless;
> Our dearest faith; our ghastliest doubt;
> He, They, One, All; within, without;
> The Power in darkness whom we guess;

> I found him not in world or sun,
>   Or eagle's wing, or insect's eye;
>   Nor thro' the questions men may try,
> The petty cobwebs we have spun.

By intuition alone, the cry of his believing heart, can he answer the negations of an apparently "Godless" nature. His faith, which thus rests on the premise of feeling, resembles that of Pascal, who likewise trusted the reasons of the heart which reason could not know. Its source, like the ground of Newman's assent, is psychological rather than logical, the will of the whole man rather a postulate of the rational faculty. And in its development, it is frequently not far removed from Kierkegaardian "existentialism," which similarly balances the demands of the inner life against the claims of nineteenth-century "knowledge."

In his *Concluding Unscientific Postscript*, which may serve as an unexpected yet oddly apposite gloss on the faith of *In Memoriam*, Kierkegaard describes his own inability to find God in the design of the objective world:

> I contemplate the order of nature in the hope of finding God, and I see omnipotence and wisdom; but I also see much else that disturbs my mind and excites anxiety. The sum of all this is an objective uncertainty. But it is for this very reason that the inwardness becomes as intense as it is, for it embraces this objective uncertainty with the entire passion of the infinite.

And to Kierkegaard "*an objective uncertainty held fast in an appropriation-process of the most passionate inwardness is the truth*, the highest truth attainable for an *existing* individual." [19] Such truth is apparently close to the faith that lives in "honest doubt," doubt that the physical order can in itself provide spiritual certainty. In a prose paraphrase of his poetic statement, Tennyson affirms the position even more emphatically than the philosopher:

God *is* love, transcendent, all-pervading! We do not get *this* faith from nature or the world. If we look at Nature alone, full of perfection and imperfection, she tells us that God is disease, murder and rapine. We get this faith from ourselves, from what is highest within us. . . .[20]

Believing that all "retreat to eternity *via* recollection is barred by the fact of sin," [21] Kierkegaard questions the possibility of a complete mystical communion. Yet his faith requires "the moment of passion" comparable to the trance experience of *In Memoriam*, for "it is only momentarily that the particular individual is able to realize existentially a unity of the infinite and the finite which transcends existence." [22] Through passionate feeling, he maintains, and not by logical processes, the individual man may unify his life and achieve the dignity of selfhood. True self-awareness, as *The Sickness unto Death* tells us,[23] is born, paradoxically, of man's despair, the possibility of which is his "advantage over the beast," since in the deepest despair the soul faces its fear of imminent annihilation, "struggles with death" but comes to know the agonizing life-in-death, the torment of "not to be able to die" as prelude to acceptance of its indestructible obligation. Having also "fought with Death" and reached the level of total or metaphysical anxiety, the poet likewise finds his acute self-consciousness an essential element in his final self-realization. Such similarities are inevitable; for Tennyson, though he differs sharply from the philosopher in his estimate of the aesthetic and moral components of life, is ultimately, according to Kierkegaard's definition, "the subjective thinker": he is one who "seeks to understand the abstract determination of being human in terms of this particular existing human being." [24]

Fortified by his personal intuition, the elegist may at last give his sorrow positive resolution. He may assimilate the apparent confusions of history; he may trust that, though all political institutions are shaken in "the night of fear" and "the great Aeon sinks in blood," "social truth" nonetheless shall not be utterly destroyed; for

> The love that rose on stronger wings,
> Unpalsied when he met with Death,
> Is comrade of the lesser faith
> That sees the course of human things.

Subjectively reappraised, natural evolution itself may now be seen as the dimly understood analogue of a possible spiritual progress; and God, whom faith has apprehended, may be construed as the origin and the end of all change, the "one far-off divine event, / To which the whole creation moves." Though the prologue addresses the Son of God as the principle of immortal Love, and thus as the warranty of the worth of human love, *In Memoriam* is seldom specifically Christian. Tennyson goes behind the dogmas of his own broad Anglicanism to discover the availability of any religious faith at all and finally to establish subjective experience as sufficient ground for a full assent to the reality of God and the value of the human enterprise. His poem accordingly is not a defense of any formal creed but an apology for a general "Faith beyond the forms of Faith." And as such it is at once universal in its implication and directly relevant to a Victorian England which was finding all dogmatic positions increasingly vulnerable.

Visiting Coniston in the summer of 1850, Coventry Patmore reported that *In Memoriam* gave a "defective notion" of Tennyson's true religious conviction.[25] Most of the reviewers, however, and a great many readers welcomed the poem as a quite adequate and deeply moving testimony of one man's triumph over the doubts that beset their whole culture. In Tennyson they recognized not so much the accomplished lyrist as the eloquent spokesman of their own fears and hopes, their will to question and their need to believe, their commitment to the advance of the new knowledge and their respect for the sanctities of a long tradition. Thus, though written as a personal confession, *In Memoriam* within a few months became a public document, and its relevance grew only the greater as the conflict between science and faith intensified.

Had the elegy never been published at all, Tennyson would of course have been among those mentioned as possible successors to Wordsworth as Poet Laureate. But its appearance shortly after Wordsworth's death greatly strengthened Tennyson's claim to serious attention. At length, then, when Prince Albert had expressed his high opinion of the poem and Samuel Rogers had vouched for the poet's respectability, the Queen on November 5 ordered that he be offered the post. With his customary diffidence, Tennyson hesitated until convinced that the office would place no constraint upon his future work. Then quietly, clearly for the moment at one with his kind, he accepted the honor. So, in the middle and most decisive year of his life, he achieved, perhaps with some reluctance, a more complete recognition than he had dared imagine.

❦ VII ❧

THE INTELLECTUAL THRONE
1850–1859

Early in the fifties Matthew Arnold was conscious both of Tennyson's authority among the new poets and of his own inability to escape so pervasive an influence. He admitted that a Tennysonian cadence had invaded the last two lines of his "Sohrab and Rustum" and that his "Tristram and Iseult" owed more than he might wish to Tennyson's descriptive reveries. "One has him so in one's head," he confessed, "one cannot help imitating him sometimes." [1] Thus, whether deliberately or not, the much admired but somewhat too elaborate close of "The Scholar-Gypsy" imitates the proem of "The Lotos-Eaters"; the new land, which is the Tyrian trader's destination,

> where down cloudy cliffs, through sheets of foam,
> Shy traffickers, the dark Iberians come,

certainly bears more than a chance resemblance to the shores reached by Ulysses, where the stream rolled down the cliffs its "slumbrous sheet of foam" and,

> Dark faces pale against that rosy flame,
> The mild-eyed melancholy Lotos-eaters came.

Indeed "The Scholar-Gypsy," perhaps the finest of Arnold's longer poems, makes a direct, though condescending, acknowledgment of Tennyson's pre-eminence:

129

> And then we suffer! and amongst us one,
>   Who most has suffered, takes dejectedly
> His seat upon the intellectual throne;
> And all his store of sad experience he
>   Lays bare of wretched days;
> Tells us his misery's birth and growth and signs,
> And how the dying spark of hope was fed,
> And how the breast was soothed, and how the head,
> And all his hourly varied anodynes.

In later years, when less eager to concede his poetic debts and frankly envious of Tennyson's fame, Arnold identified the "one" of this passage as Goethe.[2] But the description as a whole fits only the author of *In Memoriam;* the "hourly varied anodynes" are apparently the elegiac verses "Like dull narcotics, numbing pain"; and the key phrase "the intellectual throne," borrowed in fact from "The Palace of Art"[3] (where it is already used with some disapproval), may well be a half-ironic reference to Tennyson's recent assumption of the Laureateship. If the activity of the dejected monarch seems more emotional than "intellectual," Arnold himself as poet was quite self-consciously aware of the extent to which the modern mind was swayed by personal feeling; and the early-Victorian "intellectuals" who paid deepest homage to Tennyson found nothing "anti-intellectual" in his attempt to reconcile the claims of heart and head.

Tennyson, however, managed for the most part to ignore his imitators and disciples. As always he distrusted all pretension, intellectual or not, and he had no desire to ascend any sort of throne or even to serve as moral or aesthetic arbiter. If he continued to read rather widely in science and philosophy, he did so to discover the relevance of current ideas to his own life and art and not to establish himself as a master of the new knowledge. He was most reluctant to make public pronouncements as Laureate, and he avoided as far as possible the kind of "occasional" verse expected of him. Before his call to the office, he had hoped that Leigh Hunt's prospects might be brighter than his own; for he had, as he said truthfully, "no passion for courts, but a great love of privacy." [4] Shortly after assuming the post, he did bring himself to write the dedication of his collected poems "To the Queen," as a gracious tribute to a benevolent sovereign and at the same time a formal statement of his willingness to accept the honor that Wordsworth had made more honorable, "This laurel greener from the brows / Of him who utter'd nothing base." And seven years later — though he could not regard his effort as poetry — he agreed to compose two additional stanzas to "God Save the Queen" to be sung at the marriage of the Princess Royal and the Crown Prince of Prussia. But apart from these, he wrote no "Laureate" verses throughout the fifties. His other occasional pieces were all expressions of personal opinion, which might or might not run counter to accepted and official sentiment. His sonnet "To W. C. Macready" celebrated the retirement of the great Shakespearean actor, who had been one of his earliest London friends. His memorable "Ode on the Death of the Duke of Wellington" extolled attitudes and policies for the moment quite unpopular, and the ode accordingly enjoyed no immediate success with the press or public. And his "Charge of the Light Brigade" drew attention to a notorious blunder which those in authority must have preferred not to see perpetuated in rhyme.

Yet despite his independence of outlook, he received an ever-widening public acclaim. In 1853 he was asked to accept nomination as Rector of the University of Edinburgh and obliged to beg his supporters to "find another and worthier than myself to fill this office." [5] Two years later he was given an honorary doctorate at Oxford amid great applause interrupted only by an undergraduate shout, "Did your mother call you early, Mr. Tennyson?" [6] He was delighted, he said, to receive a painting of Lake Tennyson in New Zealand, though he wondered if Sir Frederick Weld, who named it, could not perhaps have had someone else in mind.[7] But he declared himself "as proud as Lucifer" to learn that Captain Inglefield had called an Arctic promontory Cape Tennyson.[8] And he was pleased no doubt to hear that another Arctic explorer, Dr. Elisha Kane, an American, remembering the simile in "The Palace of Art" of the traveler in a strange new land, had designated a great minaret of rock Tennyson's Monument.[9] Less conspicuous though more distinctly intellectual tribute came in the form of belated essays in appreciation of his early work, autographed volumes from new writers and established men of letters, and much correspondence soliciting advice and approval. Professor Ferrier begged him to examine his *History of Philosophy* and to point out anything therein that struck him as "inconsecutive in the reasoning." [10] Herbert Spencer sent his *Principles of Psychology* as a possibly useful elucidation of an evolutionary passage in "The Two Voices." [11] "Benjamin Jowett recommended that he look at Hegel's categorical exposition of a theory of history similar to that shadowed forth in *In Memoriam.*[12] Longfellow pointed out that the notes to his version of Dante's *Comedy* had been enriched by quotation from "Ulysses." [13] By the end of the fifties Tennyson was everywhere accepted as both a leader of his culture and a representative man of the nineteenth century; few poets in the mid course of their careers had ever known a comparable fame. Yet he resolutely maintained a shy defensive distance from his admirers; he seemed (as Hawthorne, observing him at an art exhibition in 1857, noted [14]) cordial but remote, intent — even in the crowd — upon preserving some inviolable right of privacy and self-possession.

From the beginning of his tenure as Laureate, Tennyson looked askance at the dominant political, social, and religious positions of his time. In politics he felt no sympathy with any of the several parliamentary factions. But he was seldom without strong political convictions of his own, and he ex-

pressed himself freely in topical rhymes — which he published either unsigned or over a pseudonym, in order perhaps
to dissociate their violence from his public office. Several of
these, written early in 1852, were vehement protests against
the policy of Lord Palmerston, then Foreign Secretary, who
had given at least tacit approval to the *coup d'état* of Louis
Napoleon. Each attempted to rouse a dormant nationalism
to resist the possibility of a French invasion. "Britons, Guard
Your Own" excitedly called for a strong military defense
and a constant readiness to mistrust even the most "peace-
ful" overtures of the new dictator, the traitor, the "liar,"
the enslaver of a once free France. "Hands All Round,"
in its first form a defiant drinking song,[15] continued the attack but now condemned France itself for capitulating to the
despot and appealed — almost prophetically — to America,
"Gigantic daughter of the West," for aid to Britain, "Should
war's mad blast again be blown" and England find herself
fighting a lonely battle against "the tyrant powers" of the
Continent. "The Third of February, 1852," the most vigorous of the group, assailed a House of Lords eager to placate
Napoleon and anxious to hush denunciations in the press;
the "fallen nobility" might, Tennyson warned, "lisp in
honeyed whispers of this monstrous fraud," but a free people
must be bold of speech:

> We dare not even by silence sanction lies. . . .

> As long as we remain, we must speak free,
>   Tho' all the storm of Europe on us break.
> No little German state are we,
>   But the one voice in Europe; we *must* speak,
> That if to-night our greatness were struck dead,
> There might be left some record of things we said.

Such pieces achieved some force of righteous indignation.
Yet their relatively low quality as poetry may be judged by a
comparison with Swinburne's dramatic lyric, "A Song in

Time of Order, 1852," inspired by a like aversion to the new autocracy. Writing some years after the event, Swinburne was able to assign his commentary to three self-exiled republicans, literally pushing away in an open boat from the shores of a reactionary Europe, disenchanted yet still confident that,

> While three men hold together,
> The kingdoms are less by three.

Too close to his subject matter, too heated to achieve perspective, Tennyson created no such dramatic situation as might transcend the unresolved debate in which he was engaged. His political verse accordingly seems merely to corroborate Walter Pater's conclusion that "good political poetry . . . can, perhaps, only be written on motives which, for those they concern, have ceased to be open questions, and are really beyond argument." [16] Tennyson himself, however, attached no high poetic value to any of his topical rhymes. Though glad that the men in the Crimea found some curious consolation in chanting — rather subversively perhaps — that "Some one had blunder'd," he privately declared the swinging dipodic "Charge of the Light Brigade" "not a poem on which I pique myself." [17] As for "The War," contributed to *The Times* in 1859 and reprinted many years later as "Riflemen, Form," he was content to know that it had been more effective than much prose exhortation in furthering the cause of a Volunteer Force to meet possible assault from the darkening south. Though frequently accused of warmongering, he sincerely believed the course of appeasement the most serious menace to a continuing peace; and he therefore made his martial rhymes, sometimes little better than doggerel, immediately quotable and strong enough in rhythm to convey his sense of public danger.

The irregular Pindaric "Ode on the Death of the Duke of Wellington" is an altogether more calculated performance than any of the political verses; and upon it Tennyson expended many of the resources of his serious art. Composed as if for a chorus of mixed voices, it captures in "ever-echoing avenues of song" the pomp and circumstance of a great state funeral. If the whole seems often too rhetorical for modern taste, it has nonetheless a firm structure and a close coherence of argument. Wellington emerges as a national hero, "a common good," "In his simplicity sublime," one whose claim to respect requires no polemical demonstration. Yet the timely and local note encroaches upon the eulogy of the man who in death has joined the ages. Credited with a selfless, wakeful sense of England's destiny, Wellington must be seen in sharp contrast to the ambitious war lords abroad and to the latter-day leaders at home who "wink . . . in slothful overtrust." Thus across the pageantry falls the shadow of Tennyson's political fears, apparent in the carefully revised final version but most evident in the pamphlet circulated on the day of the funeral ceremony:

> Perchance our greatness will increase;
> Perchance a darkening future yields
> Some reverse from worse to worse,
> The blood of men in quiet fields,
> And sprinkled on the sheaves of peace.

Since the funeral itself was a partial testimony to the "greatness" or at least the affluence of Victorian society, the forebodings of the Laureate must have seemed unnecessary, morbid, and even ill-mannered.

Insofar as he still looked to the past as a time of national purpose and integrity, Tennyson remained the political "conservative" he had been in the thirties when he wrote "You Ask Me Why" and "Love Thou thy Land." But he was now less satisfied with the social and economic relations of his own age. Even in the chauvinistic "Hands All Round" he hinted at the need for change, insisting that "That man's the true Conservative / Who lops the moulder'd branch away" and conceding that

We likewise have our evil things;
Too much we make our Ledgers, Gods.

As the "conservative," he was first of all the paternalist, ready to argue for welfare legislation, close indeed in attitude to the Tory Radicals like Lord Shaftesbury, and more and more sympathetic with the aims of the Christian Socialists as articulated by F. D. Maurice and Charles Kingsley. Convinced like these that the economic philosophy of the Manchester School was the chief source of governmental apathy toward both foreign and domestic affairs, he denounced the whole "liberal" position — the faith that a century later would seem in some respects more "conservative" than his own; and he singled out for particular attack Richard Cobden and John Bright,[18] the leading proponents of the laissez-faire credo.

Early in 1851 he read Kingsley's *Alton Locke*, in which the hero expressed singular delight in "Alfred Tennyson's poetry," especially in its "altogether democratic tendency" to be seen particularly "in his handling of everyday sights and sounds of nature." [19] And soon afterwards he in turn found stimulus in the muscular conversation of Kingsley himself, who described with vigor the shameful conditions his novel had set out to expose. With such prompting and his own concerned observation, Tennyson throughout the fifties became increasingly alarmed at the exploitation of the populace by the rugged captains of industry and all the entrepreneurs and speculators of a laissez-faire economy. Whereas Kingsley gradually tempered and then abandoned his social criticism,[20] Tennyson like Dickens grew less and less patient with the ethic of material self-help, the "lust of gain, in the spirit of Cain." "The Golden Year" of 1846 looked with hope to the extension of free trade; but *Maud*, less than a decade later, begins by giving "the golden age" a new and bitter connotation as a time

When who but a fool would have faith in a tradesman's ware or his
    word? . . .

When the poor are hovell'd and hustled together, each sex, like swine,
When only the ledger lives, and when only not all men lie.

The hero of *Maud* is, of course, rather less than sane as he inveighs against the "Wretchedest age, since Time began"; but there is often much reason in his rant, and most of his specific allusions to the malpractices of trade — for example, the adulteration of bread — are well founded in fact. At any rate, the city-clerk of "Sea Dreams" (completed by 1858), though escaping madness, is scarcely less vehement in his response to "the giant-factoried city-gloom," the inhuman avarice of his employer, and the hypocrisy of the pious swindler who has embezzled his savings. If the clerk's experience was inspired by the poet's memory of his own ill-advised investment in the wood-carving enterprise, Tennyson was now inclined to ascribe all commercial improbity to what, in a comment on *Maud*, he called "the blighting influence of a recklessly speculative age." [21] So collective an indictment is hardly to be reconciled with the conventional view that persists in regarding the Laureate as the complacent apologist for the whole order of Victorian society.

Tennyson's mood of rebellion extended to the pervasive religious orthodoxies of the ascendant middle class. Never a fundamentalist, he now outspokenly assailed a literal-minded evangelical piety as the sanction of self-righteousness and intolerance. Emily Tennyson — according to Aubrey de Vere, who visited the couple soon after their marriage — desired above all "to make her husband more religious, or at least to conduce, as far as she may, to his growth in the spiritual life." [22] Yet she made no effort to instill in him a quickened respect for dogma; she was, on the contrary, glad to see him widen his range of religious inquiry. Together they read and discussed the Bible and the classical philosophers, especially Plato and Lucretius; and alone he began a study of modern metaphysics, a more or less careful examination of the works of Spinoza, Berkeley, Kant, and the later Ger-

man idealists. To their home they welcomed the skeptical
Clough and the Broad Churchman A. P. Stanley, both much
influenced by the liberal theology of Dr. Arnold.[23] At the
time of F. D. Maurice's suspension for alleged heterodoxy
from his professorship at King's College, London, they chose
Maurice as a godfather to their son Hallam; and some months
later Tennyson penned his urbane letter "To the Rev. F. D.
Maurice," inviting the gentle "heretic" to Farringford:

> For, being of that honest few
> Who give the Fiend himself his due,
>   Should eighty thousand college-councils
> Thunder "Anathema," friend, at you,
>
> Should all our churchmen foam in spite
> At you so careful of the right,
>   Yet one lay-hearth would give you welcome —
> Take it and come — to the Isle of Wight.

He must accordingly have felt more honored than embarrassed by the dedication of Maurice's *Theological Essays* of
1854 "To Alfred Tennyson, Esq., Poet-Laureate" and the
accompanying acknowledgment of indebtedness to *In Memoriam*. Throughout the fifties he also enjoyed the company of
Benjamin Jowett, whose interest in the Higher Criticism
was already agitating the orthodox at Oxford; and it is a
telling witness to Tennyson's sympathy with new modes of
exegesis that at the end of the decade Jowett could write
part of his contribution to the controversial *Essays and
Reviews* under the poet's hospitable roof.[24]
   The influence of Maurice and Jowett undoubtedly helped
determine the course of Tennyson's later religious thought,
but for the moment it made no positive impact on his poetry.
When it touched at all on the problems of religion, his verse
in these early years of the Laureateship was concerned with
the limitations of a narrow fundamentalism rather than with
the necessity of a widened faith. In his delirium the hero of
Maud complains that "the churches have killed their Christ,"

meaning presumably that orthodoxy has forgotten the spirit of the Christian law in a desperate regard for the letter. But whereas the judgment is cryptic and incidental in *Maud*, it is quite explicit in "Sea Dreams," and central indeed to the theme of that frenetic idyl. Here the unfortunate city-clerk attends a chapel service,

> where a heated pulpiteer,
> Not preaching simple Christ to simple men,
> Announced the coming doom, and fulminated
> Against the Scarlet Woman and her creed.
> For sideways up he swung his arms, and shriek'd
> "Thus, thus with violence," even as if he held
> The Apocalyptic millstone, and himself
> Were that great angel; "Thus with violence
> Shall Babylon be cast into the sea;
> Then comes the close."

The clerk's wife is terror-stricken by this "Boanerges with his threats of doom / And loud-lung'd Antibabylonianisms"; but the clerk himself is merely repelled, for he at once associates the evangelist with the sanctimonious deceiver who has been the agent of his own ruin. The preacher obviously shares much in common with the speaker of "St. Simeon Stylites"; yet there may have been a more immediate original of the portrait. Tennyson had long resisted his mother's enthusiasm for the sermons of one Dr. John Cumming,[25] who was among the most popular and impassioned evangelists of the time. Some months before the composition of "Sea Dreams" a stringent article in the *Westminster Review* had assailed the fervent unreason and hate-stirring rhetoric of this Victorian "Boanerges" in terms that anticipated the precise language of the poem.[26] Since the author of the attack — who within a few years would call herself George Eliot — concluded by contrasting the "evangelical teaching" of Dr. Cumming with the charity of *In Memoriam*, it seems likely that the essay may have come to Tennyson's attention. But, if it did not and even if "Sea Dreams" does not indeed specifically concern Dr. Cumming, the salient fact remains that in the late fifties the Laureate's attitude toward fundamentalistic evangelism did correspond closely with that of a most articulate intellectual Radical.

Tennyson's distaste for all false convention determines the themes and penetrates the very texture of *Maud*, which is at once the most dissonant of all his major works and the most varied in its rich operatic harmonies. Dante Gabriel Rossetti, who attended a memorable reading of the "monodrama," was impressed by the intensity of the lyrics but rather shocked by the violence of the plot and astonished by the alternation of tenderness and ferocity. All in all, he told William Allingham, it is "an odd De Balzacish sort of story for an Englishman at Tennyson's age." [27] Though very few of the reviewers shared Rossetti's admiration, most agreed that *Maud* was indeed odd and un-English and most obscure; and one summed up the common reaction by suggesting that the title had one vowel too many, no matter which. But the friends of independent mind, whose opinion Tennyson should have valued, Jowett, Ruskin, the Brownings, all felt the bold strength and originality of the experiment; and at least one loyal Tennysonian, William Johnson Cory, declared that now more than ever Tennyson belonged only to those free spirits beyond the reach of a stodgy respectability:

> Leave him to us, ye good and sage,
> Who stiffen in your middle age.
> Ye loved him once, but now forbear;
> Yield him to those who hope and dare,
> And have not yet to forms consign'd
> A rigid ossifying mind.[28]

Whether the hero of *Maud* commands or repels the reader's sympathy, he at least suffers no rigidity of mind. Created to bear the burden of manifold uneasiness and turbulent emotion, he remains amorphous and unstable, less distinct than his own moods, less vivid than his melodramatic history.

"The peculiarity of this poem," as Tennyson explained (though there are other and more striking peculiarities), "is that different phases of passion in one person take the place of different characters." [29] But, unlike the speakers of Browning's best monologues, the person, from whose single and often singular point of view the whole plot must unfold, is a sensibility rather than an individual. He is — according to the poet — "a morbid poetic soul" and thus a Byronic antihero, a little like Heathcliff of *Wuthering Heights*, much like the narrator of "Locksley Hall," a kinsman of the "Spasmodic" protagonist like Alexander Smith's Walter or Sydney Dobell's Balder, a dispossessed, disconsolate young man who exists for us only in his own self-appraisals. He is, in short, the epitome of the self-conscious, sensitive, but unproductive post-Romantic, "at war with [himself] and a wretched race."

War in all its ambiguity supplies the frame of *Maud*, the point of departure and the source of resolution. The hero begins by musing on the death-stained "blood-red heath" and the fate of his father, who has been, he believes, a victim of the undeclared private war of greedy speculation. For the apparent tradesman's peace, he has decided, is in reality a "Civil war, . . . and that of a kind / The viler, as underhand, not openly bearing the sword." Deceit has reached down to the local village where "Jack on his alehouse bench has as many lies as a Czar," and perfidy has invaded his own impoverished household, where the manservant and the maid are "ever ready to slander and steal." On a higher level, "the man of science" is sedulously vain in his quest for personal glory, and even "The passionate heart of the poet is whirl'd into folly and vice." The sanction for a universal selfishness seems to be the endless war of nature, the fierce struggle for survival,

For nature is one with rapine, a harm no preacher can heal;
The Mayfly is torn by the swallow, the sparrow spear'd by the shrike,
And the whole little wood where I sit is a world of plunder and prey.

Yet Maud, yearning no doubt for a true knight of her own, sings a ballad of battles long ago when men could rise above selfish desire; and the hero, hearing, dreams of a good society in which each man no longer "is at war with mankind." But he himself implicitly accepts the rule of selfish warfare by seeking satisfaction under "the Christless code" of the duel. Then only at the depth of the madness which ensues does he recognize the horror of his guilt, "the red life spilt for a private blow," and the difference between "lawful and lawless war." The grim agent of his recovery is the "lawful" war in the Crimea, of which, as he embarks, he knows nothing except that military demand has for the moment imposed upon a dissident society the need of full cooperation. Though the war will bring its own tragedies, in it the "land . . . has lost for a little her lust of gold"; and the ending of the false peace seems essential to the establishment of any true peace. Convinced that the nation has found a worthy cause, the hero, at least temporarily, may feel one with his kind and so persuade himself, "It is better to fight for the good than to rail at the ill." Thus the war without provides a "moral equivalent" for the immoral war within.

Throughout *Maud* war in some sort is the expression of unreason in the self or the society, a restless passion which may be turned to good or evil purpose. The original alternative title of *Maud* was *The Madness*, and madness in many variations remains its central theme. From the outset the hero, even as he denounces "the vitriol madness" of the age, fears for his own sanity, since his father, he remembers, was subject to moods of insane wrath. The roaring sea and "the scream of a madden'd beach" become correlatives of the social war and his own anguish; and he resolves to find "a passionless peace" in "the quiet woodland ways" — that is, in full and deliberate retreat from all social obligation and "most of all," he insists, "from the cruel madness of love." But he senses almost immediately that his misanthropy is itself the result of an absurd and morbid ignorance of the real world. When the love of Maud overwhelms him, he yields to a complete physical and emotional intoxication, despite his awareness of love's fatality:

> What matter if I go mad,
> I shall have had my day.

Maud's beauty, however, may yet save him "Perhaps from madness," and his passion, lifting him "out of lonely hell," may seem a total good. The act of love transports him to an earthly paradise symbolized by the beloved's garden, where the cedar-tree sheltering Maud must — he imagines — know the same delight as its "Forefathers of the thornless garden, there / Shadowing the snow-limb'd Eve from whom she came." In this little Eden the rose and the lily, each imaging attributes of Maud herself,[30] commingle in passionate purity; and the hero tells the lily of Maud's faithfulness as "the soul of the rose" enters into his blood. If he is now mad, it is with the enraptured madness of pure devotion. But the murderous encounter with Maud's brother arouses once more the selfish passions of pride and rage which drive him forever from the garden and abandon him to the horror of a far different madness. The madhouse to which he is eventually confined is another hell, worse than the loneliness, peopled with dead men gabbling of their selfish obsessions in an eternal chatter "enough to drive one mad." In his delusion he has been persistently haunted by the "ghastly Wraith" of Maud, "a hard mechanic ghost," the avenging conscience, an image which his own troubled mind has distorted and desecrated. Recovery comes only when in a dream he beholds the true spirit of Maud descending "from a band of the blest" and pointing toward the cooperative war that will bring him mental peace. Then at last he may exorcise "the dreary phantom" and so escape all madness in the firm resolution that

> It is time, O passionate heart and morbid eye,
> That old hysterical mock-disease should die.

The Crimean War was, of course, a major international mistake, in which the "blunder" at Balaklava was only a characteristic incident. But if we can for the moment accept the fiction that it was a righteous social enterprise such as might effect the hero's regeneration, we may begin to appreciate the pattern of *Maud* as a poetic whole, the complex relation between the themes of war and madness and the deliberate ironic reversals. Despite the frenzy of its content, *Maud* is the most carefully constructed of Tennyson's longer poems; and the verse throughout, for all its onrush of sentiment, is calculated and controlled with great discretion. The rhetoric and even bombast of the first four sections, elaborately interweaving natural description, social comment, and self-analysis, is carried by a breathless speed of movement, largely trochaic and anapaestic, and an excited abruptness of imagery. The more colloquial recitatives that follow and later recur at frequent intervals, sometimes on the dead level of iambic prose, sometimes heightened a little by a sudden sharp thrust of satire, relax the tension and provide transitions to the great arias of the monodrama: "Go not, happy day," where the image of the rose is repeated like a full note in music and the sound conquers all sense; "I have led her home" with its rich reflective sensuality; the ecstatic aubade, "Come into the garden, Maud"; and the troubled nostalgic "O that 'twere possible." In each of these lyrics all is aesthetically ordained; no effect is accidental. The concentration of language, we may be sure, was achieved by studious revision no less than an instinctive sense of verbal rightness. The apostrophe to the stars, for instance, in "I have led her home" originally described modern astronomical knowledge as "Some cheerless fragment of the boundless plan / Which is the despot of your iron skies . . .";[31] recast slightly, the passage gains almost beyond measure — the hero is

> brought to understand
> A sad astrology, the boundless plan

That makes you tyrants in your iron skies,
Innumerable, pitiless, passionless eyes,
Cold fires, yet with power to burn and brand
His nothingness into man.

With a similar deliberation "Come into the garden, Maud" exploits to an extreme the pathetic fallacy,[32] a device normally very rare in Tennyson's work:

She is coming, my dove, my dear;
    She is coming, my life, my fate;
The red rose cries, "She is near, she is near;"
    And the white rose weeps, "She is late;"
The larkspur listens, "I hear, I hear;"
    And the lily whispers, "I wait."

She is coming, my own, my sweet;
    Were it ever so airy a tread. . . .

Appraised rationally, the conversation of the flowers invites the parodic treatment it receives in *Alice Through the Looking Glass:*

"She's coming!" cried the Larkspur. "I hear her footstep, thump, thump, thump, along the gravel-walk!"

But the lyric on its own operatic terms is indestructible and as far removed from the English common sense of *Alice* as are the verses of the Persian Hafiz, which may have suggested its imagery.[33] For the whole monodrama at its most intense moves beyond reason altogether into realms of immediate sensuous apprehension.

Maud, then, is to be judged not as a realistic case history but as a kind of "symbolist" poem, in which Mallarmé could properly find the materials and emphases of a later literature — *"romantique, moderne, et songes et passion."* [34] Tennyson, however, did strive to present dream, reverie, and even madness with a close precision of detail. He attempted a clinical accuracy in his depiction of the madhouse, and he grounded his hero's delirium on the best available knowledge of abnormal psychology. His understanding of mental unbalance dictated his invention of Maud's antitype as the perversion by a distraught mind of its real object of desire:

> 'Tis the blot upon the brain
> That *will* show itself without.

And his awareness of the quality of perception at moments of crisis, when the self must find release from agonizing subjectivity, prompted his hero's meditation on the shell thrown ashore by the Breton storm:

> Strange, that the mind, when fraught
> With a passion so intense
> One would think that it well
> Might drown all life in the eye, —
> That it should, by being so overwrought,
> Suddenly strike on a sharper sense
> For a shell, or a flower, little things
> Which else would have been past by!

The concern in *Maud* with the social forces that condition human behavior may have led Rossetti to consider the plot oddly "De Balzacish." But the psychological "realism" of the shell passage, as Rossetti should best have known, is more Pre-Raphaelite than Balzacian. It recurs poetically in "The Woodspurge" of Rossetti himself, and its effect may be traced in a great many Victorian genre paintings all more or less Pre-Raphaelite, where the distress of the subject is rendered by "an hallucinatory vividness in the natural objects around him." [35] Tennyson's practice of such realism was influenced no doubt by a common contemporary regard for detail. Yet the immediate source of the whole psychology of *Maud* was assuredly his own observation and experience, his personal melancholia and his familiarity from childhood with the darker neuroses of his father and his brothers.

The objective requirements of the monodrama as a form raise an inevitable barrier between the poet and his protagonist, so great indeed, that according to T. S. Eliot, "in *Maud* . . . the real feelings of Tennyson, profound and tumultuous as they are, never arrive at expression." [36] Nonetheless, the personal elements in the poem are considerable and ultimately decisive. As the interest in madness had its origin in Tennyson's past, so the celebration of a passion far more intense than the sentiment of his earlier love lyrics must be ascribed in large part to his present sense of complete emotional fulfillment in marriage. His close descriptions of the natural setting were directly inspired by his warm response to the landscape of the Isle of Wight and the "broad-flung shipwrecking roar" of the Channel tides. And his hero's social and political diatribes were, we know, often but heightened reflections of his own will to escape a stifling conformity. Still Tennyson himself might have accepted Eliot's criticism and yet not have understood why the masking of his "real feelings" could be considered an aesthetic defect. "The mistake," he said, "that people make is that they think the poet's poems are a kind of 'catalogue raisonné' of his very own self, and of all the facts of his life, not seeing that they often only express a poetic instinct, or judgment on character real or imagined, and on the facts of lives real or imagined." [37] One of the many hostile reviewers of *Maud*, however, who did feel that the poet's very self had reached full expression, solemnly warned, "If an author pipe of adultery, fornication, murder and suicide, set him down as the practiser of those crimes." But now Tennyson, secure in amused detachment, could meet the attack with becoming nonchalance. "Adulterer I may be," he conceded, "fornicator I may be, murderer I may be, suicide I am not yet." [38]

For all the violence imputed to him, his prevailing attitude was in fact far from suicidal. If his social commentary kept him at some distance from his growing public, his aloofness helped him to maintain a necessary perspective on his work and reputation and at the same time to establish the conditions of a full and happy private life. The attention he received as Laureate never for long distracted him from his primary concern, the making of a poetry which, regardless of its popular appeal, would satisfy the demands of his own imagination. Before *Maud and Other Poems* entered its sucond and much revised edition, he was already turning to a close study of the Arthurian matter to which he had been drawn again and again ever since his boyhood at Somersby. The better part of the next three years he devoted to the writing and rewriting of the four narratives published in June of 1859 as *Idylls of the King*. He was clearly gratified by the success of the volume, which more than retrieved the temporary loss of prestige he had suffered with *Maud*. Yet he paid little heed to fulsome eulogies of his achievement. He looked for encouragement rather to the steady sober confidence of his wife and the advice of a few intimate friends with whom he could discuss his poetic intentions.

Though his public verses of the fifties were often rebellious, his own temper was increasingly serene. Farringford, which became his home in 1853, was to afford him both the seclusion he required as artist and the peace he sought as a family man eager to give his two small sons, Hallam and Lionel, the benefit of open skies and quiet understanding. There the frequent guests who made the tedious journey from London or Oxford found him not merely the genial host but also the mature and sympathetic human being. The most telling records of his personal poise and charm that now remain are the several verse letters he wrote during his first years as Laureate, each of which attains a Horatian grace and familiarity rare indeed in English. The invitation to Maurice reveals, as we have seen, a capacity for friendship in defiance of all narrow convention. "To E. L., on his Travels in Greece," an acknowledgment of the receipt of one of Edward Lear's travel-books, is both a warm tribute to the "landscape-painter" and a pleasant evocation of a vanished Arcadia. But best of all is "The Daisy," written to Emily from Edinburgh, the "gray metropolis of the North," recalling the sun and splendor of their holiday together in Italy:

> O love, what hours were thine and mine,
> In lands of palm and southern pine;
> In lands of palm, or orange-blossom,
> Of olive, aloe, and maize and vine!

Here, in a new meter of his own invention handled with easy grace, Tennyson suffuses with the glow of shared affection his memories of a culture itself rich in the remembrance of things past. Whatever may be said of the other pieces in the troubled *Maud* volume, "The Daisy" most certainly brings the poet's "real feelings" to a full and indeed fully poised expression.

❦ VIII ❧

THE BURDEN OF SUCCESS
The 1860s

R USKIN, who had admired the violence of *Maud*, was disturbed by the "increased quietness of style" he detected in the *Idylls of the King*. Though impressed by "word-painting such as never was yet for concentration," he felt the new calm a symptom of acquiescence and considered the turn to the ancient Matter of Britain simply an unfortunate retreat from the condition of England, with which he himself was growing year by year more deeply concerned. Accordingly, with an unusual show of tact, he wrote from Strasbourg early in 1860 to inform Tennyson of his disappointment. "I am not sure," he said, "but I feel the art and finish in these poems a little more than I like to feel it. . . . It seems to me that so great power ought not to be spent on visions of things past but on the living present. . . . And I think I have seen faces, and heard voices by road and street side, which claimed or conferred as much as ever the loveliest or saddest of Camelot." [1]

Convinced as he was that his themes were universal and thus close to every present, Tennyson must have thought Ruskin's judgment a misunderstanding of his essential purpose. Yet he probably welcomed the suggestion that he might abandon — at least for a while — the domain of Arthur and speak more directly to the realm of Victoria. The completion of the *Idylls*, over which his imagination had already brooded for half a lifetime, remained the great objective of his career. But he could not yet resolve the aesthetic problems he saw inherent in his materials; and he had still to discover a principle of organization for the four tales he had executed and the others he planned to include. He realized that the Grail legend would be necessary to his final design; but, when urged to begin a Grail idyll, he merely pointed to the difficulties which the writing would entail: "I doubt whether such a subject could be handled in these days, without incurring a charge of irreverence. It would be too much like playing with sacred things. The old writers *believed* in the Sangreal." [2] The depiction of the naive Sir Gareth, on the other hand, proved no simpler, since he had not yet determined the place of innocence in the moral pattern of the poem as a whole. He had therefore scarcely well begun the Gareth idyll when he laid it aside. Until he too could believe fully in the values and symbols of his Arthurian world, he would have to work with a less intractable subject matter. And it was perhaps comforting to be told that, if Camelot failed him, he might find stimulus in settings which he could record from observation and need not imagine.

For it never occurred to him that he might rest for any great length of time from the labors of composition. Rest soon brought only restlessness. Occasionally, rather oppressed by the material success he had achieved and felt obliged to maintain, he might consider himself, as his grandson suggests, plagued "by the need . . . of writing to earn money, the penalty of his new social and domestic position." [3] But the income from his old as well as his new volumes mounted steadily — even staggeringly — throughout the sixties, and he could year by year better afford to reject the most attractive business proposals — such as the offer of twenty thousand pounds for a lecture tour of America, which he declined in 1862. Besides, however large the possible financial return, he was never to be rushed into publication. The true sanction for his activity lay deeper than any desire for reward or fame. He was driven most of all by the necessities of self-expression, the will to see his talent, the real warrant of his being, always shine in use. To an old friend he confessed "how much better he felt spiritually, mentally, and bodily, while engaged on some long poem; and how often in the intervals he found time hang heavily, and a longing came for regular work." [4] In a like mood several shorter pieces of the period, each too slight to serve the therapeutic function of the "long poem," affirm the importance of the never-ending quest and the deathfulness of retreat and passivity. "The Voyage," reminiscent in temper and imagery of "Ulysses," though much thinner in texture, is the proud chant of mariners who sail forever in pursuit of "one fair Vision" — which is by turns Fancy, Virtue, Knowledge, Hope, and Liberty — and, sailing, scorn the ease of tropic Lotos-lands, where

> At times a carven craft would shoot
> From havens hid in fairy bowers,
> With naked limbs and flowers and fruit,
> But we nor paused for fruit nor flowers.

"The Sailor Boy" patently commends the youth who, defying all cautions, cries:

> "God help me! save I take my part
> Of danger on the roaring sea,
> A devil rises in my heart,
> Far worse than any death to me."

And "The Islet," an odd exercise in romantic irony, presents a bridegroom who tempts his "sweet little wife" with a lush description of "a sweet little Eden on earth that I know" and then, as soon as the bride begs him to carry her off to this haven, declares that such peace may be bought only at the price of complete indifference to life itself,

> "For the bud ever breaks into bloom on the tree,
> And a storm never wakes on the lonely sea,

> And a worm is there in the lonely wood,
> That pierces the liver and blackens the blood,
> And makes it a sorrow to be."

Written a few years later, "Wages" translates the sentiment of all these into abstract moral statement; here the soul craves immortality not as an ultimate rest but as an extension of life's aspiration, the sort of continuum imagined by the lover in Browning's "Last Ride Together":

> She desires no isles of the blest, no quiet seats of the just,
> To rest in a golden grove, or to bask in a summer sky;
> Give her the wages of going on, and not to die.

Life in such terms was action, and the activity most meaningful to the dedicated poet was simply the making of poetry. Tennyson, however, was too much of the artist to think that the satisfaction of his need to keep busy was in itself enough; for the good poem, he knew, demanded the poet's commitment not only to the act of writing but also, and more vitally, to the thematic or emotional value of his subject matter.

As his public became more inquisitive about every aspect of his personality, Tennyson apparently grew more reluctant than ever to divulge his private feelings. Besides, with the coming of middle age the lyric impulse of his youth seems — quite naturally — to have declined. At all events, the only personal lyric of any consequence he wrote or published in the 1860s was "In the Valley of Cauteretz," a quiet ten-line memorial of his journey to the Pyrenees with Hallam, composed on his return to the region more than thirty years later. And even here the personal note is muted by reticence and resignation; whereas "Break, Break, Break" had been made poignant by the sense of immediate and irrecoverable loss, "In the Valley of Cauteretz" breathes the calm brought by time, the almost involuntary recovery of the past until now in the present "the voice of the dead" is once again "a living voice to me." In other and more typical short pieces of the period he turned his craftsmanship to difficult metrical experiments, exercises in which a dexterity of form necessarily supersedes a felt urgency of content. "On Translating Homer," for example, argues in self-consciously "lame hexameters" against the barbarity of the meter in English, while the accompanying "Specimen of a Translation of the Iliad" illustrates how a descriptive passage may be rendered effectively — if not quite Homerically — in a Tennysonian blank verse. "Milton," in a full-voweled imitation of the Greek Alcaic measure, succeeds better than most English attempts at quantitative verse and even manages to suggest something of Milton's epic range. "Boadicea," on the other hand, designed as "an echo of the metre in the 'Atys' of Catullus," sounds strangely dissonant to the untutored English ear; and the excited declamation of the ancient queen seems accordingly more factitious than dramatic. But Tennyson, who could intone its cadences "with proper force and quantity," delighted in his invention and complained that if people "would only read it straight like prose, just as it is written, it would come all right." [5] There could be no doubt, however, about the correct reading of the two Laureate poems he composed at about the same time as the experiments; each was clearly the work of the public bard commemorating a formal occasion. The "Ode Sung at the Opening of the International Exhibition" in 1862, set to music by Sir William Sterndale Bennett, canceled out some of the misunderstood belligerency of *Maud* by affirming the goodness of the dream of peace through commerce. And "A Welcome to Alexandra" sang out a warm and gallant greeting to the future Princess of Wales on her arrival from Denmark. Yet none of these verses, whether subtle in metrical innovation or simple and direct of rhythm, engaged the poet's deeper sensibilities; and none, of course, could require the sort of involvement he had come to associate with the production of a "long poem."

Though the domestic narratives to which Tennyson now turned also lacked subjective intensity, they were at least of sufficient length to occupy his protracted attention. Besides, in their concern with a society to be chronicled rather than created, they provided relief for the time being from the more troublesome ordering of the Arthurian mythology. Whether or not it adequately answered Ruskin's call for a poetry of the living present, "Sea Dreams," which appeared in January of 1860, set the pattern for the much longer poems that followed, "Aylmer's Field" and "Enoch Arden." Like the "English Idyls" of the late thirties, "Sea Dreams" moves toward a climactic picture of a small and quite unheroic group; but its movement is slowed by a heavier admixture of plot and a more complex interplay of character than the earlier pieces allowed; it is far more mindful of the economic pressures that influence bourgeois conduct; and it employs a harsher diction, in order to establish the illusion of an unromantic and indeed unpoetic "realism." In short, it attempts to adapt to verse the homely matter and manner of the mid-Victorian domestic novel, but in the process it loses the concentration and the dignity of Tennyson's best work and yet fails utterly to achieve the diversity and cumulative power of successful prose fiction.

A more ambitious effort, "Aylmer's Field" suffers from the excessive melodrama of an action which, though based on allegedly true events, could have been made credible only by a novelist able to give the characters psychological dimension and the situations a full and leisurely development. As the poem stands, however, Sir Aylmer Aylmer is a monstrous caricature of vanity and avarice; his wife is a paragon of snobbish stupidity, "Insipid as the queen upon a card"; and their only child, the fair Edith, is an impossibly anaemic yet long-suffering angel, who, thwarted in her love, must die of a broken heart and so ironically kill her father's one hope of perpetuating his position. Her lover, Leolin, whose middle-class poverty (he is a struggling young barrister) Sir Aylmer cannot countenance, is simply the impulsive virtuous young man, willing to resist the arrogance of "These partridge-breeders of a thousand years," ready even to master "the lawless science of our law" and so make his own fortune and "shame these mouldy Aylmers in their graves," and, on Edith's death, desperate enough to soak an Indian dagger (her gift) in his own life-blood. Yet the hero of the narrative is not Leolin but his brother Averill, the village rector, who remains content with a passive role until both the lovers have been destroyed. Then comes the climax of the whole unidyllic idyl: Averill, all righteous indignation, preaches a long vituperative sermon denouncing Sir Aylmer to his face before the assembled parish. Though the attack is necessary perhaps to drive the baronet to a state of hopeless incoherence, the circumstances of its delivery seem altogether improbable; its vengefulness accords ill with Averill's patient charity, and its violence — as some readers properly complained — ill becomes any respectable Anglican clergyman. Nevertheless, the sermon was clearly to Tennyson the *raison d'être* of the entire poem, the means by which he could give earnest prophetic notice that a pride of wealth and rank bespeaks a cultural decadence. Apart from the moral, the story was, he admitted, "incalculably difficult to tell, the dry facts are so prosaic in themselves." [6] But the assault on a selfish materialism engaged feelings which, if not strictly poetic, seemed to the poet urgent, vital, and far from prosaic. Though the action of "Aylmer's Field," dated 1793, was superficially historical, the moral was manifestly Victorian — relevant, that is, to all those in an affluent society who "swore / Not by the temple but the gold, and made / Their own traditions God, and slew the Lord."

"Enoch Arden," which is considerably less didactic, avoids both satire and invective. Yet the money motive is central to the plot. When an accident cuts off his steady income as fisherman, the frugal Enoch fears that his family will be reduced to "Low miserable lives of hand-to-mouth"; accordingly, to mend his resources, he sails off as boatswain on the misnamed *Good Fortune*. His wife Annie, whom he has set up as keeper of a small shop, thrives "not in her trade, not being bred / To barter," and so comes to know the miseries of want. After ten years of vain waiting for Enoch's return, and then many shorter delays, she consents to marry the ever-faithful Philip, partly because she pities him, but partly also because her daughter insists that marriage to this man "so dear to all of them" alone will "lift the household out of poverty." Enoch himself achieves financial security only in death; for "when they buried him," as the last and most prosaic lines inform us, "the little port / Had seldom seen a costlier funeral."

The economic problems of Enoch and Annie, however, though decisive in the action, have no real thematic significance; for, unlike "Aylmer's Field," "Enoch Arden" has no real social or moral theme at all. Indeed it has few larger overtones of any kind; the story, complete in itself, exists only for the several carefully arranged scenes that mark its progress. Yet the two most effective of these "little pictures" do succeed very well in registering an emotion, the mood of frustration (first in the rejected Philip and later, when the situation is reversed, in Enoch), the sense of deprivation and loss which Tennyson had always been singularly able to understand and to convey. As Philip, hidden in the shadows of a hilltop, beholds the embrace of Enoch and Annie, he experiences a depth of loneliness, the memory of which no future joy can ever quite dispel:

> Philip look'd,
> And in their eyes and faces read his doom;
> Then, as their faces drew together, groan'd,
> And slipt aside, and like a wounded life
> Crept down into the hollows of the wood;

> There, while the rest were loud in merry-making,
> Had his dark hour unseen, and rose and past,
> Bearing a lifelong hunger in his heart.

Enoch in his turn, come as from the dead like a revenant, must look with morbid fascination upon an image of light and life from which his dark misfortune has isolated him; through the dusk which shrouds him he sees the well-lit window of Philip's house, a glass protecting, as it were, a painted study of domestic bliss, in the composition of which each figure is deliberately disposed, each object related to the next:

> For cups and silver on the burnish'd board
> Sparkled and shone; so genial was the hearth;
> And on the right hand of the hearth he saw
> Philip, the slighted suitor of old times,
> Stout, rosy, with his babe across his knees;
> And o'er her second father stoopt a girl,
> A later but a loftier Annie Lee,
> Fair-hair'd and tall, and from her lifted hand
> Dangled a length of ribbon and a ring
> To tempt the babe, who rear'd his creasy arms,
> Caught at and ever miss'd it, and they laugh'd;
> And on the left hand of the hearth he saw
> The mother glancing often toward her babe,
> But turning now and then to speak with him,
> Her son, who stood beside her tall and strong,
> And saying that which pleased him, for he smiled.

Insofar as it represents Enoch's self-torturing idealization of the world he has lost, this contrived genre painting, bright against the gloom of its broad frame, has its functional validity. But to the extent that it asks to be taken as in itself an objectively true vision of reality, it appears forced and unnatural, and its every detail, in uniformly sharp focus, seems manipulated to secure the reader's sentimental response.

Throughout "Enoch Arden" the point of view we are to accept remains inconstant and uncertain; we are shifted abruptly and repeatedly from the omniscient narrator to the three naive characters, from an elevated poetic diction to the flattest colloquialism. Stylistically the confusion arises from the conflict between the desire to achieve an approximate "realism" of speech and the awareness that poetry has traditionally sought a more concentrated or heightened idiom than the language of real men. It is conceivable that a departing sailor might tell his fretful wife,

> "Keep a clean hearth and a clear fire for me,
> For I'll be back, my girl, before you know it. . . .
> Annie, my girl, cheer up, be comforted,
> Look to the babes, and till I come again
> Keep everything shipshape."

But such colloquialism is blanker than blank verse ought to be, and it jars with the studied simplicity of the lines that immediately follow:

> " . . . for I must go.
> And fear no more for me; or if you fear,
> Cast all your cares on God; that anchor holds.
> Is He not yonder in those uttermost
> Parts of the morning? if I flee to these,
> Can I go from Him? and the sea is His,
> The sea is His; He made it."

And this in turn is hardly consonant with the narrator's earlier account of Enoch's vocation, a stilted effort to lift plain fact to the level of poetry:

> Enoch's white horse, and Enoch's ocean-spoil
> In ocean-smelling osier, and his face,
> Rough-reddened with a thousand winter gales,
> Not only to the market-cross were known,
> But in the leafy lanes behind the down,
> Far as the portal-warding lion-whelp
> And peacock yew-tree of the lonely Hall,
> Whose Friday fare was Enoch's ministering.

Walter Bagehot, thinking it absurd that a fish basket should be called an "ocean-smelling osier," pointed to the ornateness

of the passage as the characteristic defect of Tennyson's art.[7]
Yet when free to exercise his imagination on less homely
materials, Tennyson actually achieved many of his strongest
effects through determined artifice. And even in "Enoch
Arden" the ornate style serves him well in the description
of the imaginary exotic setting of the shipwreck; for as he
elaborately devises "this Eden of all plenteousness," he imbues
the landscape of "the beauteous hateful isle" with a strange
terror, his own half-frightened attraction to sensuous escape
and his dread (as in "the Islet") of a lonely aestheticism.
Elsewhere, however, the narrative is so bound by the fetters
of "realism" that the self-consciously poetic diction merely
lends the commonplace a false dignity, while the colloquial
language aspires to the condition of prose.

"The Grandmother," a monologue which appeared in the
Enoch Arden volume,[8] likewise exposes Tennyson to the
danger of a bathetic literalism. With a Wordsworthian earnestness, the piece sets out to celebrate the self-possession of a
weathered old woman who has learned to accept death as
a familiar and necessary human experience. But the ballad
measure (also Wordsworthian) in which she must deliver
her wisdom gives a ludicrous lilt to the sentiment, and at
the climax the matter-of-fact mathematical rhymes simply
reinforce the bathos:

> And yet I know for a truth there's none of them left alive,
> For Harry went at sixty, your father at sixty-five;
> And Willy, my eldest-born, at nigh three score and ten.
> I knew them all as babies, and now they're elderly men.

On the other hand, the "Northern Farmer, Old Style," which
belongs to the same period and genre, is one of Tennyson's
triumphs in characterization, a wholly consistent monologue
in which the rough Lincolnshire dialect is the inevitable idiom
of the cantankerous old man who speaks it and the regular
thud of the rhyme adds a natural emphasis to the complaint.
Tennyson now permits no shadow of sentimentalism to blur

the quite unsentimental though not unsympathetic portrait; he maintains the sharp perspective of humor, an awareness of ironies his subject does not suspect — for the rustic on his deathbed, questioning God's justice in taking him and the doctor's good sense in denying him his customary pint of ale, feels entirely self-justified by the steadfastness of his faith and habits. In the "Northern Farmer, New Style," written a few years later as a companion piece, the humor yields to satire, since the new-style farmer is more vicious than crotchety, a self-seeking modern materialist, riding on rough-shod to the beat of his horse's hoofs, "Proputty, proputty, proputty." But Tennyson's control of the character and the dialect remains complete; content and style fuse so thoroughly that the question of possible conflict between the poetic and the prosaic does not arise.

Such aesthetic problems, however, were of little concern to a vast public, determined to admire even the least successful of the domestic idyls. Despite Tennyson's well-founded suspicion that his new book was not comparable in merit to his best work of the past, *Enoch Arden and Other Poems* proved, almost immediately on its publication in July 1864, the most popular of all his volumes. Meanwhile, Tennyson himself had become a national celebrity honored, envied, consulted, visited, overwhelmed with unsolicited attentions. The widowed Victoria had summoned him to Osborne to speak with him of death and immortality, and many of her humblest subjects appealed to him for advice and consolation. Gladstone, now a close friend and a great power in the land, listened patiently to his political opinions and earnestly, though often vainly, sought his approval of the Liberal program. Bishop Colenso, returning to Natal after his notorious trial for heresy, declared him "the man who was doing more than any other to frame the Church of the future." [9] The Royal Society elected him to membership. And eventually Trinity College, Cambridge, forgetting his incomplete degree, made him an Honorary Fellow. In 1868 to secure a privacy which Farringford, at least in the summer months, could no longer offer, he built Aldworth at Haslemere, a large neo-Gothic residence, "in a most inaccessible site," as Monckton Milnes (by this time Lord Houghton) remarked, "with every comfort he can require, and every discomfort to all who approach him." [10] But there was to be no escape from the burden of success. Wherever he lived, throughout the sixties and into the seventies, there came streams of callers, eager to pay their respects or merely to bask in his presence, and innumerable more distinguished guests, prepared to share with him their own talents and prestige: Garibaldi and Turgenev, Ellen Terry and Fanny Kemble and Jenny Lind, Darwin and Huxley and Tyndall, Sir Arthur Sullivan, Palgrave of the *Golden Treasury*, Pritchard the astronomer, Longfellow and Bayard Taylor, the Duke of Argyll and the Queen of the Sandwich Islands.

Tennyson was no doubt flattered by tribute so well intentioned and so various. But if he remembered at all his boyhood ambition, "Well, Arthur, I mean to be famous," he was not now to be overwhelmed by its extravagant fulfillment. Reputation, he saw clearly enough, was "only the pleasure of hearing oneself talked of up and down the street." [11] And the pleasure was as mutable as the tides of taste; the talkers, grown weary of praising, might shift without warning or reason to the malicious satisfactions of disparagement. His uneasiness had been apparent in the "Vivien" Idyll of 1859, where he established an identity of sorts with the disillusioned Merlin:

> Sweet were the days when I was all unknown,
> But when my name was lifted up the storm
> Brake on the mountain and I cared not for it.
> Right well I know that fame is half-disfame.

Now at the time of "Enoch" when his fame was rising to its peak, he was almost morbidly aware of its insecurity.

"Modern fame," he told the contentedly unpopular William
Barnes, "is nothing: I'd rather have an acre of land. I shall
go down, down! I'm up now. Action and reaction." [12] And
with the same troubled self-consciousness, he said to James
Knowles, the architect of Aldworth, as together they in-
spected the completed building: "That house will last longer
than I shall. It will last five hundred years." [13] His sensitivity
to attack explains the care [14] he wasted on an irked little piece
called "The Spiteful Letter," a reply to an envious correspondent (who deserved no answer), assuring him that even
a Tennysonian popularity is quite unstable, for

> This faded leaf, our names are as brief;
> What room is left for a hater?
> Yet the yellow leaf hates the greener leaf,
> For it hangs one moment later.

And his sense of alienation accounts for the outbursts of
intemperate spleen that punctuate one of his notebooks of the
sixties. Here in ill-finished doggerel he complains of a systematic misunderstanding of his poetic purpose:

> What I most am shamed about,
> That I least am blamed about.
> What I least am loud about,
> That I most am praised about.

His scorn of solemn admirers and his dread of future de-
tractors leads to pithy epigram:

> While I live, the owls.
> When I die, the ghouls.[15]

Self-pity mingles with self-possession:

> What I've come to, you know well;
> What I've gone thro' none can tell.

Bitterness dictates a severe moral realism with which one
must face the sordid fact beneath the fair appearance; in
the words of one jarring jingle,

> Home is home, tho' never so homely,
> And a harlot a harlot, tho' never so comely.

Life with its promise is the harlot — as the most Heinesque of these jottings reminds us — and fame the great deluder:

I ran upon life unknowing without or Science or Art;
I found the first pretty maiden but she was a harlot at heart.
I wandered about the woodland after the melting of snow.
There was the first pretty snowdrop — and it was the dung of a crow.

Such in its crudest form was the disenchantment that shadowed his real though passing delight in the evidences of his success. Such was the attitude that he expressed in more discreet terms to Frederick Locker, who was tempted for a while to play the Boswell to his Dr. Johnson. "Tennyson," Locker records, "says that as a boy he had a great thirst to be a poet, and to be a *popular* poet; . . . but that now he is inclined to think popularity is a bastard fame, which sometimes goes with the more real thing, but is independent of and somewhat antagonistic to it. He appears to shrink from his own popularity. He maintains that the artist should spare no pains, that he should do his very best for the sake of his art, and for *that* only." [16]

Yet devotion to art without regard for its current popular appeal did not, as Tennyson conceived it, release the artist from the responsibilities of communication. Despite his growing impatience with his own public, he had little sympathy with the new aesthetes who were declaring the absolute autonomy of art, the complete independence of the aesthetic object from all moral and social demand. In 1869 when a number of "aesthetic" critics objected to the persistent ethical concern in the later *Idylls of the King*, he hastily denounced the credo that had prompted their censure:

Art for Art's sake! Hail, truest Lord of Hell!
Hail Genius, Master of the Moral Will!
"The filthiest of all paintings painted well
Is mightier than the purest painted ill!"
Yes, mightier than the purest painted well,
So prone are we toward the broad way to Hell. [17]

Though the tone of this squib is merely petulant, Tennyson's hostility to aestheticism was deeply serious. From the
beginning he had been drawn to the Palace of Art by a
force stronger and more personal than any empty slogan
and yet repelled by a horror of aesthetic isolation far more
decisive than any desire for popular acclaim. The new "art
for art's sake" seemed to him but one more indication of an
increasing disregard for the ideal of an integrated culture.
In Memoriam had warned that all knowledge must be yoked
to reverence, to awareness of its human and humane obligation, lest "divine Philosophy" become — in a phrase anticipating his attack on the aesthetes — "Procuress to the Lords
of Hell." But now in the late sixties each separate depart-
ment of knowledge, including art, seemed to be losing its
sense of the social enterprise as a spiritual and moral whole
and affirming instead the inhuman self-sufficiency of its own
technical discipline.

The new Darwinian science in particular was tending, he
felt, toward the total degradation of man, insofar as it made
no provision for specifically human attributes. When Darwin
himself called at Farringford, Tennyson asked him bluntly,
"Your theory of Evolution does not make against Christianity?" And Darwin, who "seemed to be very kindly, unworldly, and agreeable," replied naively, "No, certainly
not." [18] For Darwin was indeed slow to recognize the metaphysical and moral consequences of his hypothesis. When his
old friend Adam Sidgwick, the geologist, brought him to
task for ignoring causation and "the will of God," he found
the complaint quite unintelligible. "In general," as Professor Irvine observes, "metaphysical ideas made him uncom-
fortable, and unpleasant metaphysical ideas made him ill." [19]
Tennyson had read *The Origin of Species* on its first appearance with mounting disappointment; he had hoped that Darwin might try to account in some way for the higher faculties
of man. But Darwin had no real interest in the possibility

of a human difference in kind rather than simply in degree. Unconcerned with religious or epistemological questions, he declined to consider the problem of mind. Yet mind to Tennyson by the time of Darwin's visit was philosophically the one reality, the one creative and enduring substance in a world of evolutionary change.

As he had once found — and would later again find — strong dramatic correlatives of his own emotions in classical mythology, Tennyson now looked to a favorite classical poet for oblique yet cogent commentary on the values of the new science and possibly also on the sensuality of the new art. Published in 1868,[20] "Lucretius" is both an appreciation of the *De Rerum Natura* and an indictment of the naturalism which that work so memorably expounded. The Roman subject invites and receives a more austere and less "idyllic" treatment than the Greek legend of, say, Tithonus or the Hesperides; for Lucretius is placed in a society no longer open to wonder, but bent rather upon the total destruction of the imagination and the intellect. While sane and self-controlled, the philosopher has been devoted to a way of reason, a "settled, sweet Epicurean life," withdrawn, comfortably agnostic, untroubled by mad ambition, entirely free from the prevalent "lust of blood / That makes a steaming slaughter-house of Rome." But now under the influence of a love potion, which has tickled "the brute brain within the man's," he experiences in himself an "animal heat and dire insanity," a capacity for a passion parallel to the violence of the decadent republic. After a night of storm, the appropriate symbol of his own fierce abandon, Lucretius rehearses his evil dreams: first, his vision of a cracking nature and torrential "atom-streams," such as he himself had postulated, "Ruining along the illimitable inane," clashing and recombining and flying apart forever; then the nightmare of Sulla's proscriptions and the fancy that from the meadow where the blood rained down sprang the harlots of the dictator's orgies;

and last, the terrifying image of Helen's breasts and a sword pointed at them from all directions but rebuffed by "all that beauty" and a fire, "The fire that left a roofless Ilion," shooting out of the breasts and scorching the dreamer. Now even by day his ordered thought is broken by the portents of unreason, as hideous as the grotesques in Bosch's dreadful portrayal of the temptation of St. Anthony,

> These prodigies of myriad nakednesses,
> And twisted shapes of lust, unspeakable,
> Abominable, strangers at my hearth
> Not welcome, harpies miring every dish,
> The phantom husks of something foully done.

An oread, all physical loveliness, passes before him, pursued by a satyr, an incarnate sexual lust in which the mind has been loath to believe but which the flesh knows to be real:

> A satyr, a satyr, see,
> Follows; but him I proved impossible;
> Twy-natured is no nature. Yet he draws
> Nearer and nearer, and I scan him now
> Beastlier than any phantom of his kind
> That ever butted his rough brother-brute
> For lust or lusty blood or provender.
> I hate, abhor, spit, sicken at him;

Having declared the gods — if indeed they existed at all — quite indifferent to man, Lucretius discovers no sanction in the atom-universe for the rationality he has chosen as his standard of human life; exposed suddenly and completely to the bestiality that now seems the one law of a blind evolution, he can recover his sense of the human difference only in suicide, in the deliberate assertion of the will to end like a man rather than submit to the triumph of a subhuman animalism.

Much has been made of the unlikely story that Tennyson, reading "Lucretius" aloud, paused at the description of the oread's "budded bosom-peaks" to remark, "What a mess little

Swinburne would have made of this!" [21] It is quite possible that the sensualities of the poem may reflect Tennyson's conviction that the aesthetes, for all their avowed or alleged fleshliness, had failed to understand the terror of passion and so to register its true intensity. But his basic intention in writing was surely less trivial than the effort to prove — as some critics have suggested — that he could meet the competition of the young Swinburne. His concern is to demonstrate the inadequacy of even the highest naturalistic philosophy to provide an incentive for either the humane life or the arts that embody humanity's aspiration. "Lucretius" rests by implication on the faith of the idealist that man is sustained as man only by his intuition of an order of values which transcends empirical measurement. Tennyson himself had long since achieved such a faith; the fact that in the later sixties he sought to dramatize the consequence of its decline or total eclipse is evidence of his growing sense of intellectual crisis, his fear that Victorian culture might be unable to assimilate its own scientific advances.

If he chanced upon David Masson's *Recent British Philosophy* published in 1866, Tennyson must have been surprised to find his name included in the "conspectus of the philosophic literature of the time," though he may have been quite understandably pleased by the explanation that "whatever else *In Memoriam* may be, it is a manual, for many, of the latest hints and questions in British Metaphysics." [22] The compliment fittingly acknowledged his sensitivity to the temper of his age and especially his foresight in anticipating the spiritual dilemmas posed by the new science. But no such praise could persuade him that he had been, or was now, an original or systematic philosopher. He was certainly more familiar with the main currents of nineteenth-century thought than later and less enthusiastic critics than Masson have been willing to recognize. And he was often able to sum up a complex argument in a simple image; his "Flower in the Crannied Wall," for instance, concentrates into six lines the Hegelian doctrine that the object to be understood in its full particularity has a fixed but ever-changing relation to the totality of the becoming universe:

> Flower in the crannied wall,
> I pluck you out of the crannies,
> I hold you here, root and all, in my hand,
> Little Flower — but *if* I could understand
> What you are, root and all, and all in all,
> I should know what God and man is.

But he remained consciously eclectic, convinced that no one rigid system of philosophy embraced the whole truth of experience, and eager to draw from all available sources whatever evidence of purpose or value he could find. By moderation, open-mindedness, and range of interest, he won and held the respect of the most diverse thinkers. But he was on terms of personal intimacy with the public spokesmen of the new science and the active leaders of church and state, rather than with the professional philosophers of his time, and he had little fluency in the specialized language of academic debate.

Nonetheless, philosopher or not, Tennyson was the main force behind the founding of the Metaphysical Society for the open discussion of the apparent conflicts between the new scientific rationalism and the older ethical and religious idealism. Throughout the seventies the Society brought together a remarkable assemblage of "Victorian minds in crisis," [23] agnostics, atheists, Anglicans, Roman Catholics, Unitarians; radicals, liberals, conservatives; statesmen, physicists, priests, poets. As always Tennyson was fascinated by the great argument of science and as always intimidated by its vast impersonality. But from the beginning of the Society in the spring of 1869 he was emotionally committed to the reaffirmation of a moral order as the necessary sanction for individual dignity and social well-being. Though he attended few of the gatherings and delivered no formal paper, he found some satisfaction in knowing that, even if no one abandoned the premise of faith or unfaith, neither the men of religion nor the men of science could persist in ignorance of the case for the opposition. For his own part, he sent to the first meeting the odd gnomic verses entitled "The Higher Pantheism," asking the final "metaphysical" question and quietly suggesting an affirmative reply:

> The sun, the moon, the stars, the seas, the hills and the plains, —
> Are not these, O Soul, the Vision of Him who reigns?
>
> Is not the Vision He, tho' He be not that which He seems?
> Dreams are true while they last, and do we not live in dreams?
>
> Earth, these solid stars, this weight of body and limb,
> Are they not sign and symbol of thy division from Him? ...
>
> Law is God, say some; no God at all, says the fool,
> For all we have power to see is a straight staff bent in a pool;
>
> And the ear of man cannot hear, and the eye of man cannot see;
> But if we could see and hear, this Vision — were it not He?

We have no record of the Metaphysical reaction to this statement of the limitations and even ultimate impotence of empirical knowledge. Nor can we tell whether the poet himself was fully aware that, in strict philosophic terms, the doctrine of appearances he was proposing was not a new pantheism at all but rather a quite consistent theistic idealism. The poem stands simply as witness that at the end of a decade of great material success Tennyson could assert the insubstantiality of the whole phenomenal world and the single reality of the spirit. Behind its cryptic interrogation lies the conviction that had at last made possible and indeed necessary his return to the Arthurian theme and his fashioning of the Grail legend, the meaning of which no longer eluded him, into the most compelling work of his mature imagination.

THE CITY BUILT TO MUSIC

Idylls of the King

When Tennyson at last took up the Grail theme, he composed with great speed and assurance. The complete first draft of "The Holy Grail" came, as Emily recorded, "like a breath of inspiration"; [1] it was written in less than a week in September 1868, and thereafter required little revision. A literal belief in the legend no longer seemed essential to its execution; for the poet, working in a symbolic mode, felt unconstrained by the standards of "realism" that had prevailed in the *Enoch Arden* volume. With a firm aesthetic control he boldly adapted his materials to his own vision, now sharp and coherent, of the Arthurian world. In its context the Grail quest was to prove no sacred mission, but to all except the prepared and dedicated Galahad a quite unholy mistake, the symptom and the contributing cause of a social decadence.

Though satisfied with the Idyll as a unit, Tennyson decided to withhold it until he had established its relation to the whole sequence. "I shall write three or four more of the 'Idylls,'" he told Palgrave, "and link them together as well as I may." [2] At the end of 1869, however, before he had fashioned most of the necessary links, he published "The Holy Grail" along with two other new poems, [3] "The Coming of Arthur" and "Pelleas and Ettarre," and one old one, the "Morte D'Arthur" of thirty-five years before, now expanded as "The Passing of Arthur." Then, so that his public might

171

associate these four pieces with the four parts of the *Idylls of the King* issued in 1859, he added a prefatory note to the volume explaining the order in which "the whole series should be read." But not until 1872, by which time he had written the tale of Gareth (to come in second place) and "The Last Tournament," a fine bitter version of the story of Tristram and Isolt (to be inserted near the end), did he print the *Idylls* in proper sequence and append the epilogue "To the Queen," wherein he distinguished his purpose throughout from that of Malory or of Geoffrey. And even then he had many changes still to make and several significant additions. "Balin and Balan" first appeared in 1885; and it was yet another three years before "Enid" was divided as "The Marriage of Geraint" and "Geraint and Enid" and the *Idylls* could finally be published "In Twelve Books."

The product of such long deliberation, the finished poem (or series of poems) was, not surprisingly, the poet's longest work, the most elaborately wrought, the most ambitious in scope. Yet many critics have complained that the whole, perhaps because of the protracted and intermittent composition, lacks both structural and stylistic unity. The fact that the early "Morte d'Arthur" first appeared in a modern framework as "The Epic" may suggest that Tennyson originally planned a tightly knit Arthuriad celebrating the epical exploits of the King himself rather than the trials and quests of his knights. And the title-page description "In Twelve Books" may seem to imply that the completed *Idylls* aspires to an epic status. Yet Tennyson was far too familiar with the traditional genres ever to confuse the idyl and the epic; and he must in any case have expected his title *Idylls* — in the plural — to designate not a single unified narrative but a group of chivalric tableaux selected from a great mass of available legend. The "idyl" is strictly a picture of mood, character, or gesture; and each of the Idylls moves through a series of sharply visualized vignettes toward its pictured climax, its moment of revelation. Though a few of the characters recur as links between some of the idyls, the unity of the sequence lies not in action or plot but in theme, imagery, and atmosphere.

In effect, the ten poems that constitute "The Round Table" stand as separate panels arranged in orderly progression and framed on the one side by "The Coming of Arthur" and on the other by "The Passing of Arthur." The frame defines the beginning and the end of Arthurian society, and each of the panels marks a stage in its growth or decline. Each of the parts is given an appropriate seasonal setting so that the colors of the background may accent the prevailing temper of the protagonists in the foreground and symbolize the moral condition of the realm itself. The sequence accordingly follows the cycle of the year from the fresh springtime of Arthur's marriage and Gareth's arrival at an uncorrupted Camelot, through a long summer of intense idealisms and hot destructive passions, on to the decadent October of the Last Tournament, the bleak November of Guinevere's repentance, and the winter wasteland of Arthur's defeat.[4] Far from being consistently epical or heroic, the style from idyl to idyl is as variable as the weather. The blank verse is carefully adapted in tone to the shifting subject matter, and there is an intentional difference in texture between the frame and the pictures it encloses: " 'The Coming and the Passing of Arthur,' " Tennyson explained, "are simpler and more severe in style, as dealing with the awfulness of Birth and Death."[5] The form of the *Idylls of the King* is, in short, essentially a new one which is neither to be measured nor understood by the standards of the epic.

As the "one music" of mind and soul represented the resolution of all conflict in *In Memoriam*, so the image of a musical harmony recurs throughout the *Idylls* betokening the faith in which alone a society may prosper. At the inception of Arthur's order the knights chant in unison before the King, and "for a space" he and they are "all one will." A peal of music greets young Gareth as he approaches Camelot, and at the gate the "riddling" Merlin explains the provenance of the enchanted city:

> "For an ye heard a music, like enow
> They are building still, seeing the city is built
> To music, therefore never built at all,
> And therefore built forever."

When Arthur receives Balin returning from banishment, he bids him once again "move / To music with thine Order and the King," and as Balin for the moment accepts the challenge of self-control, then

> all the world
> Made music, and he felt his being move
> In music with his Order and the King.

Vivien, however, from her first appearance is the siren of discord, and as she comes to destroy Balin's last hope of peace, the litany of hell she sings silences "the wholesome music of the wood." Later with ill-concealed irony she reminds Merlin of the truth in Lancelot's song:

> It is the little rift within the lute,
> That by and by will make the music mute,
> And ever widening slowly silence all.

By the time of the Last Tournament the Arthurian harmony has been altogether disrupted, and Dagonet the wise fool may appropriately rebuke Tristram, who has broken the music of his own life, as a source of the dissonance: "And so thou breakest Arthur's music too." In the final battle the King hears no echo of the first resolute knightly chorus but instead the jarring scream of confusion and defeat,

> And shouts of heathen and the traitor knights,
> Oaths, insult, filth, and monstrous blasphemies,
> Sweat, writhings, anguish, labouring of the lungs
> In that close mist, and cryings for the light,
> Moans of the dying, and voices of the dead.

The only music possible now must come from beyond life itself; the black-stoled figures on the funeral barge lift "as it were one voice" of lament and then, as the barge bears Arthur to his rest —

> Then from the dawn it seem'd there came, but faint
> As from beyond the limit of the world,
> Like the last echo born of a great cry,
> Sounds, as if some fair city were one voice
> Around a king returning from his wars.

Within the confines of the earthly kingdom, Arthur exacts rigorous vows of his knights but scarcely expects them to achieve the perfect or superhuman concord. He asks only that each desire it and work toward it according to his best capacity and through the common instruments of everyday experience,

> For every fiery prophet of old times,
> And all the sacred madness of the bard,
> When God made music thro' them, could but speak
> His music by the framework and the chord.

Yet "Arthur's music," his will for the good of his little world, is clearly in tune with the moral order of creation. The "score" is, ideally, to be accepted as given, not amended to suit the convenience or weakness of the individual performers. The king's authority, in other words, must be credited; it cannot be explained or proven.[6] For Arthur is presented as an ideal figure of supernatural origin and destination, as the emissary of God, and not as a realistic and therefore fallible hero. Tennyson's last change in his text, made not long before his death, was the addition to the epilogue of the line "Ideal manhood closed in real man," a description intended to clarify the design of the *Idylls* by further distinguishing the nominal protagonist from

> that gray king whose name, a ghost,
> Streams like a cloud, man-shaped, from mountain peak,
> And cleaves to cairn and cromlech still; or him

Of Geoffrey's book, or him of Malleor's, one
Touch'd by the adulterous finger of a time
That hover'd between war and wantonness,
And crownings and dethronements.

His Arthur, he wrote on the completion of "The Holy
Grail," was, in short, "mystic and no mere British Prince." [7]
Despite Swinburne's complaint — echoed by many others
— that such a conception had done violence to the Arthurian sources,[8] Tennyson found at least some medieval warrant
for the idealization of his subject. He liked to cite a passage
from Albéric des Trois-Fontaines [9] to the effect that Arthur's
character was stainless, and he drew the epigraph for the
finished sequence from Joseph of Exeter: "*Flos Regum
Arthurus.*" But whatever precedent he was following, he
gave increasing attention as his poem developed to the "ideal
manhood" at the expense of the "real man." In the
"Guinevere" of 1859 he had allowed Arthur to speak of
Modred as his nephew; but in later editions he felt it necessary
to have Arthur deny any kinship whatsoever with the traitor
knight said by Malory to have been the child of an incestuous
union between Arthur and his sister Margawse. "The Coming of Arthur" shrouds the king's unnatural birth in myth
and mystery, and the late *Idylls* make all questioning of
Arthur's absolute probity the measure of social disintegration.
Pelleas in bitter disillusion asks, "Have any of our Round
Table held their vows? . . . Is the King true?" And Tristram,
openly mocking Arthur and his code, confesses to Dagonet
that he has never espoused any ideal beyond self-interest:

"Fool, I came late, the heathen wars were o'er,
The life had flown, we sware but by the shell."

Though Tennyson resisted a rigid allegorical reading of his
poem, he admitted "a parabolic drift" — which is to say a
symbolism — in his argument. Arthur may be intended as
something more than the simple personification of conscience.[10] Yet he acts only from ethical commitment, and

his behavior consciously sets the standard by which the conduct of his whole realm is to be governed or, wanting that control, judged. In the war of Sense and Soul, which is the declared theme of the *Idylls*, he bears the banner of the Soul.

But despite his ideal manhood, or perhaps because of it, Arthur is conspicuously ineffective when brought into dramatic relation with the real men of the Round Table and the complex tumultuous woman who is his Queen. In his encounters with the marred goodly Lancelot, he seems almost wilfully naive; unwavering in his own faith, he is all trustfulness; he cannot bring himself to believe his best and strongest knight capable of deception, and he thus cannot begin to understand the meaning or even the intensity of Lancelot's recurrent dark "moods" or the "madness" that blurs his vision of the Grail. Likewise in his treatment of Guinevere he seems woodenly imperceptive. Throughout their last interview his avowed charity scarcely matches his self-approving inflexible regard for moral justice. As a man of perfect principle, he may indeed be ready to forgive "as Eternal God / Forgives," but as injured husband, he should hardly make the equation with divine mercy so explicit, and he certainly need not rehearse in detail the wrongs done to him and to his order by the wife cringing at his feet in a remorse which achieves strange dignity. Fortunately, however, he is seldom called upon to engage directly in the dramatic action of the *Idylls*. His major role is essentially recessive; as King, he is a shadowy background presence, a legendary hero off fighting the heathen, or at his own court an aloof voice of command and judgment, always a rather remote yet available standard of reference. Even in "The Coming of Arthur" he is more talked of than actually seen; he is known by his work as the bringer of civilization to a barbarous people, but his personality is no less a mystery than his origin. Not until the end does he appear at the

center of a single Idyll; but there, in "The Passing of Arthur,"
he is more completely himself than he could ever be among
real men, a ghostly figure now, "whiter than the mist that
all day long / Had held the field of battle" and unsure of his
physical identity as he approaches his ideal death:

> "Hearest thou this great voice that shakes the world,
> And wastes the narrow realm whereon we move,
> And beats upon the faces of the dead,
> My dead, as tho' they had not died for me? —
> O Bedivere, for on my heart hath fallen
> Confusion, till I know not what I am,
> Nor whence I am, nor whether I be king;
> Behold I seem but king among the dead."

First and last Arthur's vitality is of the spirit, whereas the
drama of the *Idylls* arises from the demands of passion which
he can neither experience nor fully understand. His own conduct in life and beyond it is entirely commensurate with
his vision.

But in the actual society of the Arthurian realm, with
which the body of the poem is concerned, appearance and
reality seldom coincide. As the great and greatly human
exemplars of the Order, Guinevere and Lancelot seem all
beauty and all courage; but the adulterous love between
them, the more culpable because necessarily furtive, partakes
of ugliness, suspicion, and cowardice; and the gradual discovery of their guilt destroys the idealism of others and
ultimately offers a sanction for the deliberate hypocrisies
of the whole culture. In the beginning, when faith is in the
ascendant, evil may prove but illusion; the reality may be
fairer than the appearance. Thus Gareth — followed at a
distance by the protective Lancelot, who is his hero — chal-
lenges and easily overcomes the foolish knights of the river
before the Castle Perilous and at length confronts their
brother the fearsome Death, who is really just "a blooming
boy" in grim masquerade. Geraint, on the other hand, disturbed by a vague rumor of the Queen's "guilty love for

Lancelot," questions the apparent reticence of his own Enid but learns, after needless agonies, to recognize in her a real devotion utterly beyond his deserving. So central to the theme of the *Idylls* is the problem of misapprehension that Tennyson allowed a rare intrusion of direct moral commentary to preface the narrative of Geraint's excursion into the wilderness of error:

> O purblind race of miserable men,
> How many among us at this very hour
> Do forge a lifelong trouble for ourselves,
> By taking true for false, or false for true;
> Here, thro' the feeble twilight of this world
> Groping, how many, until we pass and reach
> That other where we see as we are seen.

In taking true for false, Geraint anticipates the skeptics reluctant to believe in the actual repentance of Edyrn, the villain whose reform Geraint himself has effected; and these in turn foreshadow the cynics who will not credit even the King's goodness. Yet Geraint, living in a society still relatively pure, at least escapes the darker delusion of imputing truth to falsehood. As Arthur's Order advances in time, however, the fair appearance more and more frequently glosses over the evil reality, and the young knights who accept the fairness at face value meet an increasingly bitter disillusion. Balin, arriving at court, yearns to emulate the chivalry of Lancelot and chooses the Queen's crown as the device for his shield, the "golden earnest of a gentler life." But when he comes inadvertently upon a clandestine tryst of Lancelot and Guinevere, he cannot but feel that his old madness has returned:

> "Queen? subject? but I see not what I see.
> Damsel and lover? hear not what I hear.
> My father hath begotten me in his wrath.
> I suffer from the things before me, know,
> Learn nothing; am not worthy to be knight —
> A churl, a clown!"

Later, when Vivien confirms the truth of his worst suspi-
cions, he yields, "horror-stricken," to a brutish violence and
unwittingly fells his own brother Balan; but before both
die, "either lock'd in either's arm," Balan convinces him
that Vivien alone is false, while "Pure as our own true
mother is our Queen." Balin's fair illusion is thus ironically
restored; like Elaine, who has "lived in fantasy," he dies
deluded. For the young Pelleas, on the contrary, there can
be no recovery in life or death from a complete and shat-
tering disenchantment. Convinced like Gareth of the world's
goodness, Pelleas seeks for himself a maiden "fair . . . and
pure as Guinevere." His quest leads him to the proud Ettarre,
"a great lady in her land," whose apparent fairness belies
her essential cruelty:

> The beauty of her flesh abash'd the boy,
> As tho' it were the beauty of her soul;
> For as the base man, judging of the good,
> Puts his own baseness in him by default
> Of will and nature, so did Pelleas lend
> All the young beauty of his own soul to hers.

But though he wins the prize for her at the Tournament
of Youth, Ettarre, "affronted by his fulsome innocence,"
rebuffs his attentions. Rejected, Pelleas accepts the offer of
Gawain to plead for him with the lady, much as Gareth
once accepted the help of Lancelot. Yet whereas Gareth
proved the validity of his confident idealism, Pelleas must
learn the reality of evil. His initiation is similar to Balin's
but far more decisive. In the hot still night he discovers
Gawain sleeping with Ettarre, and in cold despair he leaves
his "naked sword athwart their naked throats." Utterly bewildered in mind, he experiences to his own disgust the
intense frustration of the body; as he rides off, he "crushes
the saddle with his thighs, and clenches his hands, and
maddens with himself." He now imputes hypocrisy to the
whole Round Table, blames the King for having made "fools
and liars" of all his subjects, and charges himself with self-

deception and blind sensuality: "I never loved her, I but lusted for her." At the last Lancelot suffers his contempt, and Guinevere quails before his pathetic fierce complaint, "I have no sword." In the madness of Pelleas, the lovers foresee "the dolorous day to be." Tristram, whose adventure immediately follows, has no illusions to lose; with a cynical "realism" he is able to exploit the now hollow conventions of a corrupt society. For by the time of Tristram only Arthur can believe in the correspondence of the fair appearance and the true reality, and even he must endure the taunt of the Red Knight, who boasts of honest evil:

> "Tell thou the King and all his liars that I
> Have founded my Round Table in the North,
> And whatsoever his own knights have sworn
> My knights have sworn the counter to it — and say
> My tower is full of harlots, like his court,
> But mine are worthier, seeing they profess
> To be none other than themselves — and say
> My knights are all adulterers like his own,
> But mine are truer, seeing they profess
> To be none other."

If the mock Round Table, so described, is founded on the defiant recognition of selfish lust, the true Round Table is destroyed by its concealed sensuality. In each of the ten Idylls within the frame, desire — usually sexual desire — determines the central action. Even in "The Holy Grail," where the quest demands complete disinterest, none but Galahad is willing to lose himself that he may find himself; Lancelot cannot wholly renounce his sin; and Gawain is easily persuaded by a bevy of "merry maidens" in a silk pavilion that an erotic satisfaction is quite sufficient. Only in the tale of Gareth does desire fully accord with duty; by persisting in the tasks assigned to him, Gareth justifies his innocent and overt love of Lynette. Elsewhere reason contends, for the most part vainly, with physical passion. Merlin's yielding to the seductive wiles of Vivien is merely the grossest example of the abject surrender of the intellect to the flesh. Lancelot refuses to accept Elaine as his paramour less from high principle than because of his physical commitment to the Queen, his "faith unfaithful" which keeps him "falsely true," and Elaine herself betrays her own purity, and indeed her life, by desperately offering her whole being on any terms to Love or else to Death — "O Love, if death be sweeter, let me die." Both Balin and Pelleas cling so intensely to the ideal of passion that no regard for the calmer way of reason remains to save them from madness when they suspect or discover that the ideal has been sullied. Tristram has achieved a modus vivendi, but only by the deliberate perversion of reason toward the rationalizing of passionate appetite. None of these characters practices or clearly recognizes the cardinal Tennysonian virtues of "self-reverence, self-knowledge, self-control." Yet the great argument of the *Idylls* as a whole is simply that, without such virtues and the faith which sanctions them, neither the individual nor the state can attain rational order or spiritual health.

In depicting the war of Sense and Soul, of passion and purity, Tennyson freely invokes the familiar color symbolism of red and white. At the outset the Lady of the Lake, "Clothed in white samite, mystic, wonderful," entrusts the sword Excalibur to Arthur; the knights, arrayed "in stainless white," attend the King's marriage; and all "the world is white with May." Soon Gareth comes in a "silver-misty morn" to a Camelot still starry-white in honor. Later he departs through "the weird white gate" to meet his adversaries, the brothers of Death: Morning-Star, from whose ornate pavilion flutters a slender crimson banner; Noonday Sun, mounted "on a huge red horse"; and Evening-Star, suffused "All in a rose-red from the west." Enid, whose love will remain innocent, seems from the first "like a blossom vermeil-white." Elaine is appropriately "the lily maid of Astolat," and in death she holds the white flower against her white robe; but the passion which destroys her is clearly represented by a scarlet sleeve that Lancelot carries to the tourney as her token. Lancelot himself, as he paces the "long white walk of lilies" in the palace garden, muses rather sadly on these "perfect-pure" emblems of the spirit; but Guinevere, who has come to meet him, declares her preference for the "garden rose / Deep-hued and many-folded." Pelleas, vexed by a song he once heard sung to the Queen, "A worm within the rose," stumbles by night through Ettarre's garden of "roses red and white," symbols of his own confused emotion, until he discovers the perfidy of Gawain. On the Grail quest the pure Galahad reaches the resolution of all contraries, when he perceives the holy vessel "Clothed in white samite or a luminous cloud" yet in itself "Redder than any rose"; but the troubled Lancelot has only a momentary glimpse of the Grail "All pall'd in crimson." The Last Tournament, which begins as "one white day of Innocence," ends with the white banners besmirched and the watching ladies eager to shed "the simple white" that they may glow in "kindlier colors." Tristram, who has won the red prize, a ruby carcanet, receives it in avariciously red hands, and carrying it to the Irish Isolt, dreams of the white-handed Breton wife he has deserted:

> He seem'd to pace the strand of Brittany
> Between Isolt of Britain and his bride,
> And show'd them both the ruby-chain, and both
> Began to struggle for it, till his queen
> Graspt it so hard that all her hand was red.
> Then cried the Breton, "Look, her hand is red!
> These be no rubies, this is frozen blood,
> And melts within her hand — her hand is hot
> With ill desires, but this I gave thee, look,
> Is all as cool and white as any flower."

Meanwhile, Arthur vanquishes the Red Knight in "blood-red armour," but the violence that ensues, the massacre and arson, "red-pulsing" up to the stars, brings but a foretaste of the madness in which his own kingdom must perish. Before long he must upbraid Guinevere as the mother of "sword and fire, / Red ruin, and the breaking up of laws." And ultimately the white abides only in the mists that shroud his retreating figure from the Queen's view or — beyond earthly things altogether — in the arm "Clothed in white samite, mystic, wonderful" that retrieves Excalibur from the reluctant Bedivere.

Closely associated with the red motif is the omnipresent animal imagery relating the unruly human passions to a nature clearly red in tooth and claw.[11] Arthur comes to "great tracts of wilderness, / Wherein the beast was ever more and more, / But man was less and less"; and Leodogran, the father of Guinevere, begs his help, "For here between the man and beast we die." The most formidable of Gareth's enemies has encased himself in hardened animal skins and made his will one with the appetite of wild beasts. Geraint contends against Edyrn, who proudly styles himself the Sparrow-hawk but who, when his pride is broken, repents having lived like a predatory creature; and he destroys the unrepentant Earl Doorm, whose bestiality is reflected in the table manners of his men, eating "with tumult in the naked hall, / Feeding like horses when you hear them feed." Balin as the Savage bears on his shield the device of a fierce beast, red-tongued ("Langued gules"), which he replaces with the Queen's crown, until, returning to the state of bestial nature, he casts aside the gentler emblem and in his violence rages with animal ferocity:

> his evil spirit upon him leapt,
> He ground his teeth together, sprang with a yell
> Tore from the branch and cast on earth the shield,
> Drove his mail'd heel athwart the crown,
> Stampt all into defacement, hurl'd it from him
> Among the forest weeds.

Vivien, who Circe-like has reduced him to this condition,

watches him assault Balan and then dismisses the dying brothers
as two "brainless bulls, / Dead for one heifer." Vivien in
fact habitually resorts to animal metaphor and in turn is
herself described in such images. If she thinks of Arthur's
knights as swine or goats or rats whose burrowings must be
"ferreted out," she feigns the helplessness of "a gilded
summer fly / Caught in a great old tyrant spider's web," but
when rebuffed she actually behaves like a snake-woman, the
lamia of classical legend: she stands

> Stiff as a viper frozen; loathsome sight,
> How from the rosy lips of life and love
> Flash'd the bare-grinning skeleton of death!
> White was her cheek; sharp breaths of anger puff'd
> Her fairy nostril out . . .

In "The Holy Grail" Percivale tells of the "four great zones
of sculpture" in Merlin's hall, each representing a stage of
ascent in the hierarchy of being, a progress in the upward
evolution of humanity:

> "And in the lowest beasts are slaying men,
> And in the second men are slaying beasts,
> And on the third are warriors, perfect men,
> And on the fourth are men with growing wings."

Galahad alone among the knights reaches the fourth level, for
by the time of the Grail quest most of the others are slipping
from the third to the second, and many have fallen to the first,
where human values have no authority. Pelleas, for instance,
whom Ettarre has likened to a dog kicked away but still
returning, finds himself degraded by passion to a state worse
than bestial when he must repudiate the civilized ideal as
mere delusion:

> "Let the fox bark, let the wolf yell! Who yells
> Here in the still sweet summer night but I —
> I, the poor Pelleas whom she call'd her fool?
> Fool, beast — he, she, or I? myself most fool;
> Beast too, as lacking human wit — disgraced,

> Dishonor'd all for trial of true love —
> Love? — we be all alike; only the King
> Hath made us fools and liars. O noble vows!
> O great and sane and simple race of brutes
> That own no lust because they have no law!"

The King is now haunted by the fear that his realm raised up from "brute violences" may before long "Reel back into the beast, and be no more"; and Dagonet the fool sadly calls him "the king of fools" to think that he could make "men from beasts." Isolt recognizes the deterioration of Tristram (to whom nonetheless she yields): "But thou, thro' ever harrying thy wild beasts / . . . art grown wild beast thyself." And all know Modred of the "narrow foxy face" to have been from the beginning merely "a subtle beast / . . . couchant with his eyes upon the throne, / Ready to spring . . ."; but at least half the kingdom joins his brutal conspiracy. Ultimately the King finds his darkest dread wholly realized, for all his realm indeed "Reels back into the beast."

As long as Arthur's Order does endure, the city stands as his protest against the bestial wasteland that constantly encroaches upon his culture. His first task as King has been to drive off the heathen, slay the beast, and fell the forest, "letting in the sun." Thereupon Camelot arises, radiant in its artifice, the triumph of rational purpose over the wilderness of desire, and Gareth as the epitome of selflessness glories in its bright urbanity. Outside its walls are no comparable shining towers or sun-etched "shadowy palaces." Yniol's manor, for instance, in the land of the Sparrow-hawk, is an image of decay, all overgrown with fern and "monstrous ivy-stems" like coiled snakes. The hall of Doorm is as uncouth and bare as the waste earldom which it dominates. And the castle of Pellam is "lichen-bearded" and "grayly draped / With streaming grass," and its battlements, "overtopt with ivy-tods," house bats and owls, the portents of a darkness as ominous as Pellam's own decadent asceticism. Camelot itself,

however, cannot survive the moral failure of its citizenry, for
the true city lives essentially in the civic ideal that must day by
day be reaffirmed. Thus, when forsaken by the seekers of the
Grail, it disintegrates so rapidly that the few knights who
return after a misspent year stumble upon

> heaps of ruin, hornless unicorns,
> Crack'd basilisks, and splinter'd cockatrices,
> And shatter'd talbots, which had left the stones
> Raw that they fell from.

In the end, when Arthur must do battle far from Camelot,
"On the waste sand by the waste sea," the city presumably has
vanished altogether, and the Order of its civilization perishes
in "the dead world's winter dawn."

The final collapse of the city-state is the inevitable result
of many earlier individual defections, for the tragedy of the
Idylls is built cumulatively in the separate episodes or panels.
Throughout the poem the wasteland serves both as setting
for personal error, passion, and self-will and as symbol of
bewilderment and frustration. Geraint, when confused by
his own jealous fears, deserts the city and the court, cries,
"To the wilds!" and forces his long-suffering Enid to lead
him by "Gray swamps and pools, waste places of the hern,
And wildernesses, perilous paths." Merlin, overcome by a
melancholy which his intellect cannot dispel, retreats to "the
wild woods of Broceliande," where at last he yields body
and soul to the libidinous Vivien as a fierce expressionistic
storm rages over "the ravaged woodland." And Lancelot, as
often as he is troubled by remorse, seeks release or self-com-
munion amid the bleak amoralities of nature:

> His mood was often like a fiend, and rose
> And drove him into wastes and solitudes
> For agony, who was yet a living soul.

Such imagery appears most effectively in "The Holy Grail,"
where the wasteland connotes the emptiness of selfish desire,
the timely recognition of which may be the prelude to spiritual

rebirth. Remembering his sins of pride, Percivale falters in the quest from a sense of deep unworthiness,

> "And lifting up mine eyes, I found myself
> Alone, and in a land of sand and thorns,
> And I was thirsty even unto death;
> And I, too, cried, 'This quest is not for thee.' "

Reduced to a searing self-awareness, Lancelot comes to a "naked shore, / Wide flats, where nothing but coarse grasses grew," and there, hearing the call of the sea, he yearns to purge himself of his guilt:

> "And in my madness to myself I said,
> 'I will embark and I will lose myself,
> And in the great sea wash away my sin.' "

But only Galahad has the full courage of self-denial, the will to face the reality of the physical death, to cross "A great black swamp and of an evil smell, / Part black, part whiten'd with the bones of men." And thus Galahad alone conquers the wasteland and at the last reaches "the spiritual city," the eternal ideal form that Camelot once strove to imitate.

Arthur concedes Galahad's title to the contemplative life and respects the validity of his heavenly vision. But he rebukes all who, without adequate preparation, would willfully confront the wasteland: "What go ye into the wilderness to see?" For to most of his knights the ascetic quest means simply an evasion of responsibility, an effort in a conscience-oppressed hour to achieve an unearned easement of the spirit. Like Tennyson himself, the King has been from the beginning open to the mystic intuition, but it has been always involuntary, unexpected, half-feared, and it has come to him only through the determined fulfillment of immediate social duties. To those few who return he explains why he could not easily have joined in the quest,

> "seeing that the King must guard
> That which he rules, and is but as the hind
> To whom a space of land is given to plow,

> Who may not wander from the allotted field
> Before his work be done, but, being done,
> Let visions of the night or of the day
> Come as they will; and many a time they come,
> Until this earth he walks on seems not earth,
> This light that strikes his eyeball is not light,
> This air that smites his forehead is not air
> But vision — yea, his very hand and foot —
> In moments when he feels he cannot die,
> And knows himself no vision to himself,
> Nor the high God a vision, nor that One
> Who rose again."

Thus, though he has known the soul's transcendence of the body, Arthur accepts the physical world all about him, the human environment, as the proper sphere for moral action. And though he himself is to be regarded as an ideal character, he values — perhaps even more highly than Galahad's unswerving virtue — the painful conversion of a man like Edyrn, who in the actual condition of this life finds himself already "halfway down the slope to hell" and learns by experience that only through humility may he retrieve his manhood. Tennyson likewise seems more concerned with the mixed middle state of human beings than with an inhuman or superhuman sanctity, for he concentrates primary attention throughout the *Idylls* on the conflicts of troubled imperfect souls, and he takes care to give his real protagonists, Lancelot and Guinevere, the sort of close psychological motivation that neither Galahad nor Arthur requires. He probes Lancelot's "remorseful pain" at the death of Elaine and at once suggests that through such suffering, Lancelot will slowly grow in stature until he die "a holy man." And to a full analysis of Guinevere's warring passions he devotes the final and climactic panel of "The Round Table."

Each of the Idylls reshapes rather than reproduces the Arthurian legends; but "Guinevere" owes less than any of the others to Tennyson's printed sources and correspondingly

more to his own creative imagination. If Arthur reflects
his mystical apprehension, Guinevere partakes of his deepest
aesthetic sensibility. She shares the poet's cherished yet mistrusted delight in the shapes and colors of material objects.
Even in her defeat she confesses to a nostalgia for the sensuous past, despite the fact that her pleasure has been her
guilt; still "half-guilty in her thoughts," she comes reluctantly
to understand that true repentance must mean

> Not even in inmost thought to think again
> The sins that made the past so pleasant to us.

Yet she has known also the familiar Tennysonian burden of
personality, and in parting from Lancelot she has cried,
"Would God that thou couldst hide me from myself!" Like
Princess Ida, whose sadness "blacken'd all her world in secret"
and made it all seem "blank and waste . . . and vain," she
is troubled by the nightmare of her own image stretching
across a surrealistic wasteland to distant ruined towers —
she dreams

> An awful dream, for then she seem'd to stand
> On some vast plain before a setting sun,
> And from the sun there swiftly made at her
> A ghastly something, and its shadow flew
> Before it till it touch'd her, and she turn'd —
> When lo! her own, that broadening from her feet,
> And blackening, swallow'd all the land, and in it
> Far cities burnt.

Like the Soul in "The Palace of Art," whom God "plagued"
with merciful despair, she is to be saved only by the awakening
conscience:

> Henceforward too, the Powers that tend the soul,
> To help it from the death that cannot die,
> And save it even in extremes, began
> To vex and plague her.

And like both of these, she ultimately recognizes her sin as
pride — though hers, as she describes it, is a "false voluptu-

ous pride, that took / Full easily all impressions from below."
Guinevere is, of course, first and last a distinct individual,
the most vivid and dramatic figure in the *Idylls*. But insofar
as she may also be considered a symbol of beauty which must
eventually come to terms with moral truth, she may (once
again like the Soul and the Princess) represent the anima,
the essential aesthetic self of the poet. As a woman she fully
indulges her selfish passions, yet seeks final atonement in a life
of service; to the nuns at Almesbury she offers the example of
the selfless dedication that Arthur vainly hoped she would
bring to his kingdom. As a counterpart of Tennyson's own
poetic struggle, she suggests not only his attraction to a
sensuous art for art's sake but also, by her last gesture, his
mature demand for a moral aesthetic.

By the end of the sixties Tennyson had made the ethical
intent of the *Idylls* sufficiently clear to alienate the new
Aesthetes. Yet within a few years the young Henry James,
who had no quarrel with moral concern, declared the
meaning of the poems less significant than the fastidious work-
manship. "If one surrenders one's sense to their perfect pic-
turesqueness," James wrote, "it is the most charming poetry
in the world. . . . It appeals to a highly cultivated sense, but
what enjoyment is so keen as that of the cultivated sense
when its finer nerve is really touched?" [12] Such a judgment
recalls Ruskin's more troubled approach to the four Idylls
of 1859, and it anticipates the censure of many later critics
less disposed than either Ruskin or James to admire the pic-
turesque in poetry. The *Idylls* have all too frequently been
dismissed — often by those who have not read them — as an
elaborate exercise in rhetoric, an ornate escape from the
realities of experience; and the relevance of their central
themes both to Victorian England and to the modern world
has been accordingly for the most part ignored.

The objection that the sequence as a whole misrepresents
medieval life and manners is hardly pertinent, for the city built

to music belongs to no society in time. The poet's method is not the way of literary realism, and the philosophy that informs his poem is itself a protest against the tyranny of fact that enslaves the realist. Though the epilogue (no doubt to the amusement of the English Aesthetes) denounced an "Art with poisonous honey stolen from France," the French Symbolists, who were most consistent in their devotion to Tennyson, immediately and quite properly recognized the *Idylls* as an antidote to the positivistic spirit that had invaded nineteenth-century poetry. In the reconstructed Arthurian mythology they found a welcome and spacious release for the poetic imagination from the narrowed materialisms of their own age.[13]

Tennyson, however, sought freedom from the momentary pressures of the time, the immediate social and economic concern, in order to interpret rather than to escape the larger spiritual crisis of his culture. By avoiding the homely local color that had sentimentalized "Enoch Arden" and the direct emotional involvement that had made his political verses of the fifties merely shrill and ephemeral, he hoped in the *Idylls* to give his vision of modern society perspective, objectivity, and dramatic substance. There are in the poem a few possible reflections of his impatience with some particular Victorian practices or attitudes. The description, for instance, of King Pellam's chapel, rich in reliquaries and thronged with plaster saints, may indicate his distaste for certain aspects of the new Anglo-Catholic ritualism; and the rough treatment of the foppish Sir Morning-Star, attended by bare-footed, bare-headed damsels in "gilt and rosy raiment," may testify to his scorn of the new dandified Aesthetes, some of whom were affecting Pre-Raphaelite gestures. But such specific parallels are neither frequent nor essential to the action. The central narratives have few contemporary referents; King Arthur is not Prince Albert, Lancelot is neither Gladstone nor Disraeli, and Guinevere is assuredly not Vic-

toria. Yet the epilogue "To the Queen" spells out the general
modern relevance in no uncertain terms:

> Take withal
> Thy poet's blessing, and his trust that Heaven
> Will blow the tempest in the distance back
> From thine and ours; for some are scared, who mark,
> Or wisely or unwisely, signs of storm,
> Waverings of every vane with every wind,
> And wordy trucklings to the transient hour,
> And fierce or careless looseners of the faith, . . .
> And that which knows, but careful for itself,
> And that which knows not, ruling that which knows
> To its own harm. The goal of this great world
> Lies beyond sight; yet — if our slowly-grown
> And crown'd Republic's crowning common-sense,
> That saved her many times, not fail — their fears
> Are morning shadows huger than the shapes
> That cast them, not those gloomier which forego
> The darkness of that battle in the west
> Where all of high and holy dies away.

Here the trust that the tempest may be averted and that the
crowned Republic may so be spared such a last great battle
in the west as destroyed the realm of Arthur seems faint and
ineffectual beside the strong forebodings of social disaster
that accompany it. In final effect, then, the *Idylls*, which
traces the rise of a purposeful order and the gradual cata-
strophic betrayal of its sustaining idealism, stands as an
oblique warning, if not a direct ultimatum, to nineteenth-
century England.

It may have been his interest in the problem and the
threat of cultural decadence that led Tennyson to regard the
bitter *Troilus and Cressida* as "perhaps Shakespeare's finest
play." [14] At any rate, the *Idylls*, read in proper sequence, builds
somewhat like *Troilus* to a tragic denouement, which the temper of a whole civilization rather than the sin of any one
individual makes inevitable. The poem no longer presupposes
the early-Victorian idea of progress, which rang through

"Locksley Hall," but a later and gloomier cyclical view of history. Could Arthur's kingdom remain true to its first principles, could it rise in time of crisis to what Arnold Toynbee would call the moral challenge, it might learn to control its successes and turn to social good its manifold selfish energies. But increasingly committed as it is to the values of expediency, sensuality, and self-interest,[15] it must face its certain doom; there can be no renewal, except in another milieu altogether, for by the fundamental law of being "The old order changeth, yielding place to new." Though few of the Victorians could see the pertinence of the analogy to their own age, Tennyson by the time of "The Holy Grail" and all the later Idylls was wholly persuaded of the soundness of his somber vision and able to write with a deeply felt urgency. His finished poem, itself a city built to music, attains its most compelling resonance in the overtones of his conviction.

UNDER THE MASK

The Plays, 1875–1882

IN THE spring of 1873 when Browning sent him a presentation copy of the long and woolly *Red Cotton Night-cap Country*, Tennyson acknowledged the gift warmly but quite self-consciously. "I have yet again to thank you," he wrote, "and feel rather ashamed that I have nothing of my own to send you back, but your Muse is prolific as Hecuba, and mine by the side of her, an old barren cow." [1] The publication of "Gareth and Lynette" the year before and with it the final ordering of the *Idylls* (except for "Balin and Balan") had indeed exhausted his best powers of invention and left him, as always when he had no new work in hand, restless and dissatisfied. The making of poetry had become so necessary to his very being that he could scarcely, even now in his mid-sixties, imagine any real living without writing. And though he might feel for the moment thoroughly written out, he had still in fact nearly twenty years of active publishing before him; in terms of volume at least, his last two decades were to be the most productive of his career. Yet he had first of all to determine the direction of his energies, and he could find little help in Browning's recent example. Whereas Browning had shifted from a dramatic to a narrative style, Tennyson was to turn from his Arthurian narratives to a prolonged experiment with the masks of drama.

Still, even had he felt no shame in silence and been content to retire from the labors of composition, he would have had little opportunity to escape the notice of a public which had long since come to expect of him a constantly renewed vitality. Though his pre-eminence was now frequently questioned, especially by young men of the "aesthetic" interest, his popularity was still extremely great. He had become a national institution; and some of his admirers regretted his unwillingness to recognize the fact, for he declined a baronetcy offered by the Queen through Gladstone in 1873 and then again through Disraeli in the following year. He was consulted as an oracle on many subjects and besieged by autograph hunters. His already enormous correspondence was increasing year by year. Thus when Emily who had long spared him the burden of letter writing (which he detested) took to her invalid's couch in 1874, it seemed necessary for his elder son Hallam to withdraw from Cambridge in order to serve as his full-time amanuensis, private secretary, and business manager, his buffer against the peremptory demands of the outside world. More than ever he complained, "I hate the blare and blaze of so-called fame," [2] but he was quite unable to avoid the acclaim showered upon him. As always, he resented published gossip about his private life at Farringford or Aldworth and was painfully aware of the attention of the journalists who followed his progress through London society. He was perhaps most irritated by the reporters who recorded in detail his appearance at the wedding in Westminster Abbey in 1878 of his younger son Lionel to Eleanor Locker, a great social event at which Browning and Gladstone and the Duke of Argyll were present as witnesses but where he himself was clearly the chief attraction, whether stumbling nearsightedly on the steps or looking round the Abbey with equanimity "as if he thought the immortals were his compeers." [3] In spite of himself, his deportment filled a public need; it coincided properly with a preconceived image of the wholly

committed poet. And it may well have been this image that
Matthew Arnold had in mind when one day late in the
seventies he remarked with solemn ambiguity to Hallam
Tennyson, "Your father has been our most popular poet for
over forty years, and I am of opinion that he fully deserves his
reputation." [4]

Tennyson, however, was not to be reduced to a popular
stereotype. Among friends he remained — sometimes discon-
certingly — his own complex self, a blunt, outspoken yet
oddly reticent man, full of excited prejudices and disinterested
sympathies, a man at once naive and ironic, troubled yet
trusting, crotchety perhaps but forever unpretentious.
Henry James, who looked forward to meeting "the poet he
had earliest known and best loved," should have been prepared, as a subtle connoisseur of conduct, for every human
and unaesthetic anomaly of character. But when at last one
evening late in the seventies he was introduced to "The
Laureate" at Eaton Place in London, he was altogether
shocked, outraged by "the monstrous demonstration that
Tennyson was not Tennysonian." [5] Whether or not, as the
novelist half suspected, he enjoyed being the source of dismay,
Tennyson had no wish at any time that the "Tennysonian"
canon (whatever the epithet might imply) should be misread
as a direct commentary on his private life or personal emotions,
nor indeed any desire that his personality should be deduced
from his published work. In an amusing though quite serious note to one of his last monologues he made what he felt
to be a necessary distinction: "The Church-warden like many
of my smaller poems is purely dramatic, and if any one following the fashion of our modern Journalism believes or con-
jectures that I myself, under the mask of my Dramatis Persona,
am sneering at any particular Bishop or casting any slur on
Baptist or Church-warden or Tradesman, I beg to remind him
that Aeschylus did not murder Agamemnon, nor Shakespeare
King Duncan." [6] James, of course, hardly needed to be re-

minded of the differences between art and life, and his use
of "Tennysonian" may have implied no simple equation of
the two. But since less-sophisticated readers clearly were
guilty of the confusion, the poet may have considered some
statement of his intention necessary to protect his own identity.

By the time of the disappointing encounter James had already written perceptive reviews of Tennyson's first two
plays. And even as a reviewer he had wondered — as indeed
others would wonder years later when he, too, turned to
the theater — why an assured artist of great attainment should
suddenly dare risk so perilous a new venture, should deliberately effect such "a rupture with a consecrated past." [7] But
the poet's decision at the age of sixty-five to enter upon the
playwright's career was rather less abrupt than James supposed. Tennyson had known the dramatic impulse as early
as *The Devil and the Lady*. He had always been a skillful
mimic and an animated raconteur, and he took great delight
in declaiming his verses, many of which had been designed
as dramatic lyrics and narratives. He had, of course, no real
knowledge of stagecraft and no acquaintance with the practical economies of the theater. But he was consistently fond of
plays, and he felt himself a competent judge of the art of
acting. Thackeray's daughter tells us how once after a performance of *Hamlet* he rallied the actors and criticized their
delivery [8] — with the memorable precedent perhaps of Hamlet's own advice to the players. Besides, though he usually
disliked stage adaptations of his poems, he may well have been
impressed by reports of a successful American version of
"Enoch Arden," and he was certainly aware of the acclaim
that the young W. S. Gilbert, not yet Arthur Sullivan's col-
laborator, had won in 1870 with "a respectful parody"
of *The Princess*.[9] In that year he himself had published
"a little song-cycle" entitled *The Window; or, The Song of
the Wrens* written in 1866 to exercise Sullivan's talents as a

serious composer. The songs were at best banal and at worst bathetic, and he was reluctant to issue so frivolous a work "in the dark shadow" of the Franco-Prussian War.[10] Yet the mere fact that he had agreed to write the verses may be taken as evidence of his growing interest in the possibility of reaching an assembled audience directly and so more or less dramatically.

Before the completion of the first draft of "Gareth and Lynette" he had grown impatient with the Idyll form as he had conceived it. He wished, he said, that he had been at liberty "to print the names of the speakers . . . over the short snip-snap of their talk, and so avoid the perpetual 'said' and its varieties."[11] He was beginning in effect to think of his poem in terms of a play. But when, after the barren rest of which he complained to Browning, he actually turned to the drama, he was ready to abandon the subject matter as well as the style of the *Idylls*. He now sought characters from history rather than from myth or legend. He was challenged by the opacity of fact, the difficulty of deducing human personality from even the most explicit of records, for — as he explained in an unpublished sonnet —

> Our age can find
> The shower that fell a million years ago,
> An ever-vanish'd Ocean's ebb and flow
> Rock-written: but no man can send his mind
> Into man past so wholly as to form
> A perfect likeness of long-vanish'd souls,
> Whate'er new light be let on ancient scrolls
> And secular perforations of the worm.[12]

Considering Shakespeare the one best able to reanimate "man past," he turned close attention to the Shakespearean history plays. And so sensitive were his readings that F. J. Furnivall, who founded the New Shakespeare Society in 1874, regularly consulted him on the authenticity of texts.[13] For his own experiments with drama he found sanction in Shakespeare's practice, and like most other literary dramatists of his time he was severely handicapped by dependence upon a master so inimitable. But he was proud to confess his indebtedness. He determined, as he himself acknowledged, to portray "the making of England" by selecting for dramatization periods of national crisis before and after the action of Shakespeare's chronicles.[14] Burdened with far more factual detail than ever oppressed Shakespeare, he began with rather extensive research into the civil and religious dissension of the sixteenth century, then moved back to the Conquest and on to the reign of Henry II. At first he thought the ill-fated Lady Jane Grey a likely subject, but before long his interest was concentrated upon her grim adversary, Mary Tudor, the least ingratiating and perhaps the most troubled of English sovereigns.

Published in 1875, *Queen Mary* was developed not as a single dramatic structure but as a sprawling panorama, a pageant unfolded with a cinematic abundance and little regard for the limitations of the theater. The twenty-three separate scenes demanded frequent and often elaborate change of sets. The "Dramatis Personae" included forty-four characters drawn from all ranks of society and listed in addition a small army of nameless supernumeraries, "Lords and other Attendants, Members of the Privy Council, Members of Parliament, Two Gentlemen, Aldermen, Citizens, Peasants, Ushers, Messengers, Guards, Pages, Gospellers, Marshalmen, etc." Though the text and cast were severely cut for the production at the Lyceum in April 1876, in which Henry Irving appeared as King Philip, no editing could impose a real coherence upon the work. James's criticism of the printed play could have been applied with almost equal force to the acted version: *Queen Mary* in either form was but "a dramatized chronicle, . . . taking its material in pieces, as history hands them over, and working each one up into an independent scene — usually with great ability." The playwright, James complained, "has embroidered cunningly the groundwork offered him by Mr. Froude, but he has contributed no new material." [15]

Tennyson indeed hewed so closely to the line of fact that he was not content to accept Froude's brilliant but biased interpretation as a full or adequate account of the sixteenth-century struggle. He carefully examined many primary and secondary sources, from Foxe's *Book of Martyrs* and the correspondence of Archbishop Parker down to the latest social and ecclesiastical histories of the period.[16] Though his own loyalties were essentially Protestant, he tried to be scrupulously fair to the claims of Catholicism, for which his new friend W. G. Ward had given him some real respect, and he strove in particular to do justice to the Queen herself, whom he felt Froude had misrepresented.[17] If his scholarly caution, his reluctance to simplify by omission, needlessly complicated the action of his play, it nonetheless gave him a sharp sense of the instability, conflict, and confusion of Marian England. Whatever his inexperience and naïveté as dramatist, he succeeded admirably in suggesting the temper of an age, the fear-shaken time described by Lord Paget on the occasion of Cranmer's execution:

> My Lord, the world is like a drunken man,
> Who cannot move straight to his end, but reels
> Now to the right, then as far to the left,
> Push'd by the crowd beside — and underfoot
> An earthquake; for since Henry, for a doubt —
> Which a young lust had clapt upon the back,
> Crying, "Forward!" — set our old church rocking, men
> Have hardly known what to believe, or whether
> They should believe in anything; the currents
> So shift and change, they see not how they are borne
> Nor whither.

Apart from its faithfulness as an historical record, which mitigates its power as a play, the strength of *Queen Mary* lies in its able characterizations. Each of the principal figures — except Philip of Spain, who in his ruthless self-sufficiency approaches caricature — emerges as a subtly rounded personality. Cranmer, in particular, is drawn in all the complexity of divided motives as politician and martyr, a man of courage, remorse, humility, and proud conviction. Cardinal Pole, driven to follow the courses of least resistance, is a convincing blend of sensitivity, fearfulness, and cruelty born of disappointment. And the princess Elizabeth, who hovers in the background as a symbol of ultimate social renewal, effectively combines sympathetic understanding with an imperious reserve willing to bide its time. But most impressive of all is the Queen herself, a real woman of tragic depth, far removed from the monster she had been in Victor Hugo's *Marie Tudor*.[18] In the beginning Mary has the capacity to rise above the wrongs she has suffered, to forgive her enemies, even to practice a measure of tolerance so long as she may retain her religious faith. In the end she is destroyed by her unreasoning passion, her obsessive love for the loveless Philip. At first her desire is simply a yearning that troubles her private dreams; "It breaks my heart," says an attendant lady, "to hear her moan at night / As tho' the nightmare never left her bed." But ultimately her frustrations determine the violence she inflicts upon her whole realm. Abandoned by the Spaniard, she loses all purpose in living and with it all true title to sovereignty. As Lord Howard explains,

> Her life, since Philip left her, and she lost
> Her fierce desire of bearing him a child,
> Hath, like a brief and bitter winter's day,
> Gone narrowing down and darkening to a close.

Here the mood recalls that of the thwarted Guinevere or, more distantly, of the abandoned Oenone. Indeed, if Tennyson had paid less heed to the political background and given the character of his protagonist more centrality, he might have found for *Queen Mary* what the play most seriously lacks, a subject, such a theme as animates many of his more vital poems: the betrayal of the social conscience by a passionate self-interest.

Harold, published a year later, shows a considerable advance in structure. Each of its scenes — the number is reduced to eleven — develops a situation which contributes directly to the action of the play as a whole; and the key scene especially, in which Harold swears under duress to support the claim of William to the English throne, attains by skillful timing a high dramatic tension. Perhaps because he had fewer records to draw upon, Tennyson introduces many fewer characters than in *Queen Mary* and much less subsidiary historical detail. He focuses the interest of the drama where it should be, on the conduct of his hero. Unfortunately, however, Harold with all his strength, courage, and (except for the one false oath) truthfulness is too uncomplicated a person to command our sustained attention, and few of the others with whom he has to contend are drawn with enough color to assume a genuine life. The women who appear as rivals for Harold's love seem particularly factitious: Edith is a frail creature of sweet and ultimately maudlin sentiment, and Aldwyth is but a villainous schemer from popular melodrama. Far inferior in characterization to *Queen Mary*, this second chronicle could not expect even the brief *succès d'estime* in the theater which greeted the first. It awaited production on a public stage for over fifty years.[19]

On a visit to Battle Abbey in 1876, Tennyson wrote a prefatory sonnet for *Harold* celebrating the field of Senlac "Where might made right eight hundred years ago." In effect the sonnet defines the theme of the play: the defeat of right by might, which may finally establish a new right but which first must demand the sacrifice of old values. Tennyson's ethical sympathies lie entirely with Harold, whose practical goodness resembles the intuitive religion of King Arthur and oddly prefigures the Victorian Broad-Church rejection of a rigid dogmatism:

> O God! I cannot help it, but at times
> They seem to me too narrow, all the faiths
> Of this grown world of ours, whose baby eye
> Saw them sufficient.

Harold instinctively resents the piety which drives Edward the Confessor, as it drove the seekers of the Holy Grail, to an ascetic withdrawal from social responsibility. Edward, who according to the "heretical" Archbishop Stigand has "A conscience for his own soul, not his realm," speaks with all the self-righteous unction of Tennyson's St. Simeon Stylites:

> I have lived a life of utter purity:
> I have builded the great church of Holy Peter:
> I have wrought miracles — to God the glory —
> And miracles will in my name be wrought
> Hereafter. — I have fought the fight and go —
> I see the flashing of the gates of pearl —
> And it is well with me, tho' some of you
> Have scorn'd me — ay — but after I am gone
> Woe, woe to England!

The woe in large part is of Edward's own making; for his indifference and indecision have irreparably weakened the English cause, and his approval — half envious and half fearful — of the disciplined Norman church has encouraged William to seek in the same assured and quite un-English orthodoxy spiritual sanction for his own quite secular designs. At the last Harold — without time enough to rally the England that Edward in his self-absorption has rebuked and neglected — must perish, resisting in vain an alien faith and a new order of despotic power.

The tension between might and right persists in *Becket*, which Tennyson had already begun before the publication of *Harold*. But now the wrong is mixed. Neither Becket himself nor Henry II, his antagonist, is blameless; both are betrayed by the external magnitude of office and the unconfessed falsity within, the personal desire for absolute dominion. Far from being a mere villain or even a ruthless self-seeker

like the Conqueror, Henry is a genial and on the whole
benevolent leader, eager for peace (on his own terms), filled
with understanding of his subjects, often impulsive and hot-
tempered, but relatively reasonable until pushed to the end of
his patience by Becket's opposition to his authority and driven
to sigh in exasperation, "Will no man free me from this pes-
tilent priest?" Becket, on the other hand, is depicted as restless,
ambitious, self-confident, able to inspire malice in his rivals
and great affection in the common people, ready to give his
all with intensity to his work whether as Chancellor at odds
with the church or as Archbishop in conflict with the state.
His sin, of which he never reaches full awareness, is pride of
spirit, an arrogance commingling with his saintly strength of
conviction. From the beginning of his tenure as primate he
knows that he will resist rather than appease the king, who
has hopefully elevated him:

> I served King Henry well as Chancellor;
> I am his no more, and I must serve the Church.
> This Canterbury is only less than Rome,
> And all my doubts I fling from me like dust,
> Winnow and scatter all scruples to the wind,
> And all the puissance of the warrior,
> And all the wisdom of the Chancellor,
> And all the heap'd experiences of life,
> I cast upon the side of Canterbury.

Before long he has exercised the power of anathema so
freely that the ironic Walter Map, who serves briefly as
Tennyson's chorus character, may warn him, "My lord, you
have put so many of the King's household out of communion,
that they begin to smile at it." Finally, as the death hour
approaches, John of Salisbury, his most faithful confidant,
must beg him to recognize the possible self-interest that may
conceal itself in sanctified attitudes:

> And may there not be something
> Of this world's leaven in thee too, when crying
> On Holy Church to thunder out her rights

> And thine own wrong so pitilessly? Ah, Thomas,
> The lightnings that we think are only Heaven's
> Flash sometimes out of earth against the heavens. . . .
> Thou hast waged God's war against the King; and yet
> We are self-uncertain creatures, and we may,
> Yea, even when we know not, mix our spites
> And private hates with our defence of Heaven.

But Becket, committed wholly to the idea of self-sacrifice, declares himself as the agent of God's will quite "prepared to die" and refuses even to hear his friend's pointed reminder that "We are sinners all, / The best of all not all-prepared to die." Thus with magnificent consistency and fortitude, but without ever achieving complete self-confrontation, he faces the doom he has anticipated since he first considered the gravity of his new position: "I may come to martyrdom. / I am martyr in myself already."

As the murderers leave the fallen Becket, a "storm bursts" over the cathedral and "flashes of lightning" illumine the stage. Lest he be accused of forcing an effect, Tennyson explains in a footnote that the elements actually did so behave at the time of the assassination. Yet no appeal to fact can guarantee that a play will enjoy an independent life of its own. Once again Tennyson is embarrassed by the raw materials of history and too cautious to take imaginative liberties. J. R. Green, the medievalist whom he consulted about matters of historical detail, was grateful for the vivid portrayal of Henry and his court. But the succession of accurate tableaux does not achieve dramatic movement. Like *Queen Mary*, *Becket* is a loose chronicle with several striking characters and some ably framed separate scenes but no real coherence of total action. The subplot, which involves Henry's love for Rosamund de Clifford and the jealousy of his wife Eleanor, is intended to provide relief from the often rather arid debate between church and crown, but it succeeds only in proving a melodramatic distraction. Eleanor of

Aquitaine is reduced to an enraged tigress. Rosamund, who appeared with some romantic grace in "A Dream of Fair Women," is scarcely more credible than the sentimental Edith of *Harold*. And the encounter between the two, where Eleanor points a dagger at Rosamund's bosom and Becket steals up from behind just in time to wrench the weapon from her hand, may have had some parallel in fact but assuredly has no place in a serious work of art.

Rebuffed in his efforts to bring *Becket* to the stage, Tennyson published the play in 1884 with an apologetic dedication declaring that it was "not intended in its present form to meet the exigencies of our modern theatre." But he never abandoned hope that, properly edited, it might one day be produced; and in the last year of his life his confidence seemed after all well placed, for Irving after many delays finally agreed to reshape the piece as a personal vehicle. On February 6, 1893 — exactly four months after Tennyson's death — *Becket* began its highly successful run of one hundred and twelve nights at the Lyceum with Irving as the Archbishop and Ellen Terry as Rosamund. Thereafter Irving repeatedly revived the role both in London and on tour, convinced, as he said, that "the play made me. It changed my whole view of life." [20] Few later actors have shared Irving's enthusiasm, and *Becket* has more and more been relegated to the low dusty shelves where it awaits the very few readers of arm-chair literary drama. Since 1935, when it has been appraised at all, it has suffered by comparison with *Murder in the Cathedral*, to which it bears little resemblance. Less varied and precise in characterization than *Becket*, Eliot's play gains from its narrowed concentration on theme and its deft use of the anonymous interpretive Chorus of Women. Less dependent on fact, it attains far greater freedom of language, a poetry uninhibited by the standards of a documentary realism and at the same time closer than Tennyson's blank verse to the rhythms of real human speech. Whereas Eliot has attempted to create a new form suited to his own idiom, Tennyson sought to adapt his gifts of style and imagination to the demands of an outmoded convention, to the "exigencies" of a theatre that had not existed since the early seventeenth century. The difference in approach helps define Tennyson's major limitation as dramatist.

Had he lived to read the published *Becket*, FitzGerald would probably have been no more satisfied with it than with the two earlier chronicles, both of which he received with marked coolness. In acknowledging the first, he carefully avoided any general estimate of the play's quality; and of the second he wrote to his "dear old Alfred": " 'Harold' came, King Harold. But I still yearn after a Fairy Prince who came from other skies than these rainy ones, with his joyful eyes, 'foxfooted step,' and his mantle glittering on the rocks." [21] FitzGerald, however, was by his own admission crotchety, and his wry demur in any case was almost drowned by the fulsome praise of other friends, Browning, Froude, Gladstone, Aubrey de Vere, George Eliot, and George Henry Lewes. So encouraged, Tennyson continued his career as dramatist. Four new plays followed the composition of *Becket* — all of them less "realistic" than the histories, yet none transfigured, as FitzGerald could have wished, by the high poetic vision.

The slightest of the four is *The Falcon*, a one-act sentimental comedy, derived from Boccaccio's tale of the Count Federigo who, having squandered all his wealth but his falcon, does not hesitate to sacrifice even the cherished bird when he must extend the hospitality of his table to the Lady Giovanna.[22] Tennyson thought his own version of the anecdote "stately and tender," [23] and the play in fact enjoyed a limited success as part of a double bill at the St. James' Theatre in the winter of 1879–80. But, apart from its gentle irony, the piece has little dramatic substance. Though the exposition is adroit, the characters are flat and the happy denouement too easy and too rapid to be convincing. The dialogue in prose achieves some fluency and humor, but the verse spoken by the Count and the Lady is stilted in its old-world formality. Nowhere do we find the mark of Tennyson's peculiar strength, the power (as in the *Idylls*, for instance) to suffuse an old story with a freshly felt emotion.

Finished in 1881 but first produced in 1892 by Augustin Daly in New York, *The Foresters — Robin Hood and Maid Marian* proved more popular than its author had any right to expect. Particularly attractive to the American audience in a mood of genial Anglophilia was the lyric which opened the second act, "There is no land like England," the "National Song" (suppressed after publication in 1830), written, as Tennyson told Daly, "when I was nineteen." [24] The bulk of the play might well have been the product of even earlier years, for the sentiment and derring-do are incredibly juvenile. The scene, for instance, in which Robin meets the disguised Marian, swears his love to her, and kneels as she shows him her sword, belongs only in the Neverneverland of Peter Pan. Robin's men dash to the rescue, and Much speaks:

> Our Robin beaten, pleading for his life!
> Seize on the knight! wrench his sword from him!
> > (*They all rush on Marian*)
> > ROBIN (springing up and waving his hand)
> > > Back!
> Back all of you! this is Maid Marian
> Flying from John — disguised.

> > MEN
> > Maid Marian? she?

> > SCARLET
> Captain, we saw thee cowering to a knight
> And thought thou wert bewitch'd.

> > MARIAN
> > You dared to dream
> That our great Earl, the bravest English heart
> Since Hereward the Wake, would cower to any

> Of mortal build. Weak natures that impute
> Themselves to their unlikes, and their own want
> Of manhood to their leader!

The less "romantic" stretches of *The Foresters* are scarcely more adult. The good bad men of Sherwood, paragons all of virtue in revolt against tyranny, retain throughout a story-book naïveté; and their attempts at humor, largely in the form of shameless punning, read like boyish imitations of the bantering of Shakespeare's clowns. Tennyson was able to persuade himself that his subject matter had a certain historical gravity, for he claimed to have sketched in the play "the state of the people in another great transition period of the making of England, when the barons sided with the people and eventually won for them the Magna Charta." [25] Such sober implications, however, are seldom apparent in the text; despite frequent hits at the villainy of Prince John, the manner of the whole is incompatible with cogent political commentary. Certainly no shadow of significance touches the Fairy Scene which Tennyson introduced at Irving's suggestion and in the stage copy transferred to the end of the third act — as his note tells us — "for the sake of modern dramatic effect." Sir Arthur Sullivan, who set all the songs to music, may have been largely responsible for making these facetious fairy rhymes the most warmly applauded lines of the play. If so, we can only wish that Gilbert had helped Tennyson furnish Sullivan a more rollicking libretto. For *The Foresters* is really a comic operetta which has failed to recognize its inherent burlesque.

Tennyson's two "tragedies," *The Cup* and *The Promise of May*, both of which were written and produced in the early eighties,[26] at least give some scope to his more serious conviction. Suggested by W. E. H. Lecky's account of a story in Plutarch, *The Cup* concerns the revenge of a Galatian priestess, Camma, who, having seen her husband slain by the covetous Synorix, feigns love for the latter and so induces

him to share with her a poisoned chalice. Lest he err in
detail, Tennyson consulted the archaeologist Sir Charles Newton of the British Museum about the worship of Artemis in
Galatia; [27] but he felt freer than in the chronicle plays to
mold his characters to his own purpose, and he strove to
make Synorix a prototype, like his Tristram, of the sensualist
who, denying the claims of a moral idealism, seeks fulfillment
in selfish passion. But again he found the dramatic medium a
distinct handicap. "The worst of writing for the stage," he
complained, "is, you must keep some actor always in your
mind." [28] He had written *The Cup* expressly for Irving, and
he could do little afterwards to change Irving's false interpretation of Synorix as "a villain, not an epicurean." [29] Once
in production, *The Cup* was Irving's own project. Irving
devised the elaborate décor, the massive sculptured pillars,
the antique lyres, and the sacred flames burning musky per-
fumes. He enlisted Ellen Terry for the role of Camma, and
he helped select the hundred beautiful girls who served as
vestal virgins, her attendants in the temple. The opening
night, which attracted "a most distinguished audience — one
of the richest in literature, art, science, and politics that has
ever been seen at the Lyceum," seemed an aesthetic event of
the first magnitude. We may guess the quality of the performance from a newspaper review which appeared the next
morning:

Not only do the grapes grow before us, and the myrtles blossom, the
snow mountains change from silver-white at day to roseate hues at
dawn; not only are the pagan ceremonies enacted before us with a
reality and fidelity that almost baffle description, but in the midst of
this scenic allurement glide the classical draperies and sea-green robes
of Miss Ellen Terry, who is the exact representation of the period she
enacts, while following her we find the eager glances of the fate-
haunted Mr. Irving.[30]

The two acts so heavily mounted must have seemed almost
static in effect, but few in the audience left the theatre

dissatisfied, for *The Corsican Brothers* by Dion Boucicault, which completed the Lyceum bill, supplied all the movement anyone could have asked. The materials from which Tennyson at another time might have made an effective classical idyl had been shaped by Irving into a lavish spectacle, and *The Cup* accordingly began its long successful run.

The Promise of May, on the other hand, fared ill from the beginning. Gladstone, who attended the opening at the Globe, thought it a good play but "above the comprehension of the vast mass of the people present." [31] On the third or fourth night the Marquess of Queensberry, who felt that he saw its drift only too plainly, rose from his seat to denounce the piece as an "abominable caricature" of free thought and a gross insult to the British Secular Union, of which he was president. The ensuing commotion in the back rows was quelled just in time to avert a riot, but not soon enough to save the play's reputation. To no avail did Herman Vezin, the actor who filled the role of Edgar the tendentious rationalist, defend the tragedy in a letter to the press as a serious drama of ideas. "So also, in time," he concluded, "will plays presenting social and moral problems crowd out dramatic trivialities which amuse for an hour and are then forgotten. Mr. Tennyson . . . has inserted the thin edge of the wedge . . . in this, the boldest experiment in the modern drama." [32] But, though the prediction was sound, the defense was not a happy one. The playwright was not Bernard Shaw; and the play, with its old-fashioned awkward plotting, stock sentiment, and melodramatic gesture, did not bring new life to the English theatre.

Nevertheless, though hastily written and poorly edited for the stage, *The Promise of May* as the only one of the seven dramas with a contemporary setting does deal in ideas which Tennyson considered of immediate relevance to his own age. The story, to be sure, is contrived and improbable: Edgar, the city intellectual, seduces and abandons a naive country

girl named Eva, then returns in disguise five years later
and professes love for her sister Dora until the disgraced Eva
reappears to expose, yet forgive with her dying breath, his
perfidy. But Tennyson was far more interested in the mo-
tivations of Edgar than in the details of the action. Despite
Queensberry's objection, Edgar is not a caricature of the
honest "secularist," though his use or misuse of the secularist
creed is plainly intended to suggest the necessity of a higher
faith. He is not perhaps a "freethinker" at all, but rather a
sensualist who, having followed the courses of self-indulgence to the point of satiation, seeks to rationalize his conduct by the logic of various disturbing new philosophies.
Toying with the proposition that man is but "an automatic
series of sensations," he denies any possible responsibility for
moral decision, yet claims for himself the right to cultivate
pleasurable sensation and to ignore the painful experience of
others. Like the hero of *Maud* before the coming of love, he
argues from the analogy of nature that amoral self-develop-
ment is the one law of an evolutionary world. When eager to
free himself from the "entanglement" with Eva, he declares
marriage "but an old tradition" and professes to find comfort
in the belief that the immanent revolution, "the storm . . .
hard at hand," will sweep away all established institutions.
He looks to the day of liberation:

> And when the man,
> The child of evolution, flings aside
> His swaddling-bands the morals of the tribe,
> He, following his own instincts as his God,
> Will enter on the larger golden age,
> No pleasure then taboo'd; for when the tide
> Of full democracy has overwhelm'd
> This Old World, from that flood will rise the New.

But later when he begins to feel the power of a remorse which
his hedonism cannot explain, he grows skeptical of his own
too easy nonconformities. Perhaps because, as he admits iron-

ically, he has now inherited his uncle's wealth, he denounces his erstwhile positions as "a Socialist, / A Communist, a Nihilist — what you will"; all these are now but

> Utopian idiotcies.
> They did not last three Junes. Such rampant weeds
> Strangle each other, die, and make the soil
> For Caesars, Cromwells, and Napoleons
> To root their power in.

But whatever their coloring, radical or reactionary, Edgar's speculations touch on many issues of real moment to Tennyson throughout his creative life, and Edgar himself is also, by endowment at least, an artist — "Born, happily, with some sense of art, to live / By brush and pencil." His intellectual crime lies not so much in the error of his opinions as in his proud aesthetic detachment from any consistent point of view. As the epigraph to the play labels him, he is "A surface man of theories, true to none." Like the Soul in "The Palace of Art," he aspires to a godlike autonomy, an independence of all social and ethical ties; and, like the Soul's, his pride must be ultimately destroyed. Yet, since he appeals to modern knowledge to redeem him from traditional reverence, his sin is more than aesthetic; he is to the poet a symbol of the self-seeker who in a world of shifting values finally cannot believe even in the self. Because it says all this much too didactically and not just because it offended the "freethinkers," *The Promise of May* fails utterly as drama. Tennyson, however, concerned almost exclusively with his theme, refused to see the disastrous limitations of the play. He had tried, he said, to give the public "one leaf out of the great book of truth and nature"; [33] and the public had rejected his effort. Bitterly disappointed, he wrote no more for the stage. [34]

None of the plays seriously altered the course of the English theater. *Becket*, the most successful on the boards and perhaps the strongest of the seven, did little more than remind

Irving and his fellow actors that there was still a place and even an audience for poetic drama. And *The Promise of May*, in most respects the weakest, demonstrated only that a playwright with ideas could stimulate controversy. But apart from their slight influence and despite their many defects, all remain a testimony to the remarkable, even if misdirected, energy that carried the aging poet into his last decade. Tennyson brought enthusiasm and resourcefulness to his dramatic experiment, and he gained from it both personal stimulus and new perspective on his work. Returning to his poetry, he found himself better able to objectify and so to release his emotion. More and more now he conceived of even the lyric as a dramatic utterance from a given situation. The dominant form of all his volumes from 1880 to the end is accordingly the monologue — the musing, the laughter, or the lament of an imagined character not to be directly identified with the author. "Under the mask of his Dramatis Persona" he could express at will the most intimate or the most alien feeling and yet maintain such detachment as would give the sentiment an independent life of its own. His experience as dramatist shows ultimately to best advantage in the vitality and abundance of his last poems.

✧ XI ✧

THE ANCIENT SAGE

The 1880s

BEFORE completing *The Cup* and while still preoccupied with plans for other dramas, Tennyson prepared a
collection of new verses, the first he had issued in eight years.[1]
For these he wrote an affectionate dedication to his namesake
Alfred, the infant son of Lionel:

> Glorious poet who never hast written a line,
> Laugh, for the name at the head of my verse is thine.
> Mayst thou never be wrong'd by the name that is mine!

But as far as the volume itself was concerned, he had no
cause to fear that any one might be ashamed of its quality.
For *Ballads and Other Poems*, published in November 1880,
was not only a remarkably vigorous book to come from a
poet already past seventy; it was in its own right a varied
and accomplished work of considerable distinction. And it
was greeted as such even by those who had regretted the
course of Tennyson's development during his long middle
period. Swinburne, who had scorned the *Idylls* and recently
had published an amusing parody of "The Higher Pantheism,"
saw evidence now of the old magic and in "Rizpah" a
veritable "new shudder." [2] And FitzGerald, still cool to
the history plays, delighted in the metrical brilliance of "The
Battle of Brunanburh," a translation of the Anglo-Saxon into
a free alliterative modern verse, which Fitz thought the proper
way at last "to render Aeschylus' Chorus." [3]

216

The only actual "ballads" in the volume were "The Revenge" and "The Defence of Lucknow," celebrations of the national honor, both of which proved immediately popular and in due course, like Campbell's "Battle of the Baltic" and Doyle's "Private of the Bluffs," became the heroic property of English schoolboys. Of the two, "The Revenge" is much the less forced in its excitement and far the more fully realized in terms of dramatic situation. The spirited rhetoric of the piece, its anapaestic swing, and heavy rhymes foreshadow the verse of Kipling, who must indeed have admired its forthright masculine irony:

So Lord Howard past away with five ships of war that day,
Till he melted like a cloud in the silent summer heaven;
But Sir Richard bore in hand all his sick men from the land
Very carefully and slow,
Men of Bideford in Devon,
And we laid them on the ballast down below;
For we brought them all aboard,
And they blest him in their pain, that they were not left in Spain,
To the thumb-screw and the stake, for the glory of the Lord.

A by-product of the research for *Queen Mary*, "The Revenge" proceeds directly toward its climax; it attains the movement of action that the drama conspicuously lacks.

The two historical monologues, on the other hand, that appeared among the *Ballads* are quite as static as some of the principal scenes in the chronicle plays. "Columbus" is a long undramatic lament of a great man in defeat, rehearsing the wrongs he has suffered from those whom he has enriched; it is less interesting as a portrait of the Admiral of the Ocean Seas (which it strives conscientiously to be) than as a reflection of the poet's own mistrust of fame and his sympathy with an aged lonely spirit, fiercely independent but aware of isolation and difference: "I am but an alien and a Genovese." "Sir John Oldcastle" is likewise a still meditation in a broken blank verse, which again extols the courage of unpopular heterodoxy, this time the Protestant faith of the "heretic" who resists to the death the superstition, reaction, and bigotry of an unenlightened society. Neither piece really transcends the factual records out of which it is shaped, and neither compares in aesthetic impact with the freshly imagined "Rizpah," wherein an intense soul once more is pitted against the cold coercions of the world.

The most vivid of all Tennyson's dramatic monologues, "Rizpah" meets most of the requirements of the genre as Browning established it. The speaker and the situation emerge gradually but sharply from the at-first bewildering flow of speech: a half-insane old woman, dying in an eighteenth-century charity ward, remembers the climactic experience of her life, the recovery and burial of the bones of her son Willy, who was hanged for robbing a mail coach on a dare. And the auditor is revealed by implication as the central action unfolds: a well-meaning evangelical lady, who has come to urge a death-bed repentance, must listen patiently to the distraught confession. Unlike Browning's major monologues, however, "Rizpah" is in effect not a character study of great psychological complexity but a lyric developing a single elemental emotion. As the Biblical title should suggest, the mother is less an individual than a type, and the passion with which she defies all constraining circumstance is simply a quintessential mother love. The rhymed stanzas in sweeping hexameters that replace the customary blank verse heighten the lyric cry, and the literal physicality of the dominant symbol adds a terror and abandon to the intensity:

Flesh of my flesh was gone, but bone of my bone was left —
I stole them all from the lawyers — and you, will you call it a theft? —
My baby, the bones that had suck'd me, the bones that had laughed and had cried —
Theirs? O, no! they are mine — not theirs — they had moved in my side.

The reality of such a relationship is so compelling that neither death nor the fear of death can destroy it. The old woman who has found her being in absolute dedication has no need now of the evangelist; she has received a direct intimation of life's meaning — "I have been with God in the dark" — and she seeks no further reassurance.

Though far removed from the stark "Rizpah" in form, style, and subject, "The Voyage of Maeldune" develops a not dissimilar theme, perhaps the most insistent motif throughout Tennyson's late poetry: the arrival through the pain and tribulation of the life journey at an ultimate recognition of moral truth. Driven by an unworthy desire for revenge, Maeldune must pass from island to island of trial and temptation until at the last, grown weary "of the travel, the trouble, the strife, and the sin," he learns the futility of recrimination and the necessity of love. Tennyson adapts the hyperbole of his ancient Celtic source to his own allegorical purpose with humor and exuberance. Each isle that comes between Maeldune and his objective represents the distractions of living and the satiety that follows indulgence: the Silent Isle, the peace that palls; the Isle of Shouting, the din of mad aggressiveness; the Flowers, the "fruitless" aesthetic delights; the Fruits, the orgies of gluttonous appetite; the Fire, the violence of all destructive passion; the undersea isle, the delusions of escape; the Bounteous Isle, a new Lotos-land where complete physical satisfaction brings misery of the spirit; the Isle of Witches, who are the sirens of sensuality; and the Isle of the Double Towers, which symbolize religious differences or the clash of science and faith or more generally the inane contentious divisiveness of human society. The description throughout is rich in detail but kept always in comic perspective; and the allegory, though clear, is unobtrusive and never solemnly didactic. In the end the hermit counsels Maeldune to desist from vengeance and "suffer the Past to be Past." But the wisdom Maeldune has attained is not suddenly thrust upon him; it is the inevitable product of his own rigorous experience.

The buoyant humor of the poem distinguishes it from Yeats's "Wanderings of Oisin," which reviewers later in the eighties could compare with it and which in its misty melancholy may or may not be more authentically Celtic.[4] But the humor of "Maeldune" is strictly functional, well suited to a fantasy of overstatement. It differs accordingly from the comedy of the two dialect pieces in the same volume, which exists for its own sake and fills no particular formal need. "The Village Wife" is little more than a clever impersonation of a tedious old gossip, a shapeless anecdote sharpened by a certain coarse folk-realism but controlled by no incisive poetic design. And "The Northern Cobbler" lacks the pattern and the verbal heightening we properly demand of either serious or comic verse. Nonetheless, the cobbler's narrative has the makings of an effective short story. His protracted struggle against alcoholism, though prosaic, is recalled with convincing vividness; and his symbol of victory, the unopened quart of gin on the window ledge above his work bench, somehow lifts his commonplace life to the level of the heroic. Dusting and polishing the bottle, half in love now with the enemy, he speculates on its extravagant size:

Wouldn't a pint a' sarved as well as a quart? Naw doubt;
But I liked a bigger feller to fight wi' an' fowt it out.
Fine and meller 'e mun be by this, if I cared to taäste,
But I moänt, my lad, and I weänt, fur I'd feäl mysen cleän disgraäced.

The comedy of character thus attains its own human pathos. If such pieces do not engage Tennyson's special gifts of style, they at least bear pleasant witness to his sense of humor, his range of sympathy, and his power of acceptance.

The consciously pathetic monologues are rather less successful, for in these the sentiment, kept at no ironic distance, lapses into sentimentalism. "In the Children's Hospital" is the trying and maudlin report, made by an unusually susceptible nurse, of little Emmie, who wills her own death rather than face "the dreadful knife" of a godless surgeon. "The First Quarrel" is a regretful widow's blank confession of how, sexually jealous without cause, she refused to bid farewell to her husband as he left home for the last time in search of work. And "The Sisters," in a more elaborate manner reminiscent of the *English Idyls,* is an old man's disturbed recollection of a diffidence in youth, which led him to abandon the girl who loved him and brought misery to the sister whom he married. All of these are based, we are told,[5] on true stories in which Tennyson apparently found some human value, but the emotion in each seems contrived and the facts are not fully translated into the self-subsistent life of poetry. "The Sisters," however, which is much the longest of the three, does reach an intense, if melodramatic, climax; Edith, the thwarted sister, represses her feelings throughout the marriage ceremony, but immediately afterwards, when she is left behind by the departing bride and groom,

> her brain broke
> With over-acting, till she rose and fled
> Beneath a pitiless rush of autumn rain
> To the deaf church — to be let in — to pray
> Before *that* altar — so I think; and there
> They found her beating the hard Protestant doors.

Here the mood with its atmospheric correlative briefly recalls similar depictions of frustration in Tennyson's best and most representative verse. Likewise familiar and Tennysonian in another vein is the speaker's insistence, elsewhere in the monologue, on an idealistic philosophy reminiscent of "The Higher Pantheism":

> My God, I would not live
> Save that I think this gross hard-seeming world
> Is our misshaping vision of the Powers
> Behind the world, that make our griefs our gains.

But apart from these two passages there is little more in "The

Sisters" than in the other narratives to suggest the special and characteristic concerns of the poet.

The one deeply personal poem of the 1880 volume was the muted debate "De Profundis," two greetings to a newborn child, each intellectually opposed to the other but both sincere and both relevant to the paradoxical middle state of human life. The first, written in 1852 at the time of Hallam's birth, is the salute of a reverent this-worldly empiricist who, valuing all the appearances of nature as the only vitality we can know, sees the child as the product of physical forces determined by an aeonian evolution. To him the earth is the source of all possible joy, and even the moon is "Touch'd with earth's light"; and it is his hope that the child may happily serve his "mortal race" and so accomplish his manhood and come at last

> in kindly curves, with gentlest fall,
> By quiet fields, a slowly-dying power,
> To that last deep where we and thou are still.

The second greeting, not completed until the late seventies, is that of the idealist who believes that "our world is but the bounding shore" of the "deep," which is the origin and destination of the human spirit and the source of all the light that the shadowy earth can glimpse. To him the child is the exile "banish'd into mystery," born into the pain of "this divisible-indivisible world" of "finite-infinite" contradictions and confusions, but gifted with a free-willed personal identity which is a fragment of the Divine consciousness and ultimately the one reality of experience,

> this main-miracle, that thou art thou,
> With power on thine own act and on the world.

Tennyson, who could sympathize with the assumptions of both greeters, finally endorses the argument of the idealist; "The Human Cry," with which "De Profundis" concludes, intimates that man cannot exist substantially at all until the

"Infinite Ideality" helps him to "be." Yet as poetry the first greeting is inevitably the more articulate, for the second involves a spiritual apprehension which, like the mystical trance of *In Memoriam*, necessarily resists statement in the matter-molded forms of speech.

During his last years Tennyson drew more and more support in his private life from the idealist's faith in the reality of spirit, his lifelong will to believe in the continuity of self-consciousness, his refusal to think that the darkening present could wholly eclipse the personal values of a past which haunted his imagination. He was distressed — to the point of physical and even mental illness — by the death of his brother Charles in the spring of 1879, and he complained for a while of hearing "perpetual ghostly voices." [6] Yet when he came to write his "Prefatory Poem" for a posthumous collection of Charles's sonnets, he could consider all their shared boyhood experience only an earnest of a perpetuity beyond death itself:

> As all thou wert was one with me,
> May all thou art be mine.

And in the summer of 1880, while in Italy (where he had been sent to recover his health), he could remember his brother without regret or lamentation as he wrote one of the finest of his late lyrics, "Frater Ave atque Vale," a tribute to Catullus and Catullus' memorable elegy to his own brother:

> Row us out from Desenzano, to your Sirmione row!
> So they rowed, and there we landed — 'O venusta Sirmio!'
> There to me thro' all the groves of olive in the summer glow,
> There beneath the Roman ruin where the purple flowers grow,
> Came that 'Ave atque Vale' of the Poet's hopeless woe,
> Tenderest of Roman poets nineteen hundred years ago,
> 'Frater Ave atque Vale' — as we wander'd to and fro
> Gazing at the Lydian laughter of the Garda Lake below,
> Sweet Catullus' all-but-island, olive-silvery Sirmio!

The emotion here is far from the "hopeless woe" ascribed to

the Roman; the living summer green encompasses the death purple, and the cry across the centuries is counterbalanced by the eternal laughter of the lake. With perfect felicity of diction and an incomparable command of assonance,[7] the poet has expressed his full acceptance of a pathos and a beauty transcending time.

Though he made new friends in the eighties of men as unlike as Thomas Hardy, Phillips Brooks, and Lord Acton, Tennyson inevitably felt the burden of age, the loss one by one of his intimates, Spedding, Dean Stanley, W. G. Ward, Carlyle, FitzGerald. To Ward, whose assured Catholic orthodoxy he admired but could not share, he addressed a warm yet incisive epitaph, every line of which is a stroke of characterization:

> Farewell, whose like on earth I shall not find,
>   Whose Faith and Work were bells of full accord,
> My friend, the most unworldly of mankind,
>   Most generous of all Ultramontanes, Ward,
> How subtle at tierce and quart of mind with mind,
>   How loyal in the following of thy Lord!

Of Carlyle he was quite possibly thinking, and perhaps also of his own not-distant death, when he wrote "The Dead Prophet," a sardonic attack on the sensation-mongers who would pry into the private affairs of a recently deceased literary genius.[8] (If so, the occasion of the piece must have been the appearance of Froude's indiscreet biography in 1882; but the attitude, of course, reflects Tennyson's own almost morbid dread of adverse publicity.)

To FitzGerald he had decided to inscribe "Tiresias," the title poem of his next volume, and in his best Horatian manner he had prepared a witty and urbane epistle of dedication. His notebooks show us something of the patience and tact with which he strove to achieve precisely the right easy and quietly modulated middle style. What is apparently the first draft ends as a personal letter:

> [I] found these lines, which you will take,
> Old Fitz, and value, as I know,
> Less for their own than for my sake
> Who love you,
> > Yours, ——

This yields to the second version:

> . . . this, which you will take,
>
> My Fitz, and value as I know
> Less for its own than for the sake
> Of me remembering gracious times
> Who keep the love of older days.[9]

And this in turn gives place to the final perfectly polished reading:

> . . . this, which you will take
> My Fitz, and welcome, as I know,
> Less for its own than for the sake
> Of one recalling gracious times,
> > When, in our younger London days,
> > You found some merit in my rhymes,
> > And I more pleasure in your praise.

But long before he was ready to publish "Tiresias," while he was still wondering whether Fitz would approve its "diffuse and opulent end," he received the melancholy news of his friend's death. Then he added to the poem an epilogue commingling his defiant idealism and his sad nostalgia:

> Gone into darkness, that full light
> Of friendship! past, in sleep, away
> By night, into the deeper night!
> The deeper night? A clearer day
> Than our poor twilight dawn on earth —
> If night, what barren toil to be!
> What life, so maim'd by night, were worth
> Our living out? Not mine to me
> Remembering all the golden hours
> Now silent, and so many dead
> And him the last.

Despite all his bereavements, however, he was no longer tempted, as in the days of early grief, to "eat his heart alone." He retained an active interest in people and a keen, though seldom sanguine, concern with public affairs. And, above all, he kept faith in the function and value of his own vocation, the making of poetry. He was constantly full of new plans for writing and publishing. He read widely in the works of other poets, and he dotted his conversation — much of which was now dutifully recorded by admirers — with pithy critical comments, remarkable for their freshness and consistent good taste. In 1882, to keep the nineteenth centenary of Virgil's death, he wrote his sensitive appreciation of the "lord of language" to whom all his life, and even in this stately encomium, he felt a deep affinity, Virgil of the "golden phrase," the pastoral poet, the visionary majestic in his sadness "at the doubtful doom of human kind." He, too, was doubtful as he pondered the human future, and he had no illusions of the permanence of even the most secure poetic fame. In the "Epilogue" to "The Charge of the Heavy Brigade," where he strove to explain his motives as a writer, he weighed all "our brief humanities" in the grim scales of modern physics. The earth — and all its poetry with it — would one day pass "In what they prophesy, our wise men, / Sun-flame or sunless frost"; and man's only hope of continuance must then be sought in some unearthly realm of spirit. But, meanwhile, the poet could play his vital part in reminding his culture of the ideal values man must live by; and even the praise of heroism in a chant like the "Heavy Brigade" might serve some worthy purpose:

> And here the Singer for his art
>   Not all in vain may plead
> "The song that nerves a nation's heart
>   Is in itself a deed."

In September 1883, Tennyson joined Gladstone on a holiday cruise to Scotland and across the sea to Scandinavia.

At Kirkwall he must have been embarrassed to hear his friend tell the welcoming throngs of the Laureate's "deathless fame" and the Prime Minister's relatively ephemeral achievement. Yet he returned home persuaded that, to honor poetry in his name and for the sake of the whole profession of letters, he must accept the highest official public recognition, a barony, though he still recoiled from the thought of any title at all. "By Gladstone's advice," he told Hallam, "I have consented to take the peerage, but for my own part I shall regret my simple name all my life." [10] On the other hand, he perhaps dimly felt that his acquiescence in the proposal would in some way be a final vindication of his father, for his proud Uncle Charles had constantly and vainly aspired to rank. [11] Emily believed that the hereditary title might prove a satisfaction to the faithful Hallam, but Tennyson was not so sure; in "the dark days" to come, he said, "a peerage might possibly be more of a disadvantage than an advantage to my sons." [12] With mixed emotions, troubled that he had been forced to reach a decision, he at last addressed a letter of formal acceptance to the Queen. But a few months later, replying to a note of congratulation from one of his French translators, he expressed his awareness of all the sad ironies of his action. "Being now in my 75th year," he wrote, "and having lost almost all my youthful contemporaries, I see myself, as it were, in an extra page of Holbein's 'Dance of Death,' and standing before the mouth of an open sepulchre while the Queen hands me a coronet, and the skeleton takes it away, and points me downward into the darkness." [13]

Reluctant to become the acknowledged legislator, Lord Tennyson declared himself past the age at which he could have joined in parliamentary debate — though he must have known that he would always have been far too diffident to speak in public. In the House he took his seat on the cross benches where he would be free of party obligation;

yet he attended too few sessions to make much use of his freedom. Though he admired Gladstone the man, he disliked most of Gladstone's policy, especially his stand on affairs of Empire; but he preferred to confine his criticisms to private letters or admonitory verses to the Prime Minister. On one occasion he did openly attack the Liberal government; the move to reduce the size and power of the navy prompted four angry stanzas to *The Times* (later reprinted as "The Fleet") in which he deplored what seemed to him a flagrant disregard for British security. In general, however, he had too little confidence in the probity of politicians even to attempt to influence their conduct. He was full of large apocalyptic fears more social than strictly political. "When I see society vicious," he remarked, "and the poor starving in great cities, I feel that it is a mighty wave of evil passing over the world." [14] Visitors to Aldworth and Farringford found him "inclined to be misanthropic" and his conversation darkened "with gloomy foreboding at the future of England." [15] And many who read his Laureate verses were distressed to see even his ode celebrating Victoria's golden jubilee invaded by his sense of possible disaster, his awareness of "thunders moaning in the distance."

In a discarded passage of the dedicatory poem to Fitz-Gerald, Tennyson complained that, if he were now to "play Tiresias to the times," he could foretell only civic disorder, lawlessness, the betrayal of old values, and "fierce Transition's bloodred morn." [16] "Tiresias" itself, published in 1885, makes the commentary oblique and incidental to the dramatic situation; the blind seer, who is doomed always to have his prophecy ignored, reviews his life of defeat and disillusion as he pleads with young Menoeceus, the son of Creon, to avert through self-sacrifice the imminent destruction of Thebes. In style the monologue, rich in classical figures of speech, recalls "Ulysses" or "Tithonus," in both of which the poet already wears "the mask of age"; and much of the composition may be assigned, as the dedication suggests, to an early date. But the theme, "the unfulfill'd desire, / The grief for ever born of griefs to be, / The boundless yearning of the prophet's heart," has a particular relevance to Tennyson in the eighties. The mistrust of anarchy as prelude to dictatorship parallels his dread of an aggressive, ill-educated democracy. Even the blindness of his protagonist must have assumed a special poignancy at a time when he himself was troubled by fears of failing vision.[17] Though he had known similar alarms (both social and personal) in his middle years, they were now far more acute. And though Tithonus also begged for release, the final longing of Tiresias rings with a new immediacy:

> But for me,
> I would that I were gather'd to my rest,
> And mingled with the famous kings of old,
> On whom about their ocean-islets flash
> The faces of the Gods — the wise man's word,
> Here trampled by the populace underfoot,
> There crown'd with worship — and these eyes will find
> The men I knew, and watch the chariot whirl
> About the goal again.

Whatever the date of the first draft, these lines from the "opulent end" seem clearly, on the evidence of the note-books,[18] to belong to Tennyson's last decade; and the mood, in any case, appropriately reflects his late disenchantment.

Of the other poems in the *Tiresias* volume, the longest by far was "Balin and Balan," the last major addition to the *Idylls of the King;* the most significant philosophically was "The Ancient Sage," to which we shall return presently. "Frater Ave atque Vale" and "To Virgil," as we have seen, both bore impressive witness to the poet's persistent strength as lyrist. Neither of the new dialect pieces, on the other hand, added much of value to the canon of his work; "To-morrow," in a stage Irishman's brogue, facetiously, and so

incongruously, tells the pathetic story of Molly Magee's
fidelity to her lover drowned in the bog; and "The Spin-
ster's Sweet-arts," in the language once more of "The Northern Farmer," pictures an eccentric (such as Dickens might
have drawn effectively in prose) who has made her tom-
cats surrogates for her rejected suitors. "The Flight," said
to be "a very early poem," [19] describes a mawkish maiden's
recoil from a *mariage de convenance*. And "The Wreck,"
apparently a very late one, depicts the misery of an aesthetic
girl married to a philistine and her ill-fated elopement with
an intellectual — in a style which anticipates the sentimental
realism of many a short story in the English nineties. None
of these, however, attracted the degree of attention already
given the lugubrious monologue "Despair," which, when
first printed four years earlier, had inspired Swinburne's
amusing parody "Disgust" and excited the protests of both
freethinkers and fundamentalists.[20] In "Despair" a man who,
according to the poet's notebook, has been "brought up in
the narrowest sect of Christianity" recounts his complete
loss of faith, his contempt for predestinarian theology, his
yielding to the logic of rationalism, and his ultimate disillusion leading to an unsuccessful attempt at suicide. Though
melodrama vitiates the recital, the poem clearly represents
Tennyson's earnest effort to argue the necessity of belief in
free will and immortality and his conviction that "in this
latter part of the nineteenth century" [21] man has been betrayed by the delusions of a vulgar half-knowledge, for — as
the would-be suicide explains in the violence of his frustration —

... these are the new dark ages, you see, of the popular press,
When the bat comes out of his cave, and the owls are whooping at
    noon,
And Doubt is lord of this dunghill and crows to the sun and the moon,
Till the sun and the moon of our science are both of them turn'd into
    blood.

Developed less shrilly than in "Despair," the mood of disillusion continues in "Vastness," a lyric which appeared separately [22] at the time of the *Tiresias* volume and was included four years later in *Demeter and Other Poems*. Originally "Vastness" seems to have consisted of but four stanzas: [23] the three with which the published version begins, bemoaning the insignificance of the human race in its cosmic setting and, within the brief span of its history, the perpetual drowning of wisdom in "a popular torrent of lies upon lies"; and a fourth which asks what can be the meaning of the struggle if we are denied the "dream" of the idealist,

What but a murmur of gnats in the gloom, or a moment's anger of bees in the hive,
Save for a hope that we shall not be lost in the Vastness, a dream that the dead are alive?

In the final version fourteen new stanzas are interposed between the opening three and the last, all of them designed to show the senseless commingling of good and evil in man's experience, "All that is noblest, all that is basest, all that is filthy with all that is fair." But even here the positive values are less vivid than the negations. Measured against the fierce lusts of a decadent society, the bourgeois ideal of marriage, for example, seems almost ironically bland and helpless: "Household happiness, gracious children, debtless competence, golden mean." Pain, on the other hand, is represented by a sharp personification:

Pain, that has crawl'd from the corpse of Pleasure, a worm which writhes all day, and at night
Stirs up again in the heart of the sleeper, and stings him back to the curse of the light.

Nevertheless, the entire catalogue of life's contradictions is as objective as the poet could make it. The private note yields everywhere to the general; accordingly an allusion in an early draft to "pigmy hates of the litterateur," which reflected Tennyson's personal battle with the reviewers, is

ultimately supplanted by a quite impersonal mention of
"pigmy spites of the village spire." What remains necessarily
subjective is the intuition of the last line, detached in several
revisions from the appalling question that is the body of
the poem: "what is all of it worth?" In what may be the
second draft, the last stanza is broken to allow the poet's
statement of faith in his own survival:

What but a murmur of gnats in the gloom, or a moment's anger of
 bees in the hive?
.   .   .   .
Peace, for I hold that I shall not be lost in the darkness, the dead are
 not dead but alive.

A later version of the last line shifts attention from the first
person singular to the second:

Nay, for I knew thee, O brother, and loved thee, and I hold thee as
 one not dead but alive.

And finally the published line makes a third-person pro-
noun the object of the love that affords an intimation of
immortality:

Peace, let it be! for I loved him and love him for ever: the dead are
 not dead but alive.

The "him" is usually taken to be a reference to Arthur
Hallam, but the earlier reading suggests that Tennyson may
have been thinking, in both drafts, of his brother Charles.
In any case, whatever the antecedent, the quiet assertion of
the one line is intended to override all the preceding doubt
and despair; as in *In Memoriam*, the persistence of love is to
make all else seem irrelevant. But the logic of the answer in
"Vastness" is elusive, and the abruptness with which it seeks
to silence the question breaks the lyric movement of the
poem.

    In "Locksley Hall Sixty Years After," the title piece of
his 1886 volume,[24] Tennyson turned from his general survey
of human confusion to a specific indictment of his own

society; he gave himself a last opportunity to play Tiresias to the times directly and at length. Remembering the first "Locksley Hall" as an ebullient early-Victorian "cry of Forward," he sought quite self-consciously to make the second a commentary on the delusions of nineteenth-century Progress. Together the two poems, he said, would one day prove of great historical interest "as descriptive of the tone of the age at two distant periods of his life." [25] He had no desire, of course, that either should be read as a personal confession, and he took pains to label the sequel "a dramatic monologue" and to explain that there was "not one touch of biography in it from beginning to end." [26] But no reader at all familiar with Tennyson's attitudes in the eighties could fail to suspect his close sympathy with the mood of the old man who is the speaker. Whereas the Byronic youth of sixty years ago found escape from personal misery in the bright promise of the "Mother-Age," the hero now seeks relief from public disillusion in personal relations and private hopes and, above all, in the good example of the rival he once grossly maligned. As before, however, the narrator's story is less important than his response to the world he lives in; and his attack on the mores of the younger generation, represented by the grandson whom he is haranguing, reflects clearly, though with considerable rhetorical exaggeration, the poet's own dissatisfaction and alarm.

The age, he is convinced, has lost its capacity for wonder until even the miracles of science are taken for granted:

Half the marvels of my morning, triumphs over time and space,
Staled by frequence, shrunk by usage into commonest commonplace! [27]

Science has indeed advanced, but the social imagination has not kept pace with its development; the proud cities have become "warrens of the poor," reservoirs of dirt and disease, monstrosities of "slated hideousness," and "There among the glooming alleys Progress halts on palsied feet." Political power has been usurped by "the practised hustings-liar," and the "old political commonsense" has been submerged in a "realm-ruining" party strife. The sanction of all such defections is a philosophy which would reverse the course of evolution by lowering "the rising race of men . . . back into the beast again." And the measure of cultural decadence is a naturalistic literature, void of reticence and reverence, eager to exploit the sordid and bestial, to deny the efficacy of reason, and at last to

Set the maiden fancies wallowing in the troughs of Zolaism, —
Forward, forward, ay, and backward, downward too into the abysm!

Tennyson was fully aware of the unpoetical hysteria into which the bitterness of his protagonist repeatedly drove the long ranting monologue. But though he strove through heavy revision of several early drafts to control the invective,[28] he himself too fully endorsed the central argument to set it in aesthetic perspective. Late in the composition of the poem he added several lines which permitted the narrator a brief self-conscious retreat from his violence:

Heated am I? you — you wonder — well, it scarce becomes mine age —
Patience! let the dying actor mouth his last upon the stage.

Cries of unprogressive dotage ere the dotard fall asleep?
Noises of a current narrowing, not the music of a deep?

The apology for the ill-tempered manner, however, was scarcely a retraction of the matter. If the fiction of dramatic objectivity was intended to disarm criticism, the speaker's moral judgments were nonetheless to be credited. "Locksley Hall Sixty Years After" was essentially the vehicle of Tennyson's own emotion, and only his intimates could have known how personal some of its sentiments were. Tennyson shared the sustaining faith of his hero as well as the disenchantment. In the one warmly assertive passage of the monologue, the narrator pays tribute to his son "early lost at sea," a man who never questioned the reality of eternal things:

Truth, for Truth is Truth, he worshipt, being true as he was brave;
Good, for Good is Good, he follow'd, yet he look'd beyond the
   grave. . . .

Truth for truth, and good for good! The Good, the True, the Pure,
   the Just —
Take the charm "For ever" from them, and they crumble into dust.

As poetry these lines suffer the burden of abstractness. But
when we learn that they were written immediately after
the untimely death of Tennyson's younger son Lionel and as
an epitaph to him,[29] they assume a poignancy quite independent of their poetic merit.

Lionel had died in April 1886 on a return voyage from
India and had been buried at sea "Beneath a hard Arabian
moon / And alien stars." The loss brought Tennyson the
deepest sorrow of his last years; the very thought of it, he
said, "tears me to pieces, he was so full of promise and so
young." [30] But no bereavement could now wholly destroy
his sense of life's meaning; for, whenever he could rise
a little above his grief, he rededicated himself mind and
heart to a philosophy which denied the finality of death.
The logic of his recovery from every personal defeat was
already apparent in "The Ancient Sage," the fullest description of his mystical intuitions and the best statement of his
late idealism.

Though eager as always to lend his poem the cast of
objectivity, Tennyson acknowledged that "The Ancient
Sage" was "very personal." [31] The piece, he explained, was
suggested by his reading of the life and maxims of Lao-tse,
but its ideas were assuredly not those of the Chinese seer.[32]
All that remains even vaguely Taoistic in the finished composition is the setting "A thousand summers ere the time of
Christ," which removes the argument altogether from the
framework of Christian revelation. After an eight-line
introduction establishing the time and place of the action,
the poem assumes the form of a monologue in a rather spare
blank verse. But in effect it soon becomes a debate between

faith and denial and thus a late counterpart to "The Two Voices." The sage, who is the speaker, reads from a scroll — and attempts to confute — the skeptical sentiments of a young poet who accompanies him as he withdraws from the city. The poet, a sensualist "richly garb'd, but worn / From wasteful living," recalls the aesthete of "The Vision of Sin," though he may have had some more immediate prototype in the Aesthetic eighties.[33] And his verses, rhyming a sweet sad agnostic hedonism, are reminiscent in mood and imagery of *The Rubáiyát* and its many late-Victorian imitations: they sing of the nightingale's self-sufficient beauty, of man as a vase of clay made and broken, of the fading rose of youth, of the pains of dotage, of wine as the agent of oblivion —

> Yet wine and laughter, friends! and set
> The lamps alight, and call
> For golden music, and forget
> The darkness of the pall.

But the sage, unlike the troubled ego that fifty years before fenced desperately with the bitter voice, is not for a moment to be shaken by the poet's doubt or tempted by the plea for soul-deadening pleasure. With deliberation and forbearance he proceeds to instruct the youth in the way of assent. The wise man, he argues (in terms of Kantian metaphysics), will act *as if* he had knowledge of the Nameless ideal, "As if thou knewest, tho' thou canst not know," for the Nameless alone gives life and meaning to the illusory world of phenomena. Knowledge is painfully limited in its reach; we cannot prove our immortality or our mortality or even our identity; indeed "nothing worthy proving can be proven, / Nor yet disproven." Pragmatically, then, faith is more availing than denial. Faith will bring us a prevision of the ultimate wholeness and harmony of experience, for

> with the Nameless is nor day nor hour;
> Tho' we, thin minds, who creep from thought to thought,
> Break into "Thens" and "Whens" the Eternal Now —
> This double seeming of the single world!

Such is the sage's philosophy, a familiar idealism, reasoned with a serene detachment. Then suddenly the poet's scroll interrupts with the ironic comment that "some have gleams, or so they say, / Of more than mortal things." And the sage at once shifts from philosophical to psychological demonstration. He appeals to his own boyhood intimations of immortality,[34] to what he called, when yet he "knew no books and no philosophies," the Passion of the Past:

> The first gray streak of earliest summer-dawn,
> The last long stripe of waning crimson gloom,
> As if the late and early were but one —
> A height, a broken grange, a grove, a flower
> Had murmurs, "Lost and gone, and lost and gone!"
> A breath, a whisper — some divine farewell —
> Desolate sweetness — far and far away —
> What had he loved, what had he lost, the boy?

And beyond this memory, which carries us back to the child on the wind-swept lawn at Somersby, the sage recollects moments of less sensuous apprehension, the mystical exhilaration celebrated long ago in "Armageddon" and known to Tennyson in some degree from time to time through all his years:

>   for more than once when I
> Sat all alone, revolving in myself
> The word that is the symbol of myself,
> The mortal limit of the Self was loosed,
> And passed into the Nameless, as a cloud
> Melts into heaven. I touch'd my limbs, the limbs
> Were strange, not mine — and yet no shade of doubt,
> But utter clearness, and thro' loss of self
> The gain of such large life as match'd with ours
> Were sun to spark — unshadowable in words,
> Themselves but shadows of a shadow-world.

With so private and unanswerable a witness to the reality of spirit, the sage closes the debate and bids the poet, perhaps now his disciple, return to the human city where he may realize his true self in a life of service. Meanwhile, he himself, having accomplished his work, will retreat to the hills for his last days of quiet contemplation.

Tennyson, of course, did not follow the example of his spokesman. But in the late eighties, after the vituperative second "Locksley Hall" had given release to his social and political anxieties, he was more and more inclined to withdraw from public affairs and correspondingly less eager to write topical verses. He retained his devotion to modern science, yet only in the belief that the proper study of nature was "a great antidote to worldliness," a corrective of all human delusions of self-importance.[35] For his real concern was now with elemental things. Though he entered no mystical state, "unshadowable in words," he turned increasingly to a calm consideration of the ultimate issues of experience. And his last two volumes accordingly seem to carry the voice of a man who like the ancient sage has already moved beyond life itself.

❧ XII ❧

THE ONE CLEAR CALL

1888–1892

In the fall of 1888 Tennyson suffered the most severe illness he had ever known. For months he remained doubtful of his recovery, and as he lay by his study window, staring across the broad landscape, he felt "as if looking into the other world."[1] Then at the crisis, when his physician considered him "as near death as a man could be without dying,"[2] he made a bold epigrammatic salute to the pains of old age which had freed the spirit of the weight of fleshly satisfaction. Later, when he had rallied beyond all expectation, he developed the epigram into the short dramatic lyric "By an Evolutionist," ending with a statement of victory not over death but over the long ordeal of sensuous life:

I have climb'd to the snows of Age, and I gaze at a field in the Past,
　Where I sank with the body at times in the sloughs of a low desire,
But I hear no yelp of the beast, and the Man is quiet at last,
　　As he stands on the heights of his life with a glimpse of a height
　　　that is higher.[3]

From such a vantage point — under the aspect, as it were, of eternity — he could now appraise, somewhat more hopefully than in the "Epilogue" to the "Heavy Brigade," the old fiction of the poet's immortality. In April 1889 he wrote "Parnassus," a meditation, in the form of a three-part Hegelian dialectic, on Horace's claim to have built for himself a monument which the passage of uncounted years could not destroy. The thesis is the classical assumption of an aesthetic fame "Sounding for ever and ever thro' Earth and her listening nations." The antithesis is the modern awareness of infinite space and ageless time, of "Astronomy and Geology, terrible Muses," the new sciences that blast the evergreen laurel and mock every human hope of survival. And the synthesis, embracing and resolving the two attitudes, is the faith that the spirit of the poet who is truly inspired, "touch'd with fire from off a pure Pierian altar," transcends the limitations of the poetic vehicle: "Let the golden Iliad vanish, Homer here is Homer there."

Meanwhile, Tennyson's own fame, ringing throughout the listening nations, seemed for the moment at least, to almost all but Tennyson himself, unshakably secure. The public regard for his work had long since extended to his person, and the course of his illness was followed with a widespread anxious concern. In August when, nearly recovered, he celebrated his eightieth birthday, he was inundated with letters and telegrams of congratulation, many embarrassingly fulsome, a few, like the generous tribute from Browning, intimate and warm-hearted. To his closest friends he wrote personal replies, but the only answer he could give scores of unknown well-wishers was an advertisement of his thanks which he sent to *The Times*. Though surely grateful for all the greetings he had received, he was no longer to be swayed as poet by expressions of approval or even of censure. "As a general rule," he told Henry Van Dyke, an American admirer, "I think it wisest in a man to do his work in the world as quietly and as well as he can, without much heeding the praise or the dispraise." [4] He himself hoped to be known only by and for his own work and, as long as men cared for what he had done, to escape the curiosity that would pry into his private life. His bibliography must stand as his biography; and for all readers who still needed to be reminded of that fact, he now — in the month of his memorable birthday — composed his "Merlin and the Gleam," a cadenced summing-up of a career in which the only significant public events were published poems.

As an allegory of Tennyson's poetic dedication, however, "Merlin" is often teasingly obscure.[5] It seeks not so much to retrace the actual course of his development as to suggest the varied forms and subjects of his verse, but it imposes upon these a definite sense of chronology and forward movement. It translates selected details of experience into topographical images and subordinates all to the melody of "the gray Magician," an alliterative meter foreshadowed by Tennyson's rendition of the Anglo-Saxon "Brunanburh" and reminiscent in rhythm of the Old Welsh lyric measures. Unlike his earlier counterpart snared by the sensual Vivien, Merlin is here steadfast in his devotion to the fairy Nimue, understood (according to Tennyson's own gloss [6]) to mean the Gleam or "the higher poetic imagination," the fugitive light that leads the singer across an ever-changing landscape. The "croak of a Raven" that decries the vision apparently represents the hostile criticism of the 1830's and probably in particular that of Christopher North (whose familiar in the *Noctes Ambrosianae* was a raven).[7] The elves, gnomes, giants, and dragons, which nowhere figure greatly in Tennyson's poetry, may symbolize the delights of fanciful escape, the attractions of the Palace of Art. The level pastures with "innocent maidens" and "rough-ruddy faces / Of lowly labour" evidently stand for the world of the "English Idyls" and all the later local-color genre studies and dialect pieces. And the "statelier" music that brings Merlin to the city and palace of Arthur is clearly the rich blank verse of the *Idylls of the King*. Then, given a new climactic place, the passing of Merlin's Arthur comes by a bold equation (as in the "Morte d'Arthur" of 1834) to signify the death of Arthur Hallam, and the loss and slow recovery of the Gleam become correla-

tives to the doubt and faith of *In Memoriam*. Thereafter the
"broader and brighter" progress of the Gleam, the singing
"thro' the world," may betoken either the mature poet's
increased social concern or simply his satisfaction in knowing
that his great elegy had brought comfort to the sorrowful.[8]
But Merlin's exultant cry of final acceptance is assuredly to
be read as the witness the aged Tennyson himself would
wish to leave, the testimony of a lifelong commitment to
poetry which partook of an ideal larger than any single
life:

> And so to the land's
> Last limit I came —
> And can no longer,
> But die rejoicing,
> For thro' the Magic
> Of Him the Mighty,
> Who taught me in childhood,
> There on the border
> Of boundless Ocean,
> And all but in Heaven
> Hovers the Gleam.

Like "the great deep" in the *Idylls*, the "boundless Ocean"
is thus both source and destination, the unknown sea from
which the singer has come and to which he now returns,
and all the while the eternity that encompasses the island
of time across which he has traveled.

In image and idea "Crossing the Bar," written two months
later, begins where "Merlin and the Gleam" ends. The
retrospect necessarily stops at the land's last limit; the death
lyric looks ahead to the point where vessel and tide reach
the open sea, to the moment

> When that which drew from out the boundless deep
> Turns again home.

As the epilogue to all editions of his work, which Tennyson
stipulated it should be, "Crossing the Bar" derives its reso-

nance from echoes of several of the earlier poems and achieves its freshness by giving familiar phrase and metaphor new connotation. The "sunset and evening star" of the opening line recalls the setting of the departure in "Ulysses," but the light is quiet now and no longer atremble with the promise of unending earthly experience. The "one clear call" resembles the "calling of the sea" brought to the dreamer in *In Memoriam* (section CIII), but the call now is far more definite, and it reaches wakeful ears prepared to understand and welcome its one purpose. The wish that there be "no moaning of the bar" suggests by negation the relentless beat of the surf in "Break, Break, Break" and the turbulence of "Ulysses," where "the deep / Moans round with many voices." And the plea that there be "no sadness of farewell," likewise by indirection, evokes the profound sadness of "Tears, Idle Tears," where all is hopeless regret as the ship "sinks with all we love below the verge."

No comparison or contrast, however, can disturb the integrity of "Crossing the Bar" as an independent unit.[9] The structure, precisely balancing the first two stanzas against the third and fourth, has its own self-sustained completeness. The metrical pattern with its repetitions and subtle variations establishes the hushed movement essential to the quietly acceptant mood. And the imagery throughout, though consciously less denotative and more figurative as the poem enters its second half, is wholly consistent and entirely functional. Those very literal readers who object to the image of the Pilot (on the assumption that voyagers may usually see their pilot *before* reaching the bar) should be reminded that the night of Tennyson's embarkation is "dark" and that the speaker, after he has crossed the bar, hopes to see his Pilot not necessarily for the first time but rather "face to face," in the full light, no longer through a mist darkly. Moreover, the Pilot is, of course, no ordinary steersman but — as the poet himself explained [10] — "That Divine and Unseen Who is always guiding us"; and by the end of the poem the secondary or spiritual level of all the metaphors has become primary. The final effect of the whole is the reverence of a quiet faith expressed in the perfect peace of a controlled art.

"Crossing the Bar" was finished [11] in time to conclude *Demeter and Other Poems*, which Macmillan issued in December 1889; and it was immediately recognized as one of Tennyson's most successful lyrics. The entire volume, however, gave evidence of his still unflagging resourcefulness as a stylist. In *Appreciations*, published in the same year, Walter Pater, discussing the diversity of modern style, had exclaimed: "Of such eclecticism we have a justifying example in one of the first poets of our time. How illustrative of monosyllabic effect, of sonorous Latin, of the phraseology of science, of metaphysic, of colloquialism even, are the writings of Tennyson; yet with what a fine, fastidious scholarship throughout!" [12] The *Demeter* volume seemed an almost deliberate corroboration of Pater's judgment. Its styles ranged from the rich formal rhetoric of the title piece to the prosy broad dialect of "Owd Roä," from the taut generalities of "Vastness" to the easy urbanity of the epistle "To Mary Boyle." The garrulous monologue "Romney's Remorse" dipped into the technical jargon of the painter, and the mournful ballad "Happy" touched in clinical detail on the horrors of leprosy. Geology and astronomy entered "Parnassus," and a roll call of exotic place names constituted "To Ulysses," an address to the much-traveled brother of Francis Palgrave. "Crossing the Bar" and "Far — Far — Away" realized the full power of the monosyllable. And "The Ring," an improbable ghost story cast in dramatic form, mingled a stilted poetic diction and the language of actual speech. Tennyson himself particularly liked "The Oak," which he thought "clean cut like a Greek epigram," [13] and indeed the sharply etched impression well represented his own latest manner, for the most striking new development in the volume was the trend toward a style of greater simplicity and economy, reduced to essentials, stripped of ornament like the winter tree:

> All his leaves
> Fall'n at length,
> Look, he stands,
> Trunk and bough,
> Naked strength.

A few of the poems — "Happy" and "Romney's Remorse," for example, each documented with a source note — required special reading and research; but, whatever the "scholarship" involved, all reflected the discipline of a "fine, fastidious" craftsman. A study of the revisions of a single heavily charged passage from the beginning of "Demeter and Persephone" should serve to indicate the arduous process by which concentration, precision, and apparent ease were attained. In an early draft Demeter had rather prosily explained her purpose in bringing Persephone back to Enna:

> ... I brought thee hither that a glance
> At thy last sight on earth, the flowery gleam
> Of Enna, might have power to disentrance
> Thy senses.[14]

This was considerably expanded to make the image more concrete and to include what seems to be a conscious echo of Milton's description of

> that faire field
> Of Enna, where Proserpin gathring flours
> Her self a fairer Floure by gloomie Dis
> Was gatherd ...[15]

> ... I brought thee hither, to the fields
> Where thou and thy sea-nymphs were used to roam
> And thy scared hands let fall the gather'd flower,
> For here thy last bright day beneath the sun
> Might float across thy memory and unfold
> The sleeping sense.

But the sea-nymphs must have seemed irrelevant, since the second line was quickly bracketed for exclusion; and the account of Persephone's awakening was clearly too elaborate. The poet began again, this time less ornately:

> . . . I brought thee hither, where thy hands
> Let fall the gather'd flowers, that here again
> Thy last bright hours of sunshine upon earth
> Might break on darken'd memories.

This was a considerable improvement, though still wordier than need be. In the final version as published, the "last bright hours of sunshine upon earth" became quite simply the "day," and the syntax of the whole acquired a new tightness:

> . . . I brought thee hither, that the day,
> When here thy hands let fall the gather'd flower,
> Might break thro' clouded memories once again
> On thy lost self.

The felicity of the changes may be appreciated here in isolation, but the full value of the reworking can be judged only in the context of the complete poem. There the late introduction of the "lost self" proves of thematic rather than merely stylistic importance: banished from love (typified by her mother Demeter), Persephone has lost her true identity, and it is the burden of the idyl to demonstrate that love can restore the self and so transcend the force of death and hell. Ultimately it is the content, the poetic meaning, that determines and justifies the technique.

Speaking of "Demeter," Tennyson told his son, "When I write an antique like this I must put it into a frame — something modern about it. It is no use giving a mere *réchauffé* of old legends." [16] Accordingly, as he re-created the myth, the Earth-Goddess remains dissatisfied with the Gods of heaven even though she has prevailed upon them to return Persephone for three of the four seasons each year; in her "deathless heart of motherhood" she yearns for a new dispensation

under "younger kindlier Gods" — essentially, that is, for a
Christian charity — which will make complete and permanent the victory of love. This new frame was obviously
Tennyson's chief interest in the old legend, his way of making it serve not so much a general "modern" purpose as a
deeply personal religious need.

A similar concern with values and emotions of special
immediacy to the poet in his eightieth year underlies most
of the other apparently objective pieces in the *Demeter*
volume. "Happy," the shrill monologue of the leper's bride,
seems contrived to show that a soul-beauty must transcend
the flesh, "This poor rib-grated dungeon of the holy human
ghost," and that the soul, as in Yeats's "Sailing to Byzantium,"
must rejoice at the destruction of its prison. "The Ring"
virtually exists for a soliloquy in which Tennyson, under the
mask of Miriam's father, examines the claims of spirit (and
perhaps of spiritualism) and concludes that the evolution of
the soul will continue in the enlightenment of death where
"utter knowledge is but utter love." And "Romney's Remorse," in much less exalted terms, quickens briefly as the
aged Romney violently repudiates his own selfish quest for
fame and his yielding, at the expense of human love, to the
seductions of art:

> This Art, that harlot-like
> Seduced me from you, leaves me harlot-like
> Who love her still, and whimper, impotent
> To win her back before I die — and then —
> Then, in the loud world's bastard judgment-day,
> One truth will damn me with the mindless mob,
> Who feel no touch of my temptation, more
> Than all the myriad lies that blacken round
> The corpse of every man that gains a name.

Though he could still grow petulant at the thought of
the world's bastard judgments, Tennyson himself now felt
none of the desire he once had known for aesthetic escape.
The frankly personal poems in *Demeter* all declared his calm

acceptance of life's imponderables. The dedication to Lord
Dufferin who had befriended Lionel in his last illness denied
any will "To question why / The sons before the fathers die.".
And the epistle "To Mary Boyle" announced his continued
wonderment at the miracle of consciousness:

> What use to brood? This life of mingled pains
>   And joys to me,
> Despite of every Faith and Creed, remains
>   The Mystery.

As "Far — Far — Away" suggests (like the retrospect in
"The Ancient Sage"), the sense of mystery had been his
from childhood when the three words had brought some
intimation "from his dawn of life" or "some fair dawn beyond the doors of death." Now, when all reality seemed of
the spirit, he could imagine — as in a suppressed stanza of
the lyric — the soul's looking back on human time from
the dimension of eternity:

> Ghost, do the men that walk this planet seem
> Far, far away, a truth and yet a dream
> Far — far — away? [17]

And now, as always when he approached such awareness,
he felt not the power but the failure of his art:

> What charm in words, a charm no words could give?
> O dying words, can Music make you live
> Far — far — away?

But whatever the inevitable limitation of language, he had
no thought of abandoning his work. Poetry remained to the
end his calling, his reason for being in the immediate physical
world. Still alert in mind and body, he continued to write
until the last. No sooner had he completed *Demeter* than
he was planning a new volume of verses. For all his "mystic
sympathies" with the far country of the soul, which passed
description, he still held literature the highest expression of
human life. He read a good deal of modern fiction, including the novels of Hardy, Meredith, and James, and he studied

the recent French poets, especially François Coppée, with unexpected interest and enthusiasm. He returned frequently
to his favorite poems in the long English tradition and explained with a craftsman's authority their distinctive merits.
And he delighted to discover an old masterpiece he had
overlooked: when the long-forgotten medieval *Pearl* was
edited in 1891 by Israel Gollancz, he contributed an intro-
ductory quatrain hailing the restoration of the poem to its
rightful place in "Britain's lyric coronet." But he was also
ready to encourage younger contemporaries. He commended
alike the decorous William Watson and the boisterous, confident Kipling and was especially gratified by the crisp reply of
the latter: "When the private in the ranks is praised by the
general, he cannot presume to thank him, but he fights the
better the next day." [18]
Even so, though responsive to verse and prose of many
kinds, he found his attention as both reader and writer drawn
increasingly to religious themes. When asked to treat of
"everyday topics," to which he once had turned with relief,
he now quietly declined: "I cannot; I must write what I am
thinking about and I have not much time." [19] And his thinking was stimulated above all by his readings in Biblical criticism and comparative religion, areas of which the typical
English parson was, he felt, woefully ignorant.[20] He was
particularly attracted to Frazer's *Golden Bough*, the first
book of which Hallam read aloud to him on its appearance
in the spring of 1890, as he sat somewhat reluctantly for
two last portraits by G. F. Watts.[21] Far from shaking his
belief, Frazer's demonstration that primitive mythologies pre-
figured Christian ritual seemed to suggest the common
ground of mankind's religious aspirations and so to general-
ize — and in a sense to certify — his own "faith beyond
the forms of faith." Sometime later, at Jowett's urging, he
began a study of Eastern history and philosophy in the hope
of finding "an Indian subject," and before long he came

upon the life and work of Akbar the Great, sixteenth-century emperor of Hindustan, who preached and practiced a broad religious toleration. Seeing in Akbar an anticipation — sufficiently remote in culture — of his own liberal theism, he at once set about the composition of what was to prove the longest and most ambitious piece in his last volume. The research behind "Akbar's Dream" remains apparent in the scholarly notes he appended to the poem. But, despite a serious effort at dramatic objectivity, the monologue of the emperor is expository and undramatic, the apology of an eclectic modernist rather than the depiction of an historical character:

> If every single star
> Should shriek its claim "I only am in heaven"
> Why that were such sphere-music as the Greek
> Had hardly dream'd of. There is light in all,
> And light, with more or less of shade, in all
> Man-modes of worship. . . .
>
> I hate the rancour of their castes and creeds,
> I let men worship as they will, I reap
> No revenue from the field of unbelief. . . .
>
> I can but lift the torch
> Of reason in the dusky cave of Life,
> And gaze on this great miracle, the World,
> Adoring That who made, and makes, and is,
> And is not, what I gaze on — all else Form,
> Ritual, varying with the tribes of men.

Akbar is much less interesting in himself than as a spokesman of the poet's undogmatic faith,[22] a reflection of what Tennyson was most often thinking about in the last months of his life.

As he moved into 1892, his last year, he continued to work on "Akbar" and the other pieces that would appear with it in the volume to be called *The Death of Oenone*. But he was now consciously working against time; in spite of himself, his pace had slowed, and the flight of days seemed ever more rapid. More and more he was driven back into his own past. He spoke frequently of his father and mother, told anecdotes of Lincolnshire, recalled conversations with Carlyle, and on a final visit to his brother Frederick in Jersey talked at length of Arthur Hallam. In "The Silent Voices," however, the best of his last lyrics, he rebuked the tyranny of such memories:

> When the dumb Hour, clothed in black,
> Brings the Dreams about my bed,
> Call me not so often back,
> Silent Voices of the dead,
> Toward the lowland ways behind me,
> And the sunlight that is gone!
> Call me rather, silent voices,
> Forward to the starry track
> Glimmering up the heights beyond me
> On, and always on!

His sense of mission as poet kept him active until the end; and he admonished himself with his own line from *In Memoriam*, "So much to do, so little done." During the summer he helped prepare the stage version of *Becket*, which Irving at long last had agreed to produce. In September he finished the manuscript of his new volume, including the prose notes. But by then he was seriously ill, suddenly exhausted, short of breath. When the proofs arrived three weeks later, he was dying. His death itself, at Aldworth just after midnight on October 6 — the full moon lighting his face and a Shakespeare in his hand — was as calm as one of his idyls; and even the attendant physician was moved to make the literary comparison: "The majestic figure as he lay there, . . ." said Dr. Dabbs in his last bulletin, "irresistibly brought to our minds his own 'Passing of Arthur.' " [23] The poet could have asked no more fitting tribute.

Sixteen days after the great state funeral in Westminster Abbey, Macmillan published *The Death of Oenone, Akbar's*

Dream and Other Poems, the slender volume that Tennyson himself had expected to stand as "his last will and testament to the world." [24] Like *Demeter*, the collection is marked by an effort to achieve variety of form and content; but since all of the more considerable pieces are of very late composition,[25] the whole leaves the dominant impression of unity, of a final overriding concern with the themes of death and the future, couched in a spare and simple language. "The Death of Oenone," far less ornate than the early "Oenone," describes the revenge for which the nymph has lived since her betrayal by Paris, and the release which she obtains when, "led by dream and vague desire" and — like a dedicated poet — "following, as in a trance, the silent cry," she plunges into her husband's pyre. "St. Telemachus," with the directness of a medieval exemplum, recounts a holier self-immolation; hearing a voice denounce him as a "deedless dreamer, lazying out a life / Of self-suppression, not of selfless love," the saint obeys "the call of God" that carries him to Rome, where he indicts, at the cost of martyrdom, the ethics of the arena. Each presents death as fulfillment, the most meaningful act of life.

Several shorter poems, on the other hand, gnarled and gnomic in style, look to the remote future for the possible resolution of human problems. "Dawn" and "The Making of Man" both suggest that "there is time for the race to grow" and so time for the spirit's complete subjugation of the ape and tiger within. "The Dreamer" urges some distant earthly hope, even though Earth herself cry out, like one in disillusioned age, "I am losing the light of my Youth / And the Vision that led me of old." And "Poets and Critics," in a similar though lighter vein, laconically bids the poet, whether underrated or overvalued, leave his work to the judgment of time, for the true artist appears but seldom "And the Critic's rarer still." Such verses, though admonitions rather than testaments, are indeed addressed, at least in part, to the world. But the true lyrics of the volume, "The Silent Voices" and the reprinted "Crossing the Bar," which in another and deeper sense do embody Tennyson's last will, speak for the solitary self facing a private and quite unworldly experience. And with them belongs the sonnet "Doubt and Prayer," the sestet of which expresses with strength and humility his ultimate aspiration beyond all the distractions of living:

> Steel me with patience! soften me with grief!
> Let blow the trumpet strongly while I pray,
> Till this embattled wall of unbelief
> My prison, not my fortress, fall away!
> Then, if Thou willest, let my day be brief,
> So thou wilt strike Thy glory thro' the day.

On the second Sunday after Tennyson's death, the Master of Trinity College, Cambridge, preached a memorial sermon in the college chapel, declaring Tennyson the greatest Trinity man since Newton.[26] The restive undergraduate of some sixty years before, who detested mathematics and had little love of any academic discipline, could hardly in his most defiant dreams have anticipated such eulogy; nor would the poet in later life on his own voyages of discovery ever have attempted to measure himself against the philosopher-mathematician "voyaging through strange seas of thought alone." But it was nonetheless an act of poetic justice that Trinity, which once had fed not the heart, should pay generous homage at a time when all England was mourning its loss. For, whatever his status in the annals of his college, Tennyson was clearly, as T. S. Eliot has adjudged him, "a great poet" — the greatest, I believe, between Wordsworth (who was, of course, a Johnian) and Yeats (who had no Cambridge connection at all).

His greatness, to be sure, has been strenuously questioned both by those who distrust the artifice of some of his many styles and by those who, regarding him as the Victorian laureate par excellence, reject his characteristically Victorian assumptions about life and art. But, if the epithet "major poet" has any meaning, Tennyson cannot be denied the essential attributes of majority: dedication to the poet's calling, command of his medium, range of vision, capacity for growth, magnitude of performance, and place in a tradition as one who, consciously indebted to a literary past, in turn influences the course of subsequent poetry. Tennyson had from the beginning the deepest sense of vocation and the awareness of a verbal power strong enough to compel his unwavering commitment. He mastered his craft by constant exercise and tireless experiment, and his technical successes in many different genres were numerous partly because his productivity was sufficiently ample to allow a large margin for error. Yet his long-sustained dexterity would have been of little avail had it not served the needs of his ever-changing sensibility. Though seldom directly subjective, his work — read as a whole and, as far as possible, in chronological order — is the faithful record of his development from the wondering child of Somersby to the ancient sage of Aldworth, from the aestheticism of the Cambridge period to the moral realism of the *Idylls of the King,* from the social confidence of "Locksley Hall" to the disillusion of its sequel, from the doubt of *In Memoriam* to the quiet assent of the last lyrics. An understanding of even the least of the verses gains from a familiarity with the total product of Tennyson's imagination. Each piece, however, must finally be assessed on its own intrinsic merits. And the longer or "major" poems, no less than the more tightly unified short lyrics, do achieve an integrity and independence: *In Memoriam* runs through a complete cycle of despair and recovery, meaningful in itself as a way of the soul; *Maud* creates its own little world, where love is the one antidote to madness; and the *Idylls* calls into new self-subsistence a mythology in which a social order rises, flourishes, and declines. Still, for all their vitality as separate entities, each of these draws freely on the established conventions of English and classical poetry; each, taking its new place in literary history, looks knowingly back to its antecedents in a similar genre. Throughout his career Tennyson maintained a sophisticated acquaintance with the work of his predecessors as a standard of aesthetic decorum and a counterbalance to his own necessary innovations. And within his lifetime he himself became the criterion by which countless younger Victorian poets evaluated their own efforts — the master, according to Swinburne, "in the sunshine of whose noble genius the men of my generation grew up and took delight." [27]

Laureate for nearly half a century to one of the world's great ages, Tennyson commanded such public attention as no English writer before or since has known. Sensitive to the moral and spiritual confusions of his time, familiar with the new sciences, aware of imminent social change and crisis, he was the voice and sometimes indeed the conscience of Victorian culture; and his work will endure, even apart from its aesthetic worth, as a mirror of his civilization. Yet the distinction that his critics have repeatedly drawn between the bard of public sentiments and the earlier poet of private sensibilities is ultimately untenable. For there was no real break in Tennyson's career; from the beginning he felt some responsibility to the society he lived in, and until the end he remained obedient to the one clear call of his own imagination. His development depended not on a sacrifice of the personal vision, but on the constant interaction between public knowledge and private feeling. From first to last his best poetry raised a psychological protest against the commonplace fact he knew with the intellect or acutely perceived with the senses. In the perspectives of evolutionary theory, he saw perpetual movement as the law of life; but with all his own passion of the past, he intuited a lost order of values, a peace — both aesthetic and religious — untouched by the bewildering changefulness and relativity of the world. Behind the roar of the London street, he could imagine what once had been "the stillness of the central sea," the elemental reality with which the spirit must once again come to terms. His response to the restless activity of his time enhanced rather than weakened his concern with the moment of insight and revelation. And his art at its highest, transcending change, invested the transitory with meaning and purpose.

Sunset & evening star
And one clear call for me!
But may there be no moaning of the bar
When I put out to sea.

But such a tide as moving seems asleep,
Too full for sound & foam,
When that is came from out the boundess deep
— Turns again home
Twilight & evening bell
And then the dark   after that
But may there be no sadness of farewell
When I embark.

Alone from out the bourne of Time & Place
Alone I sail, & far
But hope to see my Pilot face to face
When I have crost the bar.

An early draft of "Crossing the Bar" from the Harvard University Library Tennyson Papers, Notebook 54

NOTES AND SOURCES

NOTES AND SOURCES

The Eversley Edition of Tennyson's *Works*, edited by Hallam Lord Tennyson, in six volumes (New York, 1908) and later (1913) in one volume, is the standard text. W. J. Rolfe's Cambridge Edition (Boston, 1898), however, includes helpful notes and reprints many suppressed and fugitive pieces. In addition, J. C. Collins' edition of the *Early Poems* (London, 1900) remains useful and convenient. Sir Charles Tennyson edited *The Devil and the Lady* (London, 1930) and the *Unpublished Early Poems* (London, 1931) and issued a number of other verses as "Tennyson's Unpublished Poems" in the *Nineteenth Century and After*, CIX (1931), 367–380, 495–508, 625–636, 756–764. The notebooks and papers, which contain much material still unpublished, have been described by Edgar F. Shannon, Jr., and W. H. Bond in "Literary Manuscripts of Alfred Tennyson in the Harvard College Library," *Harvard Library Bulletin*, X (1956), 254–274.

Apart from the many more specific studies I have cited in the notes to each chapter, the following books and essays have proven more or less essential to my interpretation of Tennyson's development — or at least in some way stimulating and provocative.

Baker, Arthur Ernest, *A Concordance to . . . Tennyson* (London, 1914), supplemented by *Concordance to "The Devil and the Lady"* (London, 1931).

Baum, Paull F., "Alfred Lord Tennyson," Frederic E. Faverty, ed., *The Victorian Poets: A Guide to Research* (Cambridge, Mass., 1956). A survey of Tennyson scholarship and criticism.

——— *Tennyson Sixty Years After* (Chapel Hill, 1948).

Beach, Joseph W., *The Concept of Nature in Nineteenth-Century English Poetry* (New York, 1936).

Bradley, A. C., "The Reaction against Tennyson," *A Miscellany* (London, 1929), pp. 1–31.

Bush, Douglas, *Mythology and the Romantic Tradition* (Cambridge, Mass., 1937). Contains a brilliant chapter on Tennyson's ability to adapt classical materials to his own needs.

——— *Science and English Poetry* (New York, 1950). Chapter V defends Tennyson's response to the challenge of evolution.

Carr, Arthur J., "Tennyson as a Modern Poet," *University of Toronto Quarterly*, XIX (1950), 361–382.

Eidson, J. O., *Tennyson in America* (Athens, Georgia, 1943).

Fairchild, Hoxie N., *Religious Trends in English Poetry, Vol. IV: 1830–1880* (New York, 1957). Chapter V is an able though stringent assessment of Tennyson's departures from orthodoxy.

Groom, Bernard, *On the Diction of Tennyson, Browning and Arnold* (New York, 1939).

Johnson, E. D. H., *The Alien Vision of Victorian Poetry* (Princeton, 1952). Emphasizes undercurrents of protest and conflict in Tennyson's thought and work.

Langbaum, Robert, *The Poetry of Experience* (New York, 1957). Passes new and suggestive judgment on Tennyson as a writer of dramatic monologues.

Lockyer, Sir Norman and W. L., *Tennyson as a Student and Poet of Nature* (London, 1910). The distinguished astronomer estimates the poet's knowledge of science.

Masterman, C. F. G., *Tennyson as a Religious Teacher* (London, 1900).

Mustard, W. P., *Classical Echoes in Tennyson* (New York, 1904).

Nicolson, Harold, *Tennyson: Aspects of his Life, Character and Poetry* (New York, 1923).

Paden, W. D., *Tennyson in Egypt: A Study of the Imagery in his Earlier Work* (Lawrence, Kansas, 1942). An attempt at a psychoanalytic interpretation of adolescent conflicts.

Pyre, J. F. A., *The Formation of Tennyson's Style* (Madison, 1921). A study of Tennyson's metrics and diction to 1850.

Salt, Henry S., *Tennyson as a Thinker* (London, 1893). Interesting as an early anticipation of many attempts at "debunking" Tennyson.

Scaife, C. H. O., *The Poetry of Alfred Tennyson* (London, 1930).

Shannon, Edgar F., Jr., *Tennyson and the Reviewers: A Study of His Literary Reputation and of the Influence of the Critics upon His Poetry 1827–1851* (Cambridge, Mass., 1952).

Sneath, E. H., *The Mind of Tennyson* (New York, 1900). A philosopher's view of Tennyson's philosophy.

Tennyson, Sir Charles, *Alfred Tennyson* (New York, 1949). The standard and indispensable biography.

Tennyson, Hallam Lord, *Alfred Lord Tennyson: A Memoir*, 2 vols. (New York, 1897). The longest and most important record of Tennyson's reflections on his own career and his judgments of life and literature; referred to throughout the Notes that follow as the *Memoir*.

Tennyson, Hallam Lord, ed., *Tennyson and his Friends* (London, 1911). Contains many tributes to Tennyson the man and personal reminiscences by men of letters and science.

CHAPTER I: THE EYES OF WONDER

1. Quoted by Hallam Tennyson, *Memoir,* I, 11.

2. Unpublished, in Harvard University Library Tennyson Papers, Notebook 54; see also Notebook 55 for a version in the second person.

3. *Memoir,* I, 17.

4. *Memoir,* I, 323n1.

5. Cf. the role of the mother in "Supposed Confessions"; see above, p. 24.

6. Sir Charles Tennyson, "Tennyson Papers: 1. Alfred's Father," *Cornhill,* CLIII (1936), 283–305; see also Sir Charles, *Alfred Tennyson,* pp. 5–106, *passim.*

7. Sir Charles (*Tennyson,* pp. 9, 97) assumes, I think rightly, that the more melodramatic adventures in Russia and perhaps in Italy were fabrications.

8. See Sir Charles, *Tennyson,* p. 61. Dr. Tennyson was found one night "with a large knife and a loaded gun in his room." He threatened to kill his son Frederick. His wife complained to the master of the family at Bayons that her married life had been miserable for more than twenty years.

9. *Memoir,* I, 101–102.

10. See Sir Charles, *Tennyson,* p. 24 and, on Tennyson's dislike of Louth, p. 26.

11. *Memoir,* I, 318.

12. *Memoir,* I, 20.

13. One of Alfred's prose tales, "Mungo the American," dated 1823, survives in manuscript (in the Berg Collection at the New York Public Library). As compared to the early verses, the piece is in no way extraordinary. It describes the discovery by Mungo, a Panamanian Indian, of a Spaniard's sword and the subsequent effort of the Spaniard to recover his weapon, leading to the death of Mungo; at the end (rather hastily arrived at) the ruins of Mungo's hut alone remain, and all passers-by avert their eyes lest they encounter Mungo's troubled ghost. In his study of Tennyson's juvenilia (see below, note 16), W. D. Paden attempts to give the story a psychological reading.

14. Quoted from Tennyson's *Unpublished Early Poems,* ed. Sir Charles Tennyson, p. 2.

15. Sir Charles (*Tennyson,* p. 39) comments on the significance of the aphorism in view of Tennyson's attitude towards his grandfather and his later fear of criticism.

16. On *Poems by Two Brothers,* see W. D. Paden's monograph, *Tennyson in Egypt;* and on the brothers, Charles and Frederick,

see Sir Harold Nicolson, *Tennyson's Two Brothers* (Cambridge, Eng., 1947).

17. *Memoir*, I, 23.

18. Sir Charles Tennyson edited *The Devil and the Lady* in 1930.

19. At least one other drama in a similar style seems to have been lost. Hallam Tennyson quotes a fragmentary scene in the *Memoir*, I, 23–25.

20. *Memoir*, I, 172, from a letter of 1839.

21. On Wordsworth's "mystic sympathies," see Norman Lacey, *Wordsworth's View of Nature* (Cambridge, Eng., 1948).

22. *Unpublished Early Poems*, p. 25; the image recurs in "The Palace of Art," l. 86: "dewy pastures . . . softer than sleep."

23. Cf. *In Memoriam*, section LXXXIX: "Witch-elms that counterchange the floor / Of this flat lawn with dusk and bright."

24. See *Memoir*, I, 320.

25. See Jacques Barzun, *Berlioz and the Romantic Century*, 2 vols. (Boston, 1950), esp. I, 42, and II, 30.

26. Berlioz, quoted by Barzun, I, 90.

27. John St. Loe Strachey, *The Adventure of Living* (New York, 1922), p. 81. On Strachey, see Charles R. Sanders, *The Strachey Family* (Durham, 1953), esp. pp. 235–236.

28. Strachey, *Adventure*, p. 86.

29. *Memoir*, I, 170; cf. I, 316.

30. See *Unpublished Early Poems*, p. 29n. The dating of the manuscript, though not in Tennyson's hand, is probably accurate.

31. Published in the 1830 volume with the subtitle "Written very early in life." I quote from the 1830 text, which differs slightly from later versions.

32. In a Somersby notebook, Harvard Notebook 3; also quoted by Sir Charles, *Tennyson*, p. 54. But despite "the love of home," Tennyson had found life with his father at Somersby increasingly difficult by November of 1827, when he joined his older brothers at Cambridge.

CHAPTER II: THE REVEREND WALLS

1. Tennyson was admitted to Trinity College on November 9, 1827, and immediately began his period of residence (see Edgar F. Shannon, Jr., "Alfred Tennyson's Admission to Cambridge," *Times Literary Supplement*, March 6, 1959, p. 136). He withdrew at the time of his father's last illness late in February 1831 (see Sir Charles, *Tennyson*, p. 105). Darwin tells us that he "went to Cambridge after the Christmas vacation, early in 1828" (see *The Autobiography of Charles Darwin*, ed. Nora Barlow [New York, 1959], p. 58).

2. Darwin, *Autobiography*, p. 58.

3. See 253.

4. *Memoir*, I, 34.

5. When Tennyson published "The Lover's Tale" in 1879, he described the first three parts as the product of his "nineteenth year," i. e., of late 1827 or early 1828; his son dates the poem 1827 (*Memoir*, I, 48). But I assume that composition carried over well into the Cambridge period. Tennyson seems to have kept reworking the poem up until 1832 (see *Memoir*, I, 83–84, 88).

6. *Memoir*, I, 68n.

7. "To Poesy," *Memoir*, I, 60. The sonnet also appears in Harvard Notebook 3 and on a loose sheet among the Harvard papers (MS Eng 952.1, 176); the latter is marked "A. T. 1828."

8. *Unpublished Early Poems*, p. 44.

9. *Unpublished Early Poems*, p. 35. "Perdidi Diem," perhaps begun at Somersby, belongs mostly to the early Cambridge period; see Sir Charles's note to the text, p. 37.

10. "Supposed Confessions" was published in 1830, then suppressed until 1871, when all of it but seventeen lines was placed among the "Juvenilia."

11. See John Steegman, *Cambridge* (New York, 1941), p. 40.

12. Simeon, quoted by L. E. Elliott-Binns, *Religion in the Victorian Era* (London, 1946), p. 400.

13. Simeon, quoted by J. C. Pollock, *A Cambridge Movement* (London, 1953), p. 7.

14. Letter of November 7, 1827, quoted by T. Wemyss Reid, *The Life and Letters of Richard Monckton Milnes*, 2 vols. (New York, 1891), I, 51.

15. See A. T. Bartholomew, "Samuel Butler and the Simeonites," *Cambridge Magazine*, March 1, 1913, reprinted in Samuel Butler, *A First Year in Canterbury Settlement* (London, 1914); see also *The Way of All Flesh*, ch. 47; and cf. John F. Harris, *Samuel Butler* (New York, 1916), pp. 41–45.

16. The "Sims" were attacked by a Trinity man in *Alma Mater*, 1827; see Oskar Teichman, *The Cambridge Undergraduate 100 Years Ago* (Cambridge, Eng., 1926), p. 10.

17. "Saint Simeon," first published in 1842, was probably completed before the end of 1833; see Sir Charles, *Tennyson*, p. 146.

18. A more immediate source was William Hone, *The Every-Day Book* (1826), 3 vols. (London, 1838), I, 35–38.

19. H. H. Milman, ed., *The History of the Decline and Fall of the Roman Empire*, 6 vols. (Philadelphia, n.d.), III, 539.

20. Sir Charles (*Tennyson*, p. 194) sees in the poem "a reference to the Calvinism of Aunt Mary Bourne."

21. See John Connop Thirlwall, Jr., *Connop Thirlwall, Historian and Theologian* (London, 1936).

22. Kemble, quoted by Thirlwall, p. 56.

23. Kemble, quoted by Frances Brookfield, *The Cambridge "Apostles"* (New York, 1907), p. 11.

24. See *Memoir*, I, 311.

25. See *Memoir*, I, 44n.

26. See Thirlwall, p. 58.

27. Paley, quoted by Elliott-Binns, p. 361.

28. *Memoir*, I, 314.

29. See Harold A. Boner, *Hungry Generations: The Nineteenth-Century Case against Malthusianism* (New York, 1955), p. 171; Boner finds some evidence that "even in the forties" (when Malthus was generally repudiated) Tennyson "shared to some extent the fears of the Malthusians."

30. See Brookfield, p. 10; the Apostles so described the outside world.

31. Hallam's intellectual range and creative capacity could not be adequately assessed by the modern student of Tennyson and his circle until the appearance of T. H. Vail Motter's full and careful edition of *The Writings of Arthur Hallam* (New York, 1943).

32. Hallam, "Lines in Answer to a Desponding Letter," *Writings*, p. 78.

33. Cf. letter to Tennyson, July 26, 1831 (*Memoir*, I, 81): "I, whose imagination is to yours as Pisgah to Canaan, the point of distant prospect to the place of actual possession, am not without some knowledge and experience of your passion for the past. To this community of feeling between us, I probably owe your inestimable friendship." Cited also by Eleanor Mattes, *In Memoriam: The Way of a Soul* (New York, 1951), p. 31. Mrs. Mattes (pp. 12–31) gives us a useful rapid review of the friendship.

34. "To —" as in the 1833 volume, suppressed until 1872, when it was reprinted with several verbal improvements.

35. See *Memoir*, I, 38.

36. Sir Harold Nicolson tells an amusing though probably apocryphal story of the judges' decision: "it was even whispered that the first examiner had marked the lines 'V. Q.' which had impressed the second examiner as signifying 'Very good,' and not, as intended, 'Very queer.'" See Nicolson, *Tennyson*, p. 86.

37. Sir Charles, *Tennyson*, p. 76.

38. *Memoir*, I, 45, from a letter to the printer which Hallam dates "1831 probably." The original is now in the Morgan Library.

39. Hallam quoted, *Memoir*, I, 46.

40. Milnes is identified by Sir Charles (*Tennyson*, pp. 91–92). Edgar F. Shannon, Jr., though not sure of Milnes' authorship, is convinced that the reviewer was "one of the Cambridge group." The *Athenaeum* was edited at the time by the former Apostle, John Sterling. See Shannon, *Tennyson and the Reviewers*, pp. 2, 184n7.

41. Harvard Notebook 7; the fragment appears in abridged form in *Memoir*, I, 497–498; it is reproduced in facsimile in *Harvard Library Bulletin*, X (1956), 254f.

42. "To —"; this poem, "The Poet," and "The Poet's Mind" are here quoted as they appeared in 1830; later each was revised and improved. Blakesley is identified as the "clear-headed friend" in John Churton Collins, ed., *The Early Poems of Alfred Lord Tennyson* (London, 1900), p. 9, also in Sir Charles, *Tennyson*, p. 171.

43. Sometime after the Cambridge period, Sir Henry Taylor commented on Tennyson's readings: "I rather need to know what he is reading, for otherwise I find the sense to be lost in sound from time to time." Quoted by W. Macneile Dixon, *A Primer of Tennyson* (London, 1896), p. 22.

44. See Sir Charles, *Tennyson*, p. 75.

45. Brookfield quoted, *Memoir*, I, 76.

46. First published in *Memoir*, I, 59, where it is given the title "Life." The desire for knowledge and life piled on life recurs in similar phrasing but with much greater force in "Ulysses."

47. "National Song" was first published in 1830, then suppressed until it reappeared sixty-two years later as a song in *The Foresters*. See Chapter X, p. 209.

48. For instance, in addition to the poems I am discussing, the following are preoccupied with death: "The Burial of Love," "A Dirge," "Claribel," "Song" ("I' the glooming night"), "Love and Death," "The Deserted House."

49. Especially Keatsian is the use of double-barreled epithets and past-participial adjectives like "hollow-vaulted," "Laughter-stirr'd," "latticed," "mooned," "argent-lidded," "engarlanded," "shadow-chequer'd."

50. See also the unpublished poems, apparently written at about the same time, "Marion," "Lisette," "Amy," and "Lines to the Picture of a Young Lady of Fashion," *Unpublished Early Poems*, pp. 50–57.

51. *Memoir*, I, 12.

52. Sir Charles (*Tennyson*, pp. 93–96) gives us a good brief account of the mission.

CHAPTER III: THE MUSES' WALK

1. Hugh J. Schonfield, ed., *Letters to Frederick Tennyson* (London, 1930), p. 23.

2. *Memoir*, I, 81.

3. *Memoir*, I, 82.

4. Unpublished sonnet ("The Wise, the Pure, the lights of our

dull clime") of uncertain date, perhaps earlier than 1832, in Harvard Notebook 5, printed by Sir Charles, *Unpublished Early Poems*, p. 61.

5. *Unpublished Early Poems*, p. 75; the first stanza appears in *Memoir*, I, 97, under date 1832. The original is in Harvard Notebook 4.

6. See Shannon, *Tennyson and the Reviewers*, p. 5. Shannon's listing of the reviews and his discussion of their importance is of great value to all students of Tennyson.

7. *Memoir*, I, 40.

8. Hallam wrote of the poem in manuscript, "The 'Little Room' is mighty pleasant" (*Memoir*, I, 88). The piece should, I think, be regarded as a failure at humorous verse rather than an unsuccessful and bathetic serious lyric.

9. See Shannon, pp. 14–18.

10. I am indebted to G. Robert Stange's close and suggestive reading of the poem, "Tennyson's Garden of Art: A Study of *The Hesperides*," *PMLA*, LXVII (1952), 732–743.

11. "The Lady of Shalott" was the first of the Arthurian pieces to be published. Though "Sir Launcelot and Queen Guinevere" may have been written or at least begun as early as 1830 (see *Memoir*, I, 59), it did not appear until 1842.

12. Lionel Stevenson suggests such a Jungian reading in his article, "The 'High-Born Maiden' Symbol in Tennyson," *PMLA*, LXIII (1948), 242.

13. Margaret, we are told, has won her "tearful grace" from "the westward-winding flood, / From the evening-lighted wood." Like the Lady of Shalott, she hears "the murmur of the strife," but enters not "the toil of life." Rosalind of the same volume, drawn with less sympathy, is aloof and disdainful, the high-flying falcon that must "come down" to earth.

14. *Memoir*, I, 118.

15. *Memoir*, I, 35.

16. W. J. Rolfe points out that the phrase is borrowed from Hallam's "Theodicaea Novissima," where Hallam speaks of "the abysmal secrets of personality" that rest with God. See Rolfe, ed., Cambridge Edition, p. 804. The echo from the essay, unpublished until after Hallam's death, is good evidence of the impression the "Theodicaea" made on Tennyson.

17. Cf. Paden's reading of the poem (*Tennyson in Egypt*, p. 64): "Tennyson's dream embodies, explicitly, a longing for the simple world of childhood and, implicitly, a longing for the childhood of the world, before the advent of conflict between desire and denial."

18. See Shannon, p. 17, where this description of "The May

Queen" is ascribed to the young Bulwer. Cf. similar treatment of the idyls in other reviews (pp. 14, 16).

19. Hallam quoted in *Memoir*, I, 88.

20. Henry N. Coleridge, ed., *Specimens of the Table Talk of the Late Samuel Taylor Coleridge*, 2 vols. (London, 1835), II, 164; cited by Shannon, *Tennyson and the Reviewers*, p. 186n39.

21. T. S. Eliot, *Essays Ancient and Modern* (London, 1936), p. 178.

22. See *Memoir*, I, 91.

23. Hallam quoted, *Memoir*, I, 89.

24. *Memoir*, I, 104. It is possible that the brilliant image of Danaë in *The Princess* ("Now lies the Earth all Danaë to the stars") may have been inspired by the memory of Hallam's letter.

CHAPTER IV: A USE IN MEASURED LANGUAGE

1. Letter of December 30, 1833, from Henry Hallam in *Memoir*, I, 106.

2. In his fine essay on *In Memoriam*, T. S. Eliot compares the elegies to entries in a diary; see Eliot, *Essays Ancient and Modern*, p. 183. Drawing on evidence from J. M. Heath's Commonplace Book, Sir Charles Tennyson shows that at least seven sections of *In Memoriam* were probably written at least in part before the end of 1833 and that Tennyson must have been at work on several other new pieces during the first few weeks of bereavement; see *Cornhill*, CLIII (1936), 426–449.

3. *In Memoriam*, LXXXV, an early stanza, perhaps from 1833, in the Heath Commonplace Book; see Mary J. Ellmann's article on the revision of section LXXXV, *Modern Language Notes*, LXV (1950), 22–30.

4. See *Memoir*, I, 196, where Tennyson also describes "Ulysses" as "written soon after Arthur Hallam's death."

5. *Hamlet*, IV, iv, 34–39; see Douglas Bush, "Tennyson's 'Ulysses' and *Hamlet*," *Modern Language Review*, XXXVIII (1943), 38. The poem may also echo, though more faintly, the speech of Shakespeare's Ulysses to Achilles in *Troilus and Cressida*, bitterly reminding the warrior that time mocks honor as soon as the hero is content to rest from action — "to have done, is to hang / Quite out of fashion, like a rusty mail / In monumental mockery" (III, iii, 151–153); cf. "rusty mail" and "to rust unburnished."

6. This early draft, presumably the first, is in Harvard Notebook 16. For other evidence of the date, see *Memoir*, I, 196, and Sir Charles, *Tennyson*, p. 146. The Heath manuscript dates "Ulysses"

October 20, 1833; see Joyce Green, "Tennyson's Development during the 'Ten Years' Silence' (1832–1842)," *PMLA*, LXVI (1951), 670. The sadness of the early version seems to corroborate Robert Langbaum's argument (*The Poetry of Experience*, pp. 89–92) that Ulysses speaks in "enervated cadence" and "with a sense of diminished strength," but, though I agree that the poem is more meditative than blustery in tone, I cannot accept the suggestion that it expresses an obsessive death wish; Ulysses yearns not to die, but to sail on *until* he dies; to "make an end," to die in any sense, is "dull" rather than fulfilling. In any case, the very fact that Langbaum could compare Tennyson's hero to T. S. Eliot's Gerontion is one measure of the distance that separates this Ulysses from Homer's Odysseus; for a full discussion of the many adaptations between the two, see W. B. Stanford's study, *The Ulysses Theme* (Oxford, 1954).

7. See *Memoir*, I, 459, and II, 9. "Tithonus" was published in the *Cornhill* in 1860 and in the *Enoch Arden* volume in 1864. The original called "Tithon" appears in the Heath manuscript and has been published, together with a first-rate analysis and commentary, by Mary Joan Donahue (Ellmann), *PMLA*, LXIV (1949), 400–416.

8. *Memoir*, I, 193n; for manuscript title of poem, see *Memoir*, I, 139, 142.

9. Sir Charles (*Tennyson*, p. 146) believes that the poet had "probably begun the first draft of the *Morte d'Arthur*" before the end of 1833.

10. I assume that the verses were addressed to Spedding; but, if not, they are certainly very similar in tone and style to "Love Thou thy Land" and "Of Old Sat Freedom," both written about the same time and included in part or in whole in a letter of 1834 to Spedding; see Memoir, I, 141–142. Sir Charles (*Tennyson*, pp. 151–152) suggests that all three pieces were sent to Spedding. Aubrey de Vere, however, seems to assign the pieces to an earlier date, perhaps before Hallam's death; see *Memoir*, I, 506. The evidence does not support de Vere's conjecture.

11. On "Hail, Briton" see Donahue's article (cited in note 7 above), which includes a full transcript of the fifty stanzas in the Heath manuscript. Though Tennyson never published the piece, he drew lines and stanzas from it for other poems over a long period; see Donahue, pp. 394–396, and Harvard Notebooks 11, 15, 17, 46.

12. Unpublished, in Harvard Notebook 16, the same notebook that contains the early draft of "Ulysses."

13. The schedule appears undated in Harvard Notebook 10, which also contains some stanzas of *In Memoriam*, XVIII; Hallam Tennyson published it in *Memoir*, I, 124, under the running dates 1833–1835; Sir Charles (*Tennyson*, p. 149) suggests 1834 as the time of the

planned study. See also *Memoir*, I, 138, for other evidence of Tennyson's reading in 1834.

14. The poem appears in Harvard Notebook 16 in five stanzas; Hallam Tennyson, omitting one stanza, published the poem in the *Memoir*, I, 134, but changed the personal reference to "our chief resort" to an indefinite "their chief resort."

15. Quoted (in italics) in *Memoir*, I, 145.

16. See Harold G. Merriam, *Edward Moxon, Publisher of Poets* (New York, 1939), p. 170.

17. *Memoir*, I, 12.

18. *Memoir*, I, 118.

19. *Memoir*, I, 122.

20. See esp. Shannon, *Tennyson and the Reviewers*, pp. 33–45, and Joyce Green, who discounts the influence, "Tennyson's Development," *PMLA*, LXVI (1951), 662–697.

21. *Memoir*, I, 171–172.

22. Quoted by Tyndall in his reminiscences appended to *Memoir*, II, 475.

23. Esp. Rosa Baring and Sophie Rawnsley; see H. D. Rawnsley, *Memories of the Tennysons* (Glasgow, 1900), pp. 62–67, and Sir Charles, *Tennyson*, pp. 162–163.

24. Hallam Tennyson burnt most of the correspondence at his father's request but printed a few discreet extracts in *Memoir*, I, 167–176. Sir Charles rescued a few charred fragments, a good deal more personal, which he included in his *Tennyson*, pp. 180–182.

25. Though undated, "Love and Duty" was probably written in 1840 or 1841 and presumably is a commentary on the broken engagement. Sir Charles (*Tennyson*, p. 182) so regards it.

26. After a careful study of all available evidence, Professor W. D. Templeman argues that the poem was completed "during the spring and summer of 1841," by which time, he believes, Tennyson was much indebted to *Sartor Resartus*. See Templeman, "Tennyson's *Locksley Hall* and Thomas Carlyle," Hill Shine, ed., *Booker Memorial Studies* (Chapel Hill, 1950), pp. 34–59.

27. Cf. Josiah Royce's comments on the first and second "Locksley Hall," "Tennyson and Pessimism" in his *Studies of Good and Evil* (New York, 1898), pp. 76–88.

28. So reads the 1842 version; later "Let the peoples spin" was altered to "Let the great world spin."

29. Quoted by Sir Charles, *Cornhill*, CLIII (1936), 297. The *Memoir* (I, 265) quotes Dr. Ker who assigns the "dam your eyes" to a later time, the mid-forties.

30. *Memoir*, I, 158.

31. *Memoir*, I, 159.

32. Tennyson first used this label for the series in the edition of 1884.

33. *Memoir*, I, 197.

34. "Dora" was written about 1835. Tennyson comments on the "trouble" its simplicity gave him (*Memoir*, I, 196).

35. Internal evidence suggests this date, several years after the "Morte d'Arthur" itself had been completed: Tennyson, we know, read Lyell in 1837, and he enjoyed skating on the pond at High Beech during the winter of 1837–38; references in "The Epic" to the new geology and to the sport probably reflect the reading and experience of that time.

36. "The Goose" was so interpreted by William Johnson Fox in his *Lectures addressed chiefly to the Working Classes*, 4 vols. (London, 1845), I, 256. As a sentimental radical, Fox was unduly eager to picture all poets as advancing the cause of liberalism; yet there is, I believe, some warrant for his allegorical reading of this rather feeble piece. J. C. Collins (*Early Poems*, p. 139), however, gives it the opposite interpretation, construing it as an attack on the radicals.

37. FitzGerald, quoted by Sir Charles, *Tennyson*, p. 191.

CHAPTER V: A STRANGE DIAGONAL

1. See *Memoir*, I, 225.

2. See D. A. Winstanley, *Early Victorian Cambridge* (Cambridge, Eng., 1940), p. 200n2, and cf. Sir Charles, *Tennyson*, pp. 217–218. Wordsworth wrote the ode, after Tennyson declined on the ground that, though he admired Cambridge and the prince, he could find no inspiration in the event.

3. *Memoir*, I, 206.

4. *Memoir*, I, 210.

5. *Memoir*, I, 213.

6. *Memoir*, I, 187n.

7. *Memoir*, I, 188.

8. See *Memoir*, I, 269.

9. First published in 1853 but written, I should assume, in the middle or late forties.

10. See Sir Charles, *Tennyson*, p. 217.

11. See *Memoir*, I, 280–281.

12. Harvard Notebook 24 — unpublished, except in expurgated form by Hallam Tennyson (*Memoir*, I, 232–233). Hallam omits the fleas, the "infamous Swiss boy," the bad beer, the harridans, and the "other rooms," and so sacrifices most of the vitality of the stream of consciousness.

13. *Memoir*, I, 213; on the hypochondriacs, see Sir Charles, *Tennyson*, p. 199, and on the ruin, pp. 186–188, 198.

14. See Schonfield, ed., *Letters to Frederick Tennyson*, p. 81; the letter is from Tennyson's mother, who calls Dr. Gully "a very clever man." Sir Charles (*Tennyson*, p. 218) spells the name "Gulley" and locates the hospital in Birmingham. Charles Darwin speaks of taking similar hydropathic treatment at Malvern in 1848; see Darwin, *Autobiography*, p. 117.

15. The "Life" may possibly be Milnes' *Keats* (1848), though Milnes is much more respectful of his subject than Tennyson's poem would suggest. Collins (*Early Poems*, p. 250) suggests that the addressee may be Charles Tennyson, who was no longer courting a literary fame.

16. *Memoir*, I, 210, 211, and Sir Charles, *Tennyson*, p. 204.

17. *Punch* had already defended "the bard of Locksley Hall" against Bulwer's "puny darts" in " 'The New Timon' and Alfred Tennyson's Pension," an eight-line squib, *Punch*, X (1846), 64.

18. See Harvard Tennyson Papers, MS Eng 952.1, 160 and 161.

19. Harvard Papers, 160; see also Sir Charles, *Nineteenth Century*, CIX (1931), 763. Hallam Tennyson (*Memoir*, II, 165) prints these lines with slight changes but wrenched from context and assigned to a time in the 1870s. In MS 160 the lines appear as part of a poem beginning "Will no one make this man secure," written on a sheet headed "Farringford, Freshwater" and so written not earlier than the mid-fifties. I assume, however, that the lines were composed at the time of the quarrel, to which they clearly refer, since MS 161 includes part of "The New Timon and the Poets" and another version of "Will no one make this man secure." The Farringford manuscript would then be a copy of an 1846 original.

20. Harvard Papers, 126; the first stanza here does not appear either in the *Punch* version or in "Literary Squabbles"; the rest of the piece is substantially the same in these published versions, except that the person is shifted from first to third ("we," "our," "us," and "ours" become "they," "their," "them," and "theirs"). The manuscript version was first printed by Sir Charles, "Tennyson and 'The New Timon,' " *Nineteenth Century*, CIX, 763–764.

21. Both apparently were written or at least begun at Llanberis during the Welsh holiday in the summer of 1845; see Sir Charles, *Tennyson*, p. 211.

22. See Harvard Papers, 196, unpublished.

23. Harvard Notebook 23; Sir Charles (*Tennyson*, p. 220) prints the passage in *Nineteenth Century*, CIX, 634.

24. See Harvard Notebook 22. The fragment "The New University" corresponds to Part I of *The Princess*. The notebook apparently dates from the late thirties. Hallam Tennyson (*Memoir*,

I, 248n) notes, "He talked over the plan of the poem with my mother in 1839."

25. *Memoir*, I, 260.

26. *Memoir*, I, 251, 252.

27. *Memoir*, I, 251. Though Hallam does not date it, this comment was apparently made in the 1880s, and it clearly refers to the final version of the "Prologue." My own comments on *The Princess*, which follow, also concern the final text of the poem.

28. In his discussion of *The Princess*, Paull F. Baum properly calls attention to Tennyson's "exquisite comic delicacy." See his *Tennyson Sixty Years After*, p. 101.

29. See *Memoir*, I, 249. On the relation of the poem to the age, see John Killham, *Tennyson and The Princess* (London, 1958), pp. 1–169.

30. See Sir Charles, *Tennyson*, p. 164.

31. So suggests J. C. Collins, who also makes some interesting comments on the feminist movement; see his edition of *In Memoriam, The Princess, and Maud* (London, 1902), p. 148. Killham (pp. 132–133), however, thinks it unlikely that Maurice contributed anything to the poem.

32. Tennyson reopened correspondence with Emily Sellwood in November 1849 when he sent her two versions of "Sweet and Low"; their engagement was resumed apparently in April 1850. Meanwhile, at the beginning of February, the third edition of *The Princess* appeared. See Sir Charles, *Tennyson*, pp. 239–242.

33. Hallam Tennyson (*Memoir*, I, 255) prints the alternate version which Emily Sellwood rejected. In it the mother likewise soothes her infant with the promise that father will soon come "to his babe in the nest." Still another version, however, appears among the Harvard Papers, 192, and this is marked by a kind of wild Romantic terror, hardly appropriate to a cradlesong but expressive of the mother's frustration and fear:

> Who claps the gate
> So late, so late
> Who claps the gate on the lonely wold
> O were it he
> Come back from sea!
> Sleep, sleep, my blossom; the night is cold —

34. See *Memoir*, I, 253; Tennyson finds the Abbey "full for me of its bygone memories," and presumably also rich in its literary associations.

35. Cleanth Brooks analyzes the ambiguities of the poem with great subtlety in "The Motivation of Tennyson's Weeper," in his *Well Wrought Urn* (New York, 1947).

CHAPTER VI: *IN MEMORIAM*

1. See Sir Charles, *Tennyson*, p. 246.

2. *Memoir*, I, 305.

3. Tennyson sometimes felt that his poem, too, if it were to appear at all, would be posthumously published. In 1847 he wrote to his aunt concerning the elegies, which he was still revising: "Perhaps they will not see the light till I have ceased to be."

4. T. S. Eliot, *Essays Ancient and Modern*, p. 183. Other critics have, of course, been concerned with other aspects of the poem. A. C. Bradley's *Commentary* (London, 1901; rev. ed., 1930) remains the best running gloss on *In Memoriam*, its order, syntax, and often cryptic allusions. Eleanor Bustin Mattes has studied the intellectual influences on the elegy in her *In Memoriam: The Way of a Soul* (New York, 1951). Graham Hough comments on the conflict between science and religion in "The Natural Theology of *In Memoriam*," *Review of English Studies*, XXIII (1947), 244–256; and Basil Willey reviews the problem — rather more sympathetically — in *More Nineteenth Century Studies: A Group of Honest Doubters* (New York, 1956), pp. 79–105. Interesting appraisals of the scientific content will also be found in A. N. Whitehead's *Science and the Modern World* (New York, 1925) and in Georg Roppen's *Evolution and Poetic Belief* (Oslo, 1956). E. D. H. Johnson, on the other hand, has taken a fresh and rewarding approach to the poem as the record of an aesthetic development, in his essay *"In Memoriam:* The Way of the Poet," *Victorian Studies*, II (1958), 139–148. And John D. Rosenberg writes perceptively of the relation between the intellectual argument and the symbolic structure in "The Two Kingdoms of *In Memoriam*," *Journal of English and Germanic Philology*, LVIII (1959), 228–240.

5. See Sir Charles, *Tennyson*, pp. 240–241.

6. Harvard Notebook 17, dating probably from 1833–1836. The second and third stanzas of this lyric were apparently suppressed as were several other poems or stanzas (in the regular pattern), which have been preserved among the Harvard Tennyson Papers.

7. On the literary connotations of death, see Kenneth Burke, "Thanatopsis for Critics, a Brief Thesaurus of Deaths and Dyings," *Essays in Criticism*, II (1952), 369–375.

8. Milnes, "On the Death of ——," *Poems of Many Years*, 2nd ed. (London, 1844), p. 185; quoted with slight changes in Brookfield, *The Cambridge "Apostles"*, p. 233.

9. In an early manuscript, 11. 3–4 read "Door where my heart was used to beat / In expectation of his hand" (Harvard MS Eng

952.1, 104). The revision, suggesting rather than describing the feeling, is of a kind apparently quite beyond Milnes's reach.

10. In the imagery and descriptive passages of *In Memoriam* there are about fifty distinct references to water in its various forms. I here consider all as "images" insofar as they illustrate the developing emotion of the poem.

11. Some reference to the hand (or palm or finger) or the act of touching will be found in thirty of the lyrics that make up the sequence. Cf. Professor C. R. Sanders' comments on the image, "Tennyson and the Human Hand," *Victorian Newsletter*, No. 11 (1957), 5–14.

12. See Joseph Hone, *W. B. Yeats* (New York, 1943), p. 316. Yeats may be thinking of a general rhetorical heightening rather than specifically of the pastoral artifices; yet the pastoral passages do seem least like human speech.

13. See sections XXV, XXVI, XXXVIII, XL, XLVI, LXVIII, LXXIII, LXXVII, LXXXV; section LXXXIV speaks of "the flowery walk of letters," and CIX of "all the Muses' walk," but the others imply a pastoral landscape of general life.

14. Cf. lines and phrases in sections VII and CXIX; LIV (stanza 5) and CXXIV (stanza 5); the "violet" of XVIII and CXV; references to the trance of XCV in CXXII and CXXIV (stanza 6). The deepest unity, of course, lies — as we have seen — in the more spontaneous recurrence of the images.

15. *Memoir*, I, 304.

16. Like Huxley and most of the Victorian scientists, Tennyson thinks of science as entirely inductive and empirical; he has no inkling of the extent to which later science will be deductive and conceptual.

17. Editions after 1880 were revised so that "His living soul" read "The living soul," and "mine in his" became "mine in this." The change was apparently intended to facilitate the transition from the awareness of the individual dead man to the perception of the One, the ultimate reality.

18. Confessions, Book VII, chap. xvii, sec. 23, *Confessions and Enchiridion*, trans. and ed. Albert C. Outler (Philadelphia, 1955), p. 151. Tennyson's trance is compared to St. Augustine's vision by Percy H. Osmond, *The Mystical Poets of the English Church* (London, 1919), pp. 309–310. The passage in the Confessions continues: "But I was not able to sustain my gaze. My weakness was dashed back, and I lapsed again into my accustomed ways." The ecstatic experience, in other words, took place some time before Augustine's conversion and had no direct relation to his decision to become a Christian.

19. Søren Kierkegaard, *Concluding Unscientific Postscript*, trans.

David F. Swenson and Walter Lowrie (Princeton, 1944), p. 182; these passages are reprinted with an excellent brief introduction by Henry D. Aiken, *The Age of Ideology* (New York, 1956), p. 239. I have quoted them from the 1944 edition with the kind permission of Princeton University Press.

20. *Memoir*, I, 314.

21. Kierkegaard, paraphrased by Howard Albert Johnson, "The Deity in Time," pamphlet published by the College of Preachers, Washington Cathedral, Washington, D. C., reprinted from *Theology Today*, January 1945. Cf. Tennyson's comment on the mists of sin and the far planet, quoted above, Chapter IV.

22. *Concluding Unscientific Postscript*, p. 176.

23. See *The Sickness unto Death*, trans. Walter Lowrie (New York, 1954), pp. 148–154.

24. *Concluding Unscientific Postscript*, p. 315.

25. See Sir Charles, *Tennyson*, p. 245, and on the Laureateship, pp. 253–254.

CHAPTER VII: THE INTELLECTUAL THRONE

1. Quoted by Lionel Trilling, *Matthew Arnold* (New York, 1949), p. 142n, from Ernest Hartley Coleridge, *Life and Correspondence of John Duke Lord Coleridge*, 2 vols. (London, 1904), I, 210–211.

2. See C. B. Tinker and H. F. Lowry, *The Poetry of Matthew Arnold: A Commentary* (New York, 1940), p. 209; Tinker and Lowry comment that Tennyson rather than Goethe was perhaps originally the "one" (see pp. 209–211). Arnold's resentment of Tennyson, we may add, sometimes interfered seriously with his critical judgment — as when he told Gerald Massey, who published a new volume of verse in 1869, that Tennyson's *Holy Grail* (which appeared at the same time) could not prove "a dangerous competitor" (see Massey, *My Lyrical Life* [London, 1889], p. ii). Arnold, however, continued to "imitate" Tennyson's verse — as, for example, in "Palladium" (cf. "Then we shall rust in shade, or shine in strife" with the "To rust unburnish'd, not to shine in use" of "Ulysses") or "Growing Old" (cf. "And weep and feel the fullness of the past / The years that are no more" with the terminal line of each stanza of "Tears, Idle Tears").

3. Cf. "The Palace of Art," ll. 215–216: "Yet not the less she held her solemn mirth / And intellectual throne."

4. *Memoir*, I, 336. On Leigh Hunt's prospects and his own, see Tennyson's unpublished letter of April 1850 to John Forster, manuscript in Berg Collection, New York Public Library.

5. *Memoir*, I, 363.

6. See T. Herbert Warren, *The Centenary of Tennyson* (Oxford, 1909), p. 9.

7. See *Memoir*, I, 406.

8. See Tennyson's letter of December 9, 1852, to his brother Frederick, in Schonfield, ed., *Letters to Frederick Tennyson*, p. 109.

9. See Charles W. Shields, "The Arctic Monument Named for Tennyson by Dr. Kane," *Century*, LVI (1898), 483–492.

10. *Memoir*, I, 381.

11. See *Memoir*, I, 411.

12. See *Memoir*, I, 425.

13. See *Memoir*, I, 444.

14. See Sir Charles, *Tennyson*, pp. 305–306.

15. "Hands All Round," as it first appeared in the *Examiner* (February 7, 1852), is reprinted in Rolfe's Cambridge Edition, p. 868. Tennyson included a much less hysterical version of the song in his *Tiresias* volume (1885).

16. Walter Pater, "Coleridge," *Appreciations* (1889; London, 1931), p. 93.

17. *Memoir*, I, 409–410.

18. Unpublished verses beginning "O where is he the simple fool" name Bright and Cobden as triflers with national security (see Harvard Notebook 26). These must also be the "niggard throats of Manchester" in "The Third of February, 1852."

19. *Alton Locke*, 2 vols. (New York, 1898), I, 263.

20. The preface to the fourth edition of Kingsley's *Yeast* in 1859 indicates that conditions in society have changed for the better since the first publication of the novel (1848).

21. *Memoir*, I, 396.

22. Quoted by S. M. Paraclita Reilly, *Aubrey de Vere* (Lincoln, Neb., 1953), p. 49.

23. If not directly derivative from Clough's moral verses, Tennyson's "Will," written early in the fifties, expounds a quite Arnoldian philosophy of duty. The brilliant image of the wasteland in the second stanza, however, is quite beyond Clough's poetic reach: the man of little will

> . . . seems as one whose footsteps halt,
> Toiling in immeasurable sand,
> And o'er a weary sultry land,
> Far beneath a blazing vault,
> Sown in a wrinkle of the monstrous hill,
> The city sparkles like a grain of salt.

24. See Evelyn Abbott and Lewis Campbell, *The Life and Letters of Benjamin Jowett*, 2 vols. (London, 1897), I, 276.

25. See Sir Charles, *Tennyson*, p. 234.

26. See "Evangelical Teaching: Dr. Cumming," *Westminster Re-*

view, NS VIII (1855), 436–462, reprinted in George Eliot's *Essays* (New York, 1884), pp. 115–156. Tennyson's descriptions of "the heated pulpiteer's" fulminations against the "Scarlet Woman" and talk of the "Apocalyptic millstone" should be compared with George Eliot's attack on Cumming's violent anti-Romanism and his apocalyptic prophecies. The tone of George Eliot's essay may be inferred from such a passage as this: "But reassure yourselves! Dr. Cumming has been created. Antichrist is enthroned in the Vatican; but he is withstood by the Boanerges of the Crown Court."

27. Quoted from a suppressed letter by M. L. Howe, "Dante Gabriel Rossetti's Comments on *Maud*," *Modern Language Notes*, XLIX (1934), 291.

28. Quoted in *Memoir*, I, 393, from Cory's *Ionica*. Cf. Cory's acknowledgment that Tennyson was "the light and joy of my poor life"; see A. C. Benson, ed., *Ionica* (London, 1905), p. xviii.

29. *Memoir*, I, 396.

30. Cf. E. D. H. Johnson, "The Lily and the Rose: Symbolic Meaning in Tennyson's *Maud*," *PMLA*, LXIV (1949), 1222–1227.

31. Unpublished, Harvard Notebook 30.

32. Ruskin's well-known essay, "On the Pathetic Fallacy," approvingly cites this lyric as an example of the justified use of the "fallacy"; see *Modern Painters*, Part IV, ch. 12.

33. See J. D. Yohannan, "Tennyson and Persian Poetry," *Modern Language Notes*, LVII (1942), 89–90, and cf. W. D. Paden's reply, *MLN*, LVIII (1943), 652–656.

34. Stéphane Mallarmé, *Divigations* (Paris, 1897), p. 112, from his obituary, "Tennyson vu d'ici," contributed to Henley's *National Observer*, VIII (1892), 611–612.

35. Graham Reynolds, *Painters of the Victorian Scene* (London, 1953), p. 23.

36. Eliot, *Essays Ancient and Modern*, p. 182. By "arrive at expression" Eliot may mean "find an adequate objective correlative," but the comment seems to me ambiguous. The feelings do not "arrive at expression," Eliot suggests, because Tennyson "neither identifies himself with the lover, nor the lover with himself." But again the meaning eludes me: were Tennyson to identify himself fully with his fictitious lover, would he not necessarily have altogether to suspend his own "real" feelings?

37. *Memoir*, I, 402.

38. Quoted by Sir Charles, *Tennyson*, p. 286.

CHAPTER VIII: THE BURDEN OF SUCCESS

1. Ruskin, quoted in *Memoir*, I, 452–454.

2. Letter of October 3, 1859 (about three months after the publication of the *Idylls*) to the Duke of Argyll, who had told Tenny-

son that Macaulay had suggested the Grail theme; quoted in *Memoir*, I, 456–457.

3. Sir Charles, *Tennyson*, p. 367.

4. Conversation reported by Mrs. Bradley, *Memoir*, II, 51.

5. *Memoir*, I, 459; see also I, 436.

6. *Memoir*, I, 495.

7. See Bagehot's essay, "Wordsworth, Tennyson, and Browning; or Pure, Ornate and Grotesque Art in English Poetry" (1864), reprinted in Edmund D. Jones, ed., *English Critical Essays, Nineteenth Century* (London, 1916), pp. 460–461, 467–468.

8. "The Grandmother" was first published as "The Grandmother's Apology" in July 1859 in *Once a Week*, where it was illustrated with a drawing by Millais.

9. Colenso's opinion, quoted by Mrs. Woolner, *Memoir*, II, 23.

10. Quoted by Dixon, *Primer of Tennyson*, p. 31.

11. From a conversation of 1860 reported by Mrs. Bradley, *Memoir*, I, 468.

12. From Allingham's report of a conversation between Tennyson and Barnes in October 1863, *Memoir*, I, 513.

13. Dixon, *Primer*, p. 31.

14. See Harvard Notebook 37. The verses that follow the stanza from "The Spiteful Letter" are also drawn from this notebook, though the first, slightly altered, and the last of the five passages have been published by Sir Charles, *Nineteenth Century*, CIX, 630–631.

15. This couplet is quoted by Frederick Locker (Lampson) in the chapter he contributed to the *Memoir*; see II, 74.

16. *Memoir*, II, 79–80.

17. *Memoir*, II, 92.

18. From a rather cryptic entry in Emily Tennyson's journal for August 17, 1868, *Memoir*, II, 57.

19. William Irvine, *Apes, Angels and Victorians* (New York, 1955), p. 113.

20. "Lucretius" was first published in *Macmillan's Magazine*, May 1868, but was begun and perhaps finished in first draft as early as the fall of 1865; see *Memoir*, II, 28.

21. See Sir Charles, *Tennyson*, p. 375, and Nicolson, *Tennyson*, p. 230. But "Lucretius" (see note 20) was written before most of the so-called "aesthetic poetry" in English, perhaps before the appearance of Swinburne's *Poems and Ballads* (1866), and it was published three years before Buchanan made explicit the charge of "fleshliness" in his notorious "Fleshly School." Though it may be directed in part against some new aesthetic tendencies becoming apparent by 1865, "Lucretius" is not, I believe, written as an answer to Swinburne.

22. David Masson, *Recent British Philosophy* (New York, 1866), pp. 26–27. I am grateful to Dr. Martha Salmon for calling my attention to this work.

23. This is the apt subtitle of Alan Willard Brown's thorough study, *The Metaphysical Society* (New York, 1947).

CHAPTER IX: THE CITY BUILT TO MUSIC

1. Passages from Emily Tennyson's journal, *Memoir*, II, 57.

2. Letter to Palgrave, December 24, 1868, *Memoir*, II, 62.

3. The second part of the *Holy Grail* volume consisted of seven non-Arthurian poems, most of which I have examined: "The Northern Farmer. New Style," "The Victim," "Wages," "The Higher Pantheism," "Flower in the Crannied Wall," "Lucretius," and "The Golden Supper" (this last is a continuation of the early and then still unpublished "Lover's Tale").

4. The seasonal symbolism foreshadows the "natural" metaphor used by Spengler in his theory of rising and falling civilizations. As Reinhold Niebuhr paraphrases Spengler, "All civilizations pass through ages analogous to spring, summer, autumn and winter; which is to say that historical organisms are equated with natural ones." But, says Niebuhr, this means that the freedom of history is illusory and that all moves by necessity. From Niebuhr's *Nature and Destiny of Man*, quoted by Hans Meyerhoff, ed., *The Philosophy of History in our Time* (New York, 1959), pp. 314–315. Despite the metaphor, however, Tennyson is much closer to Toynbee than to Spengler, insofar as he believes that civilizations are free to make mistakes.

5. *Memoir*, I, 483n; cf. II, 133, 133n.

6. In my interpretation of Arthur's character and function, I am much indebted to F. E. L. Priestley's fine essay, "Tennyson's *Idylls*," *University of Toronto Quarterly*, XIX (1949), 35–49. On various aspects of the sequence, several other articles may be cited as of particular value: T.P. Cross, "Alfred Tennyson as a Celticist," *Modern Philology*, XVIII (1921), 485–492; S. C. Burchell, "Tennyson's 'Allegory in the Distance,'" *PMLA*, LXVIII (1953), 418–424; and Sir Charles Tennyson, "The Idylls of the King," *Twentieth Century*, CLXI (1957), 277–286. In addition to these, two older studies may still be consulted with profit: M. W. MacCallum, *Tennyson's Idylls of the King and Arthurian Story from the Sixteenth Century* (Glasgow, 1894) and Richard Jones, *The Growth of "The Idylls of the King"* (Philadelphia, 1895).

7. From a letter to Drummond Rawnsley, Harvard Tennyson Papers, MS Eng 952.2, 11.

8. See Swinburne's 1872 pamphlet *Under the Microscope* (Portland, Me., 1909), p. 35; cf. Swinburne's *Miscellanies* (London, 1895), p. 246f.

9. See *Memoir*, II, 129, but Hallam Tennyson seems to have confused the passages his father quoted.

10. Cf. Tennyson's comment on the early "Morte d'Arthur," *Memoir*, I, 194.

11. One of my former students, Edward Engelberg, has commented on this imagery in a perceptive article, "The Beast Image in Tennyson's *Idylls of the King*," *ELH*, XXII (1955), 287–292. In the paragraph that follows I draw on some of the illustrations which Engelberg has described in fuller detail, and I add a number of others which did not so directly serve his purpose.

12. Henry James, in a review of Tennyson's *Queen Mary*, 1875, *Views and Reviews* (Boston, 1908), p. 178.

13. See Marjorie Bowden, *Tennyson in France* (Manchester, 1930), esp. pp. 116–117, 153.

14. Quoted by Sanders, *The Strachey Family*, p. 257.

15. Cf. Niebuhr (Meyerhoff, ed., pp. 316–317). Niebuhr divides the causes of cultural decline into "the two general categories of the sins of sensuality, and the sins of pride. In the former the freedom of history is denied and men creep back to the irresponsibility of nature." The sins of pride may engender a false "mystic other-worldliness" which may make "the human spirit, not the master of history but the agent of its own emancipation from history."

CHAPTER X: UNDER THE MASK

1. *Memoir*, II, 146.

2. *Memoir*, II, 165.

3. One of the wedding guests, quoted by Sir Charles, *Tennyson*, p. 440.

4. Arnold quoted, *Memoir*, II, 225.

5. Henry James, *Autobiography* (New York, 1956), ed. F. W. Dupee, pp. 585, 587.

6. An unpublished note, apparently in another hand but with corrections by Tennyson, probably written in 1890, in Harvard Notebook 56.

7. James, "Tennyson's Drama," *Views and Reviews*, p. 167; pp. 165–204 of this volume reprint James's reviews of *Queen Mary* for the *Galaxy* of September 1875, and of *Harold* for the *Nation*, January 18, 1877.

8. See Anne Thackeray Ritchie, *Records of Tennyson, Ruskin, Browning* (New York, 1892), p. 59.

9. See Sir Charles, *Tennyson*, p. 411. The Gilbert and Sullivan operetta *Princess Ida* appeared in 1884.

10. See Tennyson's own prefatory note to *The Window*, excusing the appearance of the volume only by his obligation to fulfill his agreement with the composer.

11. *Memoir*, II, 113n.

12. From a sonnet of undetermined date which appears along with other material relating to the historical plays in Harvard Notebook 59. Sir Charles includes it among the "Unpublished Poems," *Nineteenth Century*, CIX, 628.

13. See Oscar Maurer, "Swinburne *vs.* Furnivall," *University of Texas Studies in English*, XXXI (1952), 86–96.

14. See *Memoir*, II, 173–174.

15. James, *Views and Reviews*, pp. 183, 184. With James's comments cf. Harley Granville-Barker's "Tennyson, Swinburne, Meredith and the Theatre," Granville-Barker, ed., *The Eighteen-Seventies* (Cambridge, Eng., 1929), pp. 161–191.

16. Tennyson drew up a rather erudite list of books which he consulted as sources for *Queen Mary;* see *Memoir*, II, 176.

17. Tennyson liked to tell a story of how Froude after the publication of his *History of England* was frightened, when visiting the crypt of Westminster Abbey, by the sudden waving of the banner of Queen Mary, whom he had maligned. See Sir Charles Tennyson, "Tennyson's Conversation," *Twentieth Century*, CLXV (1959), 42.

18. Tennyson described Hugo's 1833 drama as "a mere travesty," *Memoir*, II, 422.

19. Sir Charles (*Tennyson*, p. 435) tells us that *Harold* was given its first public performance in 1928; he does not say whether or not there were earlier private presentations.

20. Irving, quoted by Sir Charles, *Tennyson*, p. 535n. Irving died on October 13, 1905, just after a performance of *Becket* at Bradford.

21. Letters from FitzGerald, quoted in *Memoir*, II, 182–183, 192.

22. See *The Decameron*, Day the Fifth, Ninth Story. The tale had served as the basis of a narrative poem by Coventry Patmore, published in 1878, which may have directed Tennyson's attention to Boccaccio's original.

23. Tennyson, quoted by Sir Charles, *Tennyson*, p. 447.

24. *Memoir*, II, 390.

25. *Memoir*, II, 173.

26. *The Cup* was planned early in 1879 and completed late in 1880 (see *Memoir*, II, 256–257). It opened at the Lyceum on January 3, 1881, and ran for one hundred and twenty-seven nights. *The Promise of May* was written in the summer of 1882 and presented at the Globe on November 11 (see Sir Charles, *Tennyson*, pp. 463–464).

27. See *Memoir*, II, 257.

28. *Memoir*, II, 260.

29. *Memoir*, II, 385.

30. "Mr. Tennyson's New Play," *Daily Telegraph*, Tuesday, January 4, 1881. The preceding comment on the audience is also from this review.

31. Gladstone quoted, *Memoir*, II, 279.

32. From a clipping dated November 17, 1882 (I have not succeeded in identifying the newspaper), which Tennyson — with apparent approval — pasted in his notebook (Harvard Notebook 66).

33. *Memoir*, II, 269.

34. Tennyson wrote no plays after *The Promise of May*, but he did make changes in his texts for the productions of *The Foresters* and *Becket*.

CHAPTER XI: THE ANCIENT SAGE

1. I exclude the early piece, *The Lover's Tale*, which Tennyson, annoyed at attempts at piracy, released in 1879 along with its sequel, "The Golden Supper." See above, Chapter II, note 5, and Chapter IX, note 3.

2. Swinburne, "Tennyson and Musset," *Miscellanies*, p. 220.

3. FitzGerald quoted, *Memoir*, II, 272.

4. Yeats was especially annoyed by a comparison to his disadvantage in the *Manchester Guardian*; see Allan Wade, ed., *The Letters of W. B. Yeats* (New York, 1955), pp. 105–106. I am grateful to my student Louis Cornell for calling my attention to the similarities between the two poems.

5. See *Memoir*, II, 234–235, 249, 252, 253.

6. *Memoir*, II, 244.

7. Sir Harold Nicolson (*Tennyson*, pp. 285–286) has given us a most suggestive analysis of the vowel patterns in the poem.

8. "The Dead Prophet" was first published in 1885, but I have been unable to determine exactly when it was written. I have assumed that it belongs to the eighties both in composition and in subject, but I am unable to interpret the subtitle "182–" (if indeed it is not a deliberate attempt to mislead). An earlier draft of the poem appears along with parts of *The Promise of May* in Harvard Notebook 68, which apparently dates from the early eighties. We do know that Tennyson disliked Froude's biography of Carlyle; see *Memoir*, II, 301.

9. Unpublished, Harvard Notebook 46.

10. *Memoir*, II, 300.

11. Sir Charles (*Tennyson*, p. 471) suggests the possibility of such motivation.

12. *Memoir*, II, 302.

13. *Memoir*, II, 305.

14. *Memoir*, II, 337; cf. II, 303, 395.

15. See *Memoir*, II, 296, and E. A. Horsman, ed., *The Diary of Alfred Domett, 1872–1885* (London, 1953), p. 283.

16. See Harvard Notebook 46; Sir Charles (*Tennyson*, p. 483) quotes a slightly altered version of the same lines.

17. On Tennyson's eye troubles in the eighties (never quite as serious as he supposed), see *Memoir*, II, 304, 311.

18. The lines appear in Harvard Notebook 46 along with the 1883 dedication of the poem to FitzGerald. They may, of course, have been written earlier and entered in the notebook in revised form. It is impossible to tell how much of the early part of the poem was recast to make it serve Tennyson's late purposes.

19. *Memoir*, II, 319.

20. Sir Charles (*Tennyson*, pp. 460–461) describes the reception of "Despair." A representative rationalistic attack (which he does not mention) is G. W. Foote's pamphlet, *Atheism and Suicide*, issued in 1881 by the Freethought Publishing Company. Foote argues that atheism does not lead to suicide, since the great poet James Thomson (a rather unhappy example!) has not yet taken his life.

21. From an unpublished note to the poem, Harvard Notebook 49. Neither this phrase nor the reference to the "narrowest sect" appeared in the prose epigraph which headed the poem when it appeared in the November 1881 number of the *Nineteenth Century*.

22. "Vastness" first appeared in *Macmillan's Magazine* for November 1885; Macmillan and Co., Tennyson's new publishers, issued the *Tiresias* volume in December.

23. In discussing the revisions and variants of "Vastness," I draw on the unpublished Harvard Notebook 52.

24. *Locksley Hall Sixty Years After, Etc.* was published in December 1886, though dated 1887. Besides the title poem, the volume contained *The Promise of May*, "The Fleet," and a Laureate piece on "Opening of the Indian and Colonial Exhibition by the Queen."

25. Hallam's account of his father's attitude, *Memoir*, II, 329.

26. The dedication describes the poem as "this dramatic monologue." A letter (quoted in *Memoir*, II, 331) denies the presence of "biography."

27. The "commonest commonplace" may possibly echo a conversation between the young Tennyson and the aged Wordsworth. When Tennyson suggested that in a future time people would land in shoals on the mountains to see nature's wonders, Wordsworth replied, "Ah, I do not like to look into the common-placing future."

See Sir Charles, "Tennyson's Conversation," *Twentieth Century*, CLXV (1959), 40.

28. See Harvard Notebook 51, and also a separate draft, Harvard Papers, 128. The lines attacking Zolaism seem to have given particular trouble, and the word "Zolaism" itself was apparently a late and euphonic substitute for "Realism."

29. See *Memoir*, II, 329.

30. *Memoir*, II, 324.

31. *Memoir*, II, 319.

32. See Tennyson's MS note, *Memoir*, II, 476n. Tennyson's notebook shows him trying and discarding several titles, "Laotze," "The Way of Life," "The Venerable Master."

33. Possibly Oscar Wilde or George Moore. Moore sent Tennyson a presentation copy of his *Pagan Poems* (1881), inscribed "To Alfred Tennyson the poet who never fails, from George Moore a contemporary versifier." The copy was offered for sale several years ago by C. A. Stonehill, Ltd., London and New York.

34. Tennyson told Alfred Domett in 1883 that he sometimes thought of writing an ode on the same subject as Wordsworth's "Intimations" ode. See Domett, p. 269.

35. See the report of Tennyson's conversation in the eighties by his niece, Agnes Grace Weld, in her *Glimpses of Tennyson and of some of his Relations and Friends* (London, 1903), p. 112.

CHAPTER XII: THE ONE CLEAR CALL

1. See *Memoir*, II, 348.

2. Sir Andrew Clark's opinion, *Memoir*, II, 354; see also II, 508.

3. The "evolution" of these lines is scarcely of the sort that Swinburne had in mind when a few months earlier he published his burlesque "Dethroning Tennyson," in which he argued that the work of the Laureate should properly be ascribed to Charles Darwin. The squib is clearly a hit at the Baconians, but as such it pays Tennyson the subtle compliment of an implied comparison with Shakespeare; it is therefore interesting as an additional testimony to Tennyson's place in Victorian poetry. It was published in *Nineteenth Century*, XXIII (1888), 127–129, and reprinted as "Tennyson or Darwin?" in Swinburne's *Studies in Prose and Poetry* (London, 1894), pp. 141–145.

4. Letter of August 19, 1889, *Memoir*, II, 361.

5. See Gordon S. Haight's elucidation of the poem, "Tennyson's Merlin," *Studies in Philology*, XLIV (1947), 549–566.

6. See *Memoir*, II, 366.

7. Haight (pp. 564–565) argues that "croak" is a pun on "Croker"

and that J. W. Croker was accordingly the hostile reviewer Tennyson had in mind; but since the raven was associated with Christopher North and since Tennyson believed that North had not only attacked in his own review but had also instigated Croker's attack, I prefer my own reading of the line. Sir Charles (*Tennyson*, p. 517n) suggests that the raven is Tennyson's grandfather.

8. Haight (p. 563) believes that this section of "Merlin" (stanza VIII) refers only to the reception of *In Memoriam;* I am inclined to think its application more general.

9. I am much indebted to the critical explication and analysis by Thomas J. Assad, "Analogy in Tennyson's 'Crossing the Bar,'" *Tulane Studies in English,* VIII (1958), 153–163.

10. *Memoir,* II, 367.

11. "Crossing the Bar" was apparently a quite "spontaneous" composition, and Tennyson told his son, "It came in a moment" (*Memoir,* II, 367). Yet like all his poems it was subject to careful revision. What Hallam prints as "the Original MS" (*Memoir,* II, facing 432) must be a clean copy of the final draft, for it is clearly later than the notebook version (which I have reproduced in facsimile, following chapter XII, from Harvard Notebook 54), where line 3 begins with "But" rather than "And," line 7 reads "came" instead of "drew," and the last stanza runs:

> Alone from out the bounds of Time and Place
> Alone I sail, and far
> But hope to see my Pilot face to face
> When I have crost the bar.

The superiority of the final draft is surely considerable. The "face to face" (though clearly an echo of I Corinthians, 13:12) and the "Time and Place," found in both versions, recall the rhyme and imagery of the last stanza of H. F. Lyte's hymn, "Praise, my soul, the King of heaven," a familiar early-Victorian paraphrase of Psalm 103:

> Angels, help us to adore him;
> Ye behold him face to face;
> Sun and moon, bow down before him,
> Dwellers all in time and space.

12. Walter Pater, "Style," *Appreciations,* p. 13.

13. *Memoir,* II, 366.

14. I quote the unpublished drafts of this passage from Harvard Notebook 53.

15. In his stimulating critical essay, "Tennyson's Mythology: A Study of Demeter and Persephone," *ELH,* XXI (1954), G. Robert Stange compares these lines from *Paradise Lost* with the published "Demeter," ll. 34–51.

16. *Memoir*, II, 364. On the "frame" see also Curtis Dahl, "A Double Frame for Tennyson's Demeter?" *Victorian Studies*, I (1958), 356–362.

17. Unpublished, in Harvard Notebook 55. On "Far — Far — Away" see above, Chapter I, pp. 1–2.

18. Kipling quoted, *Memoir*, II, 392.

19. *Memoir*, II, 394.

20. See *Memoir*, II, 401.

21. Cf. *Memoir*, II, 378, and Sir Charles, *Tennyson*, pp. 520–521.

22. Tennyson was also attracted to the death of Giordano Bruno as a likely subject for a new poem. In Bruno's heterodoxy he saw yet another parallel to his own faith. "His view of God," he said, "is in some ways mine" (*Memoir*, II, 424).

23. G. R. Dabbs, quoted in *Memoir*, II, 429.

24. Tennyson's view of the volume, according to Hallam, *Memoir*, II, 419.

25. "The Tourney," a very slight romantic ballad, probably belongs to a much earlier period. "Riflemen, Form!" appeared, as Tennyson's endnote says, in *The Times* in 1859. And "Mechanophilus" is a reduction (from thirteen to nine stanzas) of "Aeonophilus," an unpublished piece apparently from the 1830s, which appears in Harvard Notebook 17. I have excluded several other poems, none of which is a striking addition either to this volume or to the Tennyson canon. Among these, "The Church-Warden and the Curate" is yet another monologue in Lincolnshire dialect; "The Bandit's Death" is a rhymed monologue based on a melodramatic story by Scott; "Charity" is a sentimental confession of a wronged woman's debt to the widow of her seducer; and "Kapiolani" is an attempt to celebrate a Hawaiian heroine in an imitation of a Hawaiian chant.

26. See the pamphlet by H. Montagu Butler, "A Sermon preached in the Chapel of Trinity College, Cambridge, on October 16th, 1892, in reference to the Death of Lord Tennyson, Honorary Fellow of the College" (Cambridge, 1892).

27. Swinburne, *Under the Microscope*, p. 42; this praise immediately follows Swinburne's fierce attack on the "Morte d'Albert" (*Idylls of the King*) in the same essay.

INDEX

Note: Each of the works by Tennyson cited in the text is here listed separately. Writings by others are entered under the names of the authors concerned.